Commitment to Sustainability

Ooligan Press is committed to becoming an academic leader in sustainable publishing practices. Using both the classroom and the business, we will investigate, promote, and utilize sustainable products, technologies, and practices as they relate to the production and distribution of our books. We hope to lead and encourage the publishing community by our example. Making sustainable choices is not only vital to the future of our industry—it's vital to the future of our world.

OPEN BOOK

OpenBook Series

One component of our sustainability campaign is the newly created OpenBook series. *Brew to Bikes: Portland's Artisan Economy* is the forth book in the series, so named to highlight our commitment to transparency on our road toward sustainable publishing. We believe that disclosing the impacts of the choices we make will not only help us avoid unintentional greenwashing, but also serve to educate those who are unfamiliar with the choices available to printers and publishers.

Efforts to produce this series as sustainably as possible focus on paper and ink sources, design strategies, efficient and safe manufacturing methods, innovative printing technologies, supporting local and regional companies, and corporate responsibility of our contractors.

All titles in the OpenBook series will have the OpenBook logo on the front cover and a corresponding OpenBook Environmental Audit inside, which includes a calculated paper impact from the Environmental Defense Fund.

More About Sustainability in Publishing

The OpenBook series is only one element of Ooligan Press's Sustainable Publishing Initiative, which began with our first OpenBook, *Rethinking Paper and Ink: The Sustainable Publishing Revolution*. A collaboration among Ooligan students, the Green Press Initiative, and sustainable publishing professionals, *Rethinking Paper and Ink* is an examination of sustainable publishing practices and includes an comprehensive account of the choices we made in producing the book itself as sustainably and responsibly as possible.

OpenBook Audit

Brew to Bikes: Portland's Artisan Economy

Figures below relate to a print run of 2,000 books.

	Chemicals	Greenhouse Gases	Energy	Fiber	Waste
Paper†					
Cover paper: 10pt. Mohawk Kromekote C1S, 30% PCW, FSC-certified. 259 lbs. used.	Less than 1-lb. reduction in volatile organic compounds; Less than 1-lb. reduction in hazardous air pollutants.[5]	98-lb. reduction in carbon dioxide equivalent.[5]	Less than 1 million BTU reduction in net energy[5]; Manufactured by Mohawk Fine Papers, Inc. in NY state in a carbon-neutral facility using wind-generated electricity.	Less than 1-ton reduction in virgin fiber use.[5]	32-lb. reduction in solid waste; 371-gal. reduction in wastewater.[5]
Text paper: 60-lb. Rolland White Enviro100 Print, 100% PCW, PCF, FSC-certified. 5,040 lbs. used.	4-lb. reduction of volatile organic compounds; 2-lb. reduction of hazardous air pollutants.[5]	6,200-lb. reduction of carbon dioxide equivalent.[5]	21 million BTU reduction in net energy[5]; Manufactured by Cascades in Quebec, CN, using recycled biogas energy.	9-ton reduction in virgin fiber use, the equivalent of about 65 trees.[5]	1,813-lb. reduction in solid waste; 29,855-gal. wastewater reduction.[5]
Printing & Binding					
23" x 35" sheets were printed on a Man Roland 702 press by United Graphics Incorporated in Mattoon, IL.	Aqueous coatings reduce volatile organic compound emissions since they are water-based instead of petroleum-based.	UGI uses Printcom Wash 211p to clean their presses, which is free of chlorinated hydrocarbons, aromatic hydrocarbons, and hazardous air pollutants.	Since 1998, Henkel has reduced their total energy consumption by 40% and plan to lower their current consumption by another 15% by 2012.	Insufficient data.	Printcom Wash 211p is water-emulsifiable, and, once used, qualifies as non-hazardous waste. All cleaners and washes are recycled over multiple jobs.
Perfect bound with Henkel Purmelt QR 3365. 4 lbs. used.					
Covers were finished with an aqueous coating (1347C) manufactured by Coating & Adhesives in Leland, NC. 5 lbs. used.	Polyurethane (PUR) adhesives are not water-soluble, meaning they are easier to remove during recycling than ethylene vinyl acetate (EVA) adhesives.				Since 1998, Henkel has reduced their waste output by 37% and plan to lower their current output by another 10% by 2012.
Ink					
HyPlus 100 offset printing ink manufactured by Toyo Ink in Japan.	HyPlus 100 ink is soy oil-based and petroleum solvent-free.	HyPlus 100 contains up to 3% volatile organic compounds.	Insufficient data.	N/A	Toyo implements ink recycling and solvent recovery systems to minimize waste output.

This OpenBook Audit—performed by Ooligan Press—stems from our commitment to transparency in our efforts to produce a line of books using the most sustainable materials and processes available to us.

All quantities and material specifications were supplied by United Graphics Incorporated.

†Environmental impact estimates were made using the EDF Paper Calculator tool at http://www.papercalculator.org.

§Compared to paper made with 100% virgin fiber.

"*Brew to Bikes: Portland's Artisan Economy* leaves the non–Portland-based reader feeling a little envious of what is established and unfolding in their city, but also provides the research and groundwork for one to take steps toward turning their city into a more supportive, people- friendly environment."

—Faythe Levine, Director and Co-author of
Handmade Nation: The Rise of D.I.Y. Art, Craft & Design

"This new book examines the organization of Portland's artisan economy at the ground level, and then places it in the broader context of the changes facing cities and policy makers. The core of the book is the rich and nuanced description, supported by qualitative research, of the many different sectors that make up the artisan economy. The authors of these chapters describe an alternative to the mainstream economic model by focusing on diversity, sustainability, and the development of social wealth as key organizing factors. While retaining a critical perspective, this book suggests that Portland's artisan economy not only promises the possibility of a more humane and sustainable city, but also of viewing consumption as an export-oriented activity. *Brew to Bikes* is a fun and thought-provoking read."

—Greg Andranovich, Department of Political Science,
California State University, Los Angeles

"Charles Heying and his army of student researchers provide a ground tour of Portland's artisan economy. These case studies illustrate how a mostly DIY community of craft brewers, independent designers, and many more contribute to the city's economy and shape the very space and character of the city itself. This is a creative economy defined by independent, small-scale, and locally-rooted enterprises that seek 'social wealth' rather than 'professionals and knowledge workers' in search of lifestyle amenities."

—Carl Grodach, Department of Urban and Public Affairs,
University of Texas at Arlington

"Loaded with vivid detail and rich history, this fine book conveys the spirit of one of America's most unique and progressive cities. An antidote for those who decry the hegemony of large corporations and the leveling of local culture in the era of globalization, this is a must-read for all who care about the future of American cities and the future of American work."

—Richard Lloyd, Author of *Neo-Bohemia: Art
and Culture in the Postindustrial City*

BREW TO BIKES

PORTLAND'S ARTISAN ECONOMY

Brew to Bikes

Portland's Artisan Economy

Charles Heying

Ooligan Press
Portland State University
Portland, Oregon

Brew to Bikes: Portland's Artisan Economy
Charles Heying
Portland State University
Copyright © 2010 Charles Heying

Ooligan Press
Department of English
Portland State University
P.O. Box 751, Portland, Oregon 97207
503.725.9748; fax 503.725.3561
ooligan@ooliganpress.pdx.edu
www.ooliganpress.pdx.edu

Library of Congress Cataloging-in-Publication Data
Brew to bikes : Portland's artisan economy / [edited by] Charles Heying.
    p. cm.
Includes bibliographical references and index.

ISBN 978-1-932010-32-9 (alk. paper)

1. Artisans—Oregon—Portland. 2. Portland (Ore.)—Commerce. 3. Portland (Ore.)—Economic conditions. I. Heying, Charles H.
HD9999.H363U622 2010
331.7'94—dc22

2010016221

Cover & Interior Design by Ellery Harvey
Cover Photo by Whitney Gayer

Contents

BACK TO THE FUTURE

For Lois.

Brew to Bikes:
Portland's Artisan Economy

INTRODUCTION

Charles Heying

IT'S SATURDAY MORNING and my granddaughter Sophie and I are heading to breakfast while her mom is at Pilates. We decide against Genie's, our usual spot, where tattooed wait staff serve huevos rancheros and morning cocktails. We drive up Division Street looking for the place where we ate with her cousins, Emma, Hans, and Amelie, when they were in town. What was the name? It had those big sliding windows that opened to the street. We catch a glimpse of the retro chic Caffe Pallino as we drive by, but the traffic is moving us along so I am reluctant to stop. Sophie is disappointed. She won't get her favorite dish, Bob's Red Mill oatmeal with walnuts. "Let's try Petite Provence," I offer. "It's just up the street."

A sidewalk café and artisan bakery, Petite Provence, with its exposed ceiling joists and stately black and gold paneling, suggests something vaguely French, refined but inviting. We arrive before the morning rush. The drift of fresh baked bread and coffee prepares us for a great breakfast. A mature waitress, with continental bearing and hint of an accent, seats us at a table where Sophie can see kitchen workers prepare crème brûlée and fruit tarts. We order, then chat—school, friends, sleepovers, the week's history of small triumphs. The plates arrive; we unfold our cloth napkins and enjoy, for a moment, the arrangement of the food, the inviting colors and textures. Then we eat. My two poached eggs on basil pesto and roasted tomato with a side of polenta are wonderful. Sophie's French toast topped with fresh cranberries, blueberries, and a touch of cream cheese is more than she can handle. I slide a bit onto my plate—excellent! The waitress serves coffee, Nossa Familia, an interesting choice since Portland's iconic Stumptown Coffee Roasters is just down the street. But Nossa Familia is finding supporters among those who prefer milder blends. And then the teaser from the kitchen: would we like to sample the crème brûlée? How can we not? Just a taste, so good with the last sip of coffee. We check the bread on the way out. "Fennel and Raisin or Walnut Currant? Sophie, you choose."

A wonderful morning, a meal distinct enough to remember, and fresh baked bread to take home. And the cost for this experience? Only a few dollars more than two Grand Slam breakfasts from Denny's and a loaf of Wonder bread.

Welcome to Portland's artisan economy and to our book about it. In these pages you will encounter many experiences like the one just described while learning about the many artisan enterprises that populate Division Street and other neighborhoods in Portland. You will also be presented with a thesis that explains how post-industrial economic transformations have created a space for artisan enterprises to flourish.

Not everything about the artisan economy is as sweet as the breakfast at Petite Provence. One of the more controversial manifestations of what we are calling the artisan economy is the conversion of spaces of our industrial past into new spaces of elite consumption. Sociologist Sharon Zukin has long lamented the transformation of New York City's working-class districts into bohemian arts enclaves and gentrified neighborhoods with chic boutiques and pricey restaurants.[1] Zukin is troubled about the loss of an authentic economy that produced real things, and its replacement by a consumption economy of professionals and "knowledge workers" that "lack a producer's knowledge to change a cucumber into a pickle, but have a consumer's knowledge of how a good pickle tastes."[2]

It's a valid concern, but somewhat misdirected. Zukin and others have focused so much on the "spaces of consumption" that they have largely ignored the "people who produce." Besides, that's not how things seem to work in Portland. We are more DIY (do-it-yourself) than shop and buy. If an item is too expensive, we surely have something we can barter for it, or we know someone who will show us how to make it. That's not to say we don't have our upscale neighborhoods, loft conversions, high-rise waterfront condos, and tensions over displacement. I have my own love/hate relationship with Portland's Pearl District, and deep reservations about the San Francisco weekenders who own the fancy condos with views of the Willamette River and Mount Hood. But beyond that, we have a burgeoning artisan economy that lives happily alongside an older Portland of working class businesses and regular neighborhoods. Perhaps the size and scale of Portland make it seem so much less contentious. Perhaps I am willfully avoiding all the heavy-weight concerns of class analysis, urban cultural theory, and more. Perhaps it doesn't seem to make sense here. Perhaps it's just too nice a morning.

Let's leave Petite Provence, check out a few blocks of Division, and see what Portland's artisan economy looks like at street level. Perhaps this can help explain this seemingly comfortable mix of hip and homespun. Next door west of Petite Provence is the Scoreboard Sports Pub, with two giant roof-top dish antennae, dingy gray siding, and armory style gun slot windows. Next door east: Beads at Dusti Creek; Urban Wellness Group, "Massage, Acupuncture, Natural Medicine"; Bearly Worn/Vintage Voodoo, "clothes for the modern hippy, from near and far"; and then Ace's Quick Cash pawn shop. Across Division Street and occupying the bays and office of a converted gas station is the Bike Exchange—one of Portland's ubiquitous bike shops. On the same lot is Taqueria los Gorditos, a Mexican food cart that has become so popular one can honestly describe their weekend clientele as a crowd. With its newly built patio, it is inching toward semi-permanence. Next to

Various baked goods on display at Petite Provence in southeast Portland. Photo © Rachel Moore

Petite Provence, Division Street. Photo © Rachel Moore

it: Oregon Transmission Center, a white block building that handles shift kits, clutches, and all types of domestic and foreign transmissions. On the day I was scoping the street, a customer arrived in a jacked-up pickup with his scruffy dog riding shotgun. It was a non-event when he left the service center, crossed the street to Petite Provence, and got his coffee and croissant.

Right up against Oregon Transmission, its plant shed tucked under a massive Clear Channel billboard, is Oscar Albert, "garden nursery, wine bar, and bottle shop." Next door to them: The Guiding Tree, featuring "Tarot, Astrology, Reiki, Crystals"; then Nomad Precision Body Adornment and Tribal Art Museum; and finally, Aaron's Shoe Repair, with its only decoration a free calendar from Oregon Leather Co. and a working gumball machine that isn't there for ambience. But even Aaron's has been infiltrated by the hipsters. Taped to the back of his cash register is a flyer for the Rose City Rollers, a non-profit that has fostered the rebirth of the roughhousing women's sport of roller derby, and that is drawing crowds of more than two thousand to its events.

And so it goes, up and down Division Street. Disaster Restoration shares a warehouse with upscale Lauro Mediterranean Kitchen and Stumptown Coffee's central roasting. Across from Division Hardware is the nondescript Egyptian Club, a hallmark dive bar and place of historical importance for Portland's lesbian community. And down the street is Loprinzi's Gym, started by Sam Loprinzi, runner-up for Mr. America in 1948, with all its equipment designed and built by the Loprinzi brothers. It is a place where people have worked out for forty years, with some of its first patrons still pumping iron. A bit further down is another Portland icon, Langlitz Leathers, a family business for fifty years that boasts an international reputation for its handmade motorcycle leathers.

What do these have in common? They are all part of Portland's emerging artisan economy. Other cities have their bohemian districts, but Portland stands alone as an urban economy that has broadly embraced the artisan approach to living and working. Scholars including Elizabeth Currid,[3] Richard Lloyd,[4] and Richard Florida[5] have told part of the story of arts economies and the creative class, but it all comes together here in Portland. It's localism without parochialism; it's back to the future, the Jetsons on bikes.

Rich in detail and theory, *Brew to Bikes: Portland's Artisan Economy* describes how the transformation from an industrial to a post-industrial economy is being articulated in the trend-setting edges of Portland's artisan production. For example, the microbrew renaissance, for which Portland can justifiably claim leadership, established a foothold in a U.S. beer market where four major brewing companies control over 95 percent of the market.[6] The metro area of Portland now has thirty-eight breweries, the largest per capita concentration of microbrew establishments for any metro area in the world. Twelve percent of beer consumed in Oregon is craft brewed, three times the national average. Statewide, there are ninety-six brewing facilities directly employing five thousand Oregonians.[7] In artisan foods, Portland has been discovered. A story in the *Los Angeles Times* magazine noted that "it's in the food-savvy city of Portland that the new food economy has taken root, and where the future may be taking shape."[8] Regarding cycling in Portland, a *New York Times* article explained how the nexus of planning, passion, and artisan skills is creating a new industrial cluster: "Cyclists have long revered Portland for its bicycle-friendly culture and infrastructure.... Now, riders are helping the city build a cycling economy."[9] Handcrafted frames, precisions parts, specialty bikes, and numerous organized bicycling activities add $90 million to Portland's economy.[10] Even Portland's fashion sector has thrived, despite the city's reputation for zen casual couture and its distance from traditional fashion centers. Ninety local designers sell their clothing in twenty-six retail shops found in neighborhoods throughout the city. And Portland designers are building reputations beyond the city. Leanne Marshall, who then lived in Portland, won the fifth season of the reality television show, *Project Runway*.

My colleagues and I begin *Brew to Bikes* by exploring the scholarly literature that contributes to our understanding of the artisan economy. More than a review, we integrate diverse strains of scholarly thinking about the economic transformations that are changing how we work and live. We examine contemporary scholarship on the arts and cultural industries as economic engines and how tourism and arts amenities intersect with the growth of a creative workforce. We consider grassroots movements that emphasize local self-reliance, sustainable living, and the integrity of craft work. We argue that these diverse literatures, taken together, logically lead to conceptually rich artisan economy synthesis.

We take up this synthesis in Chapter 2, which distills the base concepts and thematic core of the artisan economy. We compare the characteristics of a mass-production economy to an artisan economy in terms of product qualities, work life, organizational structure, and complex moral orientation. We consider how our artisan economy thesis challenges traditional thinking about economic development and wealth creation.

Having established the origins of the artisan economy concept and presented our theoretical synthesis, we test our theory using case studies of Portland's four signature sectors: brew, food, fashion, and bikes. These chapters constitute the book's second part. We identify these as Portland's signature sectors because they are known to be significant contributors to Portland's economy, they exhibit complex evolutionary histories, and they have attracted the attention of the national news media. The inclusion of bike artisans in this section also provides an example of artisan production that lies outside the traditional definition of handcrafts or artisanal foods.

In the book's third part, we present additional case studies that cumulatively reveal the breadth and depth of artisan production in Portland and the common themes of artisan industry. The rich narratives and detailed descriptions provide a glimpse inside the many vibrant enterprises and communities that constitute Portland's artisan economy. In the last chapter, we consider the spatial aspects of the artisan economy. As the artisan sector has grown, so has the need for live/work spaces to accommodate the special lifestyle and space needs of the new artisans. We describe how the city and developers have worked with artisans to develop creative spaces.

In the final part of *Brew to Bikes*, we consider the lessons learned from the various case studies and the 118 artisans who graciously answered our questions. We discuss the special contribution of the book and consider the larger questions that are posed by the success of Portland's artisan economy. Is Portland a frontier in the transformation of urban economies, or a cultural anomaly representing a romantic, populist turn away from the global? Is artisan production limited to a narrow range of expensive, high-end retail products, or are we observing a broader shift from homogeneous, mass-produced, mass-marketed products to handcrafted, limited-production products that engender a more personal relationship between producer and patron? If the artisan economy is part of a seismic shift in how we do things, is this transformation grounded in a larger moral shift in values toward local, sustainable, self-reliant systems of making and using? In the chapter on economic development, we recognize that Portland's artisan economy has grown organically because of the fortuitous intersection of many variables, but that public decisions were relevant. We suggest some strategic interventions that could be integrated into the larger project of building a good city.

Brew to Bikes represents our shared love of Portland. It is a celebration of the artisans of the city and an analysis of economic change. It has been written to appeal to popular readers, professionals, and academics. Locals who love Portland—and those beyond the city borders who look to Portland for leadership in planning, civic life, and livability—will now discover the relevance of its economic transformation. Popular readers will appreciate the vibrant details of urban living and the creative subcultures that energize our city. Professionals, including city planners, consultants, and developers who work in the arts, tourism, and development should appreciate our insights into economic change. The book's academic audience is found in many disciplines. *Brew to Bikes* would be an engaging supplemental text for undergraduate and graduate courses in popular culture, community and economic development, urban sociology, arts economics, and sustainable cities.

Brew to Bikes offers something different than similar books on arts, culture, and economic development. Where they focus on the iconic first-tier cities such as New York, London, or Los Angeles, *Brew to Bikes* takes as its subject one of the fast-growing medium-sized cities where most urban growth in the United States is currently taking place.[11] It also provides a richly detailed examination of artisan activity across an entire city rather than within an atypical neo-bohemian neighborhood. And it brings attention to the production aspects of the new economy rather than an exclusive focus on consumption. More than other books of this genre, our book provides a comprehensive and accessible framework (the artisan approach to working and living) for understanding the changing nature of work in a post-industrial economy. This framework integrates a traditional artisan worldview with new insights about the role of cultural industries in urban development, a new moral orientation to sustainability, and the paradoxical emergence of local distinctiveness in a global economy. In other texts, artisans are the backdrops for structural changes in the larger economy, in *Brew to Bikes* they are conscious agents of the change they embody. Lastly, this book describes a second wave of doing things differently in Portland and in Oregon, a place that has, for two decades, held reader interest. That wave builds on values embodied in Oregon's land-use planning and Portland's revitalization, and helps explain people's continued attraction to this place.

CREATING *BREW TO BIKES*

MANY HANDS, HEADS, AND HEARTS helped create *Brew to Bikes*. It began as a research project about Portland's independent fashion industry, undertaken by Marianne Ryder, Shanna Eller, and myself, and supported by an Institutional Career Support grant from Portland State University. As we presented our findings at academic conferences, we realized our research was leading us to a broader conceptual thesis about working and living in a post-industrial economy. Progressively, a book emerged as the proper vehicle to investigate what we had begun calling the artisan economy. Realizing that such a project required more help, I applied for and received a Faculty Enhancement Grant to broaden the research. At the end of spring term, 2008, we put out a general call to students, enticing them with food, local beer, and the possibility of becoming a chapter author in a book about Portland's artisan economy.

The response was surprising, even overwhelming. Over forty students expressed interest in the project, a good sign that the artisan economy concept was addressing something essential and relevant. At the first organizational meeting, twenty-two students committed to the project with a full understanding of their responsibilities. They committed to weekly seminars on research protocols and writing techniques, understood that their chapters would be subject to serious review and editing, and accepted the reality that their only reimbursement would be a small honorarium for expenses. They did all this knowing that the prospect of getting their names in print was dubious given that we did not yet have a publisher.

It was a good summer project, but as expected, opportunities took some students in other directions. In the end, fourteen students submitted chapters either as sole or joint authors: Renée Bogin, Tracy Braden, Melissa Cannon, Laura Cesafsky, Lauren Larin, Moriah McSharry McGrath, Serenity Madrone, Joshua Roll, Oliver Smith, and Bridger Wineman.

The summer work got the book on track and during the next academic year, one that coincided with my sabbatical leave, we began to hit our stride. My latent talent as a promoter was stirred to the surface. Students who dropped in for a chat were promptly enrolled in the project. The first was Alison Briggs, who volunteered to write a chapter on entrepreneurial non-profit organizations, including Free Geek, where she worked. When some research assistant money became available, I brought her and Laura Cesafsky on to do several more chapters each. Their work was stellar. Next was Talia Jacobson, who needed a research course to finish her planning degree. She worked with Tracy Braden and Lauren Larin to reframe and rewrite the food chapter. Serendipitously, I connected with Rebecca Ragin, a freelance author with considerable experience writing for coffee trade journals. She agreed to write the coffee chapter. Amanda Hess was between internships and volunteered to do the information technology chapter. Bridger Wineman was enticed into taking on a second chapter to fill the gap on artisan live/work spaces for artisans. During all this, I was personally encouraged by Ethan Seltzer, Director of the Nohad A. Toulan School of Urban Studies and Planning, who saw great promise in the project and supported it with tuition remission funding for student researchers.

In a planned and piecemeal way it all came together, much like the process of improvisation and assemblage that is characteristic of artisan work. But one piece was still missing—no book contract. Surprisingly, most of the chapters were in draft form before we found a publisher; a great leap of faith for those contributing to the project. Finally, in spring of 2009, Ooligan Press agreed to publish *Brew to Bikes*, mainly due to the enthusiastic promotion by acquisition editors Megan Wellman, Parisa Zolfaghari, and Logan Balestrino, who sold the project to Dennis Stovall, Coordinator of the Publishing Curriculum, and the Ooligan Press executive committee. Thus began our fruitful collaboration with Ooligan Press. Working with graduate students who are learning the craft of publishing has truly been rewarding and inspiring. I was looking for editors with an eye for detail and a good sense of what could be trimmed to bring the book down to a manageable size. I was rewarded with a fine team who were both fun to work with and learn from. Thanks to managing editors Katie Shaw, Dehlia McCobb, and Julie Franks. I was also invited to participate with the graphic design group. What other author has a team of ten designers competing to create the cover design and having the privilege of participating in the final selections? Every author should have so much fun. Thanks to Ellery Harvey, Cory Freeman, and the rest of the Ooligan Design team, and thanks to all who have made this project a reality.

CHAPTER 1
GENESIS OF THE CONCEPT

Charles Heying
Marianne Ryder

PORTLAND'S ARTISAN ECONOMY is a particular and local response to the larger economic forces that are changing our world. In this chapter, we describe these economic forces and how urban elites and grassroots activists have responded to them. We show how urban elites largely focus on policies to attract mobile capital and creative workers to their communities. Alternatively, we show that the grassroots response is grounded in self-reliance and sustainable development, and is reclaiming the integrity of work. The purpose of this chapter is to situate the artisan economy within the context of these responses and prepare the ground for the artisan economy synthesis presented in Chapter 2. We begin with two concepts, Fordism and post-Fordism, which academics have used to describe distinct periods of capitalist development.

FORDISM

FORDISM REFERS TO the economic and institutional forms that became dominant in the late nineteenth century and reached maturity in the post–World War II period. It is an economic system organized around mass production and mass consumption, and is so named because important aspects of the revolutionary restructuring of economic organization were introduced by Henry Ford. Hallmarks of the Fordist system are standardization of component parts and assembly line manufacturing in which each worker performs a single task. Fordism also describes a centralized organizational structure in which information flows "up the chain of command" and where roles within the firm, such as management, accounting, marketing, and personnel, are specialized and professionalized. A Fordist system is one in which significant advantages can be realized by increasing the scale of operations as per-unit costs for equipment and overhead are reduced by increased output. In its more mature form, Fordism also involves an increase in the scope of operations as the standard managerial and distributional functions are mobilized for new product lines and services.[1] For example, General Electric began in electrical generation and appliances but now is diversified into infrastructure, finance, and media.[2] Other characteristics of the Fordist system are huge manufacturing complexes that anchor the urban economies of iconic locations such as Detroit and employ large numbers of unionized laborers who expect to be working for the company through most of their employed lifetimes.

The mirror of mass production is mass consumption of standardized output. As more workers move from rural occupations to the urban wage labor force and receive a share of the benefits of productivity through higher wages, they are able to purchase the products that keep the factories running. These products became part of their lives, shaping their behaviors, attitudes, and expectations. The attitudes of mass consumption reflect naïve optimism about a better future in which new products alleviate the drudgery of everyday tasks and new options in mobility and connectivity are made available to all. This faith in progress is created and reinforced through mass marketing techniques that set the standards for taste and fashion and create the demand and expectation for more and better products and services.[3]

The conflicts of Fordism are resolved in what is called the welfare state consensus. This includes an activist nation-state that uses legislation, money management, and investment power to create urban growth regimes and full employment. It also includes a negotiated settlement between industry leaders and unions to share productivity gains.[4] The Fordist period is generally recognized as fostering urban prosperity, increased real wages and standard of living, and decreased wealth differentials between income groups.

POST-FORDISM

POST-FORDISM DESCRIBES THE PHASE SHIFT in the market/industrial system in which the success and contradictions of the Fordist system are resolved in a new set of economic and institutional relationships. The watershed of this period of crisis and transformation is generally set around 1970. The factors that create and define the shift are many.

Decentralization: Disruptive technologies, especially in transportation, communications, and information technologies lowered transaction costs and eased the friction of space, thereby reducing the advantages of hierarchical control and central location. Processes that formerly were most efficiently done in-house and at a central location could now be done at a distance, hived off to independent units, or sourced out to specialized producers. Functions requiring routine operations, back office, and line manufacturing were transferred to low-cost locations, first from central cities to suburbs, then from north industrial to sunbelt locations, later from U.S. to international locations, always in search of new markets, lower-cost labor, and reduced regulatory oversight.[5]

Networked forms of organization: In the post-Fordist era, centralized command-and-control organizations give way to networked forms of organization. Networked organizations are characterized by permeable boundaries, multiple loose associations, and customizable resources provided by specialized providers. Communication is point-to-point rather than through formal organizational channels. Collaboration within networks requires higher levels of trust and commitment and is reinforced through repeated interactions. Firms within a network are more autonomous, and authority in the network derives from specialized local knowledge rather than position in the hierarchy. Networks of organizations are believed to be more flexible and responsive to risk and opportunity.[6]

Rise of knowledge and service economy: The increasing complexity and sophistication of society needed to build and service infrastructure, move products, and plan and manage organizations creates a space for new independent knowledge industries and knowledge workers in finance, media, education, marketing, planning, legal services, development, and more. This complexity also greatly increases non-professional service work as a part of the economy; jobs such as those of apartment managers, day care workers, elevator service technicians, and truck drivers. Increasingly these knowledge industry and service firms operate independently, providing services on contract.[7]

Flexible specialization: The accumulation of knowledge in science, engineering, and design applied to production processes has increased the scope and complexity of all forms of manufacturing, but it has also lowered the barriers to entry. Specialized, single-purpose machines and systems that required large investment are being replaced by sophisticated and programmable machines that can be repurposed for short runs of specialized products. These machines are particularly suited to smaller innovative firms, who specialize in quick turnaround, short-run, customizable services.[8] Flexible specialization also refers to the clusters of independent skilled craft workers or subcontracting firms, like those in the film industry, who can be assembled on a project-by-project basis.[9]

Bringing place back in: Scholars across disciplines have evolved in their understanding of the importance of place in a globalized economy. At first they suggested that place would become irrelevant. As evidence, they noted the proliferation of global franchise operations in food, hospitality, and entertainment that make world cities nearly indistinguishable from each other. Similarly, they observed how footloose firms making standardized products were able to assemble the raw materials, technology, and labor wherever costs were lowest, thereby muting traditional location-specific advantages. But recently, scholars have rediscovered the importance of place. Clusters of innovative firms—like those in Silicon Valley or the London financial district—that have special skill sets, access to specialized resources and labor, and benefit from face-to-face informal interactions to generate new ideas and coordinate projects, demonstrate that place remains relevant in a globalizing economy.[10]

Breakdown of the welfare state consensus: As globalized firms become fully embedded in source and marketing networks, faith in the regulatory power of the state has given way to faith in the coordinating power of free markets. This has fundamentally undermined the welfare state consensus that guaranteed full employment and the equal sharing of productivity gains between capital and labor. Also, it reduced the commitment of the federal government to funding social welfare and urban revitalization programs.[11]

RESPONSE FROM URBAN ELITES

City as an entertainment machine: As urban economies shifted from Fordist industrial production to post-Fordist knowledge, and service industries and globalization increased competition between cities, a consensus developed that central cities had increasingly become sites of consumption rather than production. In a global economy, cities are thrust into competition to attract not only the mobile capital of multinational financial, technological, and entertainment industries, but also the educated and mobile workers who have the skills required by these industries. These sought-after educated and new-economy workers do not necessarily go where the jobs are located. The combination of technological changes, globalization and widely available internet connections means that workers with the right set of skills and education can choose where they want to live, and these workers seek out places that offer a mix of urban amenities and "quality of life." To attract these high-income workers and the footloose new-economy industries to the city, many urban policymakers focus their entrepreneurial efforts on remaking the city into what Lloyd and Clark label "an Entertainment Machine."[12] An important aspect of the entertainment machine strategy is to elevate the role of arts and culture in the economic and redevelopment efforts of central cities.

Stevenson[13] analyzes the "reimaging spectrum" of ideas underlying the emphasis on entertainment and culture in urban development since the 1980s. At one end of the place-making spectrum are the cities that depend upon what Stevenson labels the "Americanization" strategy, based on urban spectacles and shopping. Americanization-style projects are designed to create an image of a particular city as an attractive and fun place to visit and conduct business. These cities launch urban rebuilding projects, often near harbors or on former industrial sites identified as blighted or decayed, to create urban consumption zones that will attract tourists. Urban entertainment venues constructed during the 1980s and 1990s include sports arenas, arts facilities, and festival malls—all of which were promoted as ways to appeal to mobile capital and labor as well as to generate new city revenues and jobs through related businesses such as restaurants, hotels, and retail shops. The resulting spaces, such as Baltimore's Harborplace, Boston's Quincy Market, or London's Docklands, tend to have a sameness about them that marks them as global place-making spaces.

At the opposite end of the spectrum are cities that enact a set of development strategies focused on "local cultural identity, the promise of 'authenticity' and the idea of creativity."[14] This strategy of "cultural planning" or "Europeanization" combines local cultural activities with social and economic policies to improve the quality of life and foster economic development. Cultural planning is broadly designed to include cultural resources, activities, processes, and products—anything that constitutes local culture as defined by urban residents. In spite of the language of authenticity and creativity, the cultural planning strategy in practice is not very different from the Americanization version. Like the Americanization strategy, cultural planning tends to rely on image-creating projects, such as historical building renovations and new cultural events to draw people into the city, while investing little in activities focused around current city residents. Stevenson concludes that both Americanization and Europeanization place-making strategies rely more upon symbolic and idealized notions of cities than they do upon people's actual experiences of the cities.

Creative class: Richard Florida's creative class thesis introduced a new phase in the evolution of the entertainment/entrepreneurial city strategy.[15] While Florida also highlights the importance of quality of life for attracting highly skilled workers, he goes further in suggesting that cities abandon traditional strategies to attract corporations (even high tech) with tax abatements, incentives, and land assembly. Instead, Florida argues that industry and innovation will follow the creative class. Florida defines the creative class as "scientists and engineers, university professors, poets and novelists, artists, entertainers, actors, designers and architects," basically anyone involved "in work whose function is to 'create meaningful new forms.'"[16] He emphasizes that creative workers are an increasingly large and important segment of the workforce, now exceeding 30 percent. They are also more likely to be footloose and willing to seek out places where there are others who share their interests and values. The places they seek will be more urban and bohemian in outlook, more participatory and open, more diverse and tolerant. The willingness to welcome new people and new ideas creates "low entry barriers for people" and "a place where newcomers are accepted quickly into all sorts of social and economic arrangements."[17] Cities that have the cultural ambience that resonates with the creative class will enter into a virtuous cycle of growth, attracting or growing clusters of new-economy industries that, in turn, become thick with opportunity and possibility for change.

Florida's creative class thesis has produced a flurry of interest from urban elites anxious to attach their growth agendas to his thesis. Cities like Milwaukee, Wisconsin, attempted to rebrand themselves as cool and hip, updating their websites and promotional materials with references to their indie music scene and bohemian neighborhoods and pushing downtown redevelopment with new urbanist live/work/play appeal. Beyond the hype, the success of these efforts is questionable. Like Stevenson's critique of the cultural strategies of the 1980s and 1990s, rebranding efforts are quickly mirrored by cities elsewhere and are remarkable only in their similarity. More tellingly, Milwaukee sustained accelerated job loss, increased poverty, and continued racial and economic polarization during the rebranding campaign.[18]

Neo-bohemias: Milwaukee's failed attempt to rebrand itself as a hip location appealing to the creative class suggests that "coolness" is something that bubbles up from below rather than being imposed from above. The case of the Wicker Park neighborhood in Chicago demonstrates that spontaneous growth can ignite the virtuous cycle of creativity described by Florida. Richard Lloyd conducted a long-term case study of Wicker Park, a "neo-bohemian" neighborhood in Chicago, to analyze how an artistic community of visual artists, performers, and musicians developed within the neighborhood and how the environment stimulated artistic production. Artists began moving to Wicker Park in the 1980s but remained fairly isolated from one another until the establishment of a few key restaurants, coffee shops, and clubs that provided places for local artists to meet one another, socialize, and network. The presence of local "quasi-public" gathering spots helped foster creative collaborations and artist networks and supported an active and visible artistic presence in the city. These social spaces also provided jobs to young artists and venues for local musicians and performers. Neighborhood events and activities attracted media attention, which brought more artists to the area, along with others who were interested in the arts and the neighborhood. This concentrated pool of artists in one location also proved attractive to national cultural industries who were scouting new talent. Lloyd concludes that artist enclaves like Wicker Park serve as sites of "research and development" for mass-market cultural industries in film, television, and popular music, along with newer industries like web design.[19]

Creative cities: In 1995, Charles Landry and Franco Bianchini introduced the idea of the "creative city."[20] While it draws from a similar stream of creative class thinking, it provides a more nuanced and empowerment-based model of development. In their book *Creative City*, Landry and Bianchini assert that in a rapidly shifting economy, the creativity of urban residents is the one resource that cities can depend on to survive and adapt. Rather than advocating that cities spend resources and effort on attracting foot-loose corporations or members of specific occupational classes, they pro-pose an approach to urban planning that builds upon the unique potential of city residents, human creativity, and innovation to spur urban develop-ment. In his later work, Landry offers a toolkit to generate new ways of approaching urban problems and to stimulate relevant debates and urban policy.[21] When creative people and creative organizations work together in an urban setting, they create a "creative milieu" that fosters the formation of urban "innovative hubs."[22] Landry defines creative milieu as a specific location with the right "preconditions in terms of 'hard' and 'soft' infra-structure to generate a flow of ideas and inventions."[23] Hard infrastructure includes roads and other aspects of the built environment, as well as the organizational structures that support learning and networking, such as universities, community meeting places, and cultural facilities. Soft infra-structure refers to "the system of associative structures and social networks, connections, and human interactions" that constitutes the informal learning and social environment.[24] As part of the toolkit, Landry recommends a set of strategies to support a creative milieu, including a strategic planning process, establishment of indicators to measure urban creativity, and techniques to foster "creative thinking and planning."[25] Landry also offers suggestions for supporting creative processes in city planning, and includes case studies of various creative city projects.

Allen J. Scott's 2006 article on creative cities provides an overview of the concepts and characteristics of the creative city and discusses some of its pos-sibilities and pitfalls. Scott first provides a brief overview of the "historically specific forms of the creative city" that are emerging within the framework of the new economy.[26] He then describes some potential policy strategies to support economic development and creativity and discusses how creative cities fit within the larger global economy. He concludes with some caveats for those who see the creative cities' growth as the solution for all urban problems. According to Scott, local interconnected structures of work and production are the core components around which "social, cultural, and political" activities develop and interact with each other to define the geographically and historically unique identities of urban areas.

Competition and cooperation between urban areas also shape cities' unique characters and help foster local agglomerations and economic specializations which tend to create "a virtuous circle of agglomerated growth."[27] These agglomerations then become associated with specific geographic locations. The so-called new economy is notable for its tendency to create geographical agglomerations for certain industries, such as can be found in Silicon Valley and Hollywood. The new economy represents a recent phase of capitalism, and like other economic phases that preceded it, has created new urban structures that represent its unique characteristics. Some of the more prominent characteristics of this new economy include a predominance of networks of small firms that specialize in different aspects of production output and work to specifications that change frequently; project-based hiring practices that rely upon a labor force of "part-time, temporary, and free-lance" workers; and products that compete "not only on the basis of cost but also increasingly on the basis of their qualitative aspects."[28] In the social and political realm, the new economy produces sharp social divisions between the highly skilled workers at the top levels of the economic hierarchy and the unskilled, low-wage-earning workers at the bottom of the production hierarchy.

Creative cities share many new economy characteristics as they "are typically organized around production systems marked by shifting inter-firm networks and flexible labor markets"[29] that facilitate communication and learning between firms and workers while supporting creativity and innovation. These production systems also spawn a tendency for firms and workers from related sectors to cluster in specific locations. Another notable characteristic of the new economy is a connection between economic agglomerations that employ large numbers of creative workers and local quality of life and culture. Therefore, one part of a creative-city strategy combines economic development strategies with cultural development or "place-making and place-promotion activities."[30] While a creative-city economic development approach has been linked to Florida's creative-class argument, Scott critiques Florida's argument that cities should be attempting to attract the members of the creative class to spur economic development. He also warns against the notion that a creative-cities approach to economic development can work in all cases or that it will lead to some sort of "creative utopia."

RESPONSES FROM THE GRASSROOTS

WHILE URBAN ELITES are attempting to remake cities into lively entertainment locales or are promoting the more nuanced creative-cities or creative-clusters approach to economic development, grassroots activists are proposing quite a different response to the challenges of the post-Fordist era. Their response is grounded in self-reliance, sustainability, and artisan sensibilities. In this section, we examine the main streams of grassroots resistance: going local, going green, challenging the tyranny of work and consumption, rediscovering place and local knowledge, and rediscovering craft and the integrity of work.

Going local: Scholars in the "going local" tradition make a case for a more systemic shift to local self-reliant economies that will be more stable and resilient in a globalizing world.[31] In the world described by these authors, there is a moral imperative, an economic rationale, and gathering evidence that sustainable economies will develop local and renewable food, transportation, energy, and financing systems. Increasingly, they will substitute locally produced goods for imported goods.

Those who advocate for economies based on local production confront the prevailing neo-liberal orthodoxy that favors capital and corporate mobility over the welfare of workers and community. Going-local advocates challenge three core beliefs of market fundamentalists. The first belief is that the sole responsibility of corporations is to maximize profits for shareholders. The second belief is that competition for profits drives productivity and innovation so, in the long run, everyone will benefit through lower costs for goods and services even if some workers and communities are hurt in the short run. The third belief they challenge is that in a global world of mobile capital and labor, government regulation of the economy is an ineffective and anachronistic impediment to the efficient working of the market. Going-local advocates also challenge the prescription for survival proposed by market fundamentalists. That prescription says that the correct response to this global free-for-all is to attract mobile capital and increase exports in industries where the community has some competitive advantage. In short, the community should do anything it must to bring in export-oriented corporations that will create jobs, increase incomes, and support the local tax base.

Going-local advocates believe that the benefits of unfettered free markets are oversold and the costs are ignored. They argue that cities that attempt to attract firms through tax abatements, land assembly, lax regulatory oversight, and the suppression of wage expectations are engaged in a competitive "race to the bottom."[32] The collective outcome of this destructive competition, even for the winners, is communities saddled with debt, tax shifting from corporations to individuals, underfunded public institutions, stranded infrastructure, environmental degradation, and the demise of civic trust as citizens feel victimized by paying higher taxes for fewer services.

Supporters of self-reliant communities identify the period of ascendancy of neo-liberal orthodoxy as one of increasing stratification of wealth and income. During this period, quality-of-life indicators fall as mobile corporations increasingly offload their responsibilities for taxes, health care, and pensions. They attribute the increase in child poverty and family stress to the forced participation of more household members in a lower-paying labor market. They argue that the free market strategy has not halted job losses; it has only freed corporations to shift or outsource production to sites of lower labor costs. They observe how big-box retailers undermine small businesses that have served the community for generations as employers, civic leaders, and supporters of charitable causes. They note the resurgence of income, age, and racial segregation as the less mobile have been stranded in declining communities. They see cheap goods and labor insecurity encouraging the rise of wasteful consumption and worker disempowerment.

But the most substantive loss, according to going-local advocates, is that the control of decisions that affect workers, civic institutions, and cities moves out of the councils of community and into the boardrooms of absentee corporations. Likewise, the economic surplus created by the labor and ingenuity of local workers is taken from the pockets of community members and put in the hands of anonymous corporations. As the goals of community and mobile capital have separated, the transfer of wealth and control has greatly increased the risk to the community and decreased its ability to respond.

Advocates of going local offer an alternative model, what they call "economics as if community mattered."[33] They urge communities to stop the destructive competition for footloose firms and instead build resilient local economies based on community-owned enterprises and locally distinct, homegrown, socially responsible businesses. Because their equity is anchored in community, they believe that cooperatives, housing trusts, employee-owned enterprises, community-development banks, credit unions, and public-owned utilities will sequester wealth for the community rather than the owners of capital. They suggest that communities experiment with local currencies and small-scale energy production. They urge local governments to adopt living-wage ordinances and building codes that require use of local contractors, labor, and locally sourced materials. Local governments should also provide space and seed money for community gardens, farmers' markets, small business incubators, and neighborhood storefront renovations. Going-local advocates understand that trade with other areas is both necessary and beneficial, but they urge citizens to be socially conscious consumers and localities to form global networks with like-minded communities. Advocates of self-reliant communities believe that changing the paradigm from capital supremacy to community benefit will unlock many more avenues of innovation that will take full advantage of local markets and talent to build capacity at the local level.

Going green: The movement for sustainable cities arises from a similar concern with the consequences of unfettered free markets.[34] The mission of the movement is to identify and strengthen the tools available to cities to reduce the social and environmental impacts of unregulated urban development. The movement seeks to encourage livable communities that are supportive of human interaction and that respect the limited carrying capacity of the natural environment, both locally and in terms of the resources and energy that cities draw from distant hinterlands. The ideal sustainable city is compact and designed to encourage pedestrian, bike, and transit travel. It is a mixed-use city with less-rigid boundaries between working, living, and social spaces. Within neighborhoods, residential options are available for the full spectrum of groups, classes, and needs. Housing is located on narrow, tree-lined streets with sidewalks to encourage interaction and reduce heat-island effects. Neighborhoods have shops, offices, schools, and public spaces within walking distance.

Sustainable cities are closed-loop systems where recycling, deconstruction, and repurposing of materials are the cultural norm. In sustainable cities, local governments offer incentives to reduce water runoff through green roofs, rain gardens, and reduction of impervious surfaces. Residents are given incentives to replace overwatered, chemically treated lawns with low-maintenance native landscapes and productive home gardens. Sustainable cities implement environmental zoning to preserve stream buffers and generously fund restoration of polluted wetlands, rivers, and urban streams. They rewrite building codes to encourage green building practices and utilize their power of procurement to jumpstart alternative energy and conservation practices. They support efforts such as farmers' markets and community-supported agriculture that substitute local products for imports.

Challenging the tyranny of work and consumption: At the heart of industrial capitalism is the promise of freedom—a release from a predictable life trajectory, traditional frames of thinking, and from the security and social responsibility of community. This liberation fires the drive for innovation and accumulation and starts the engine of productivity that produces a seemingly endless variety of new things. As capitalism kills old social forms, it creates new ones to serve the engine of production and provide a means of social cohesion in the unsettled environment. One of these new social forms is the consumer.[35]

Liberation from traditional culture leaves a deeply felt insecurity. One function of consumption is to becalm social insecurity with the promise of egalitarian progress and perpetual abundance. Buying the latest gadget creates a sense of inclusion with what's happening, of being a part of the incremental innovations that are reshaping the brave new world. Buying and consuming are part of an individual's continual social surveillance, the universal project of self-betterment to prepare one to ride the wave of the next big thing. This process is powerfully reinforcing because innovation creates a world in which success depends on the mastery of new modes of operation.[36]

A second function of consumption is to create class and lifestyle distinctions in a society where the old forms of status and distinction have been undermined. In the leveling created by mass production, the conspicuous consumption of elite early adopters soon becomes the aspirational consumption of the bourgeois, and eventually the imitative consumption of the masses.[37] This inescapable cycle of product devaluation propels successive rounds of innovation and consumption. Cultural mediaries drive this process with ever more aestheticized products and experiences connected with new presentations of self and lifestyle.[38]

In creating the consumer, capitalism links several powerful psychological drivers: a balm for insecurity, the illusion of distinction, and the promise of abundance. The downside of this social invention is the creation of a culture of insatiable needs and unfettered growth, a destructive cycle of work-and-spend that ultimately creates wage slavery, exploits the environment, and undermines autonomy.

Voluntary simplicity: As industrial capitalism took off in the late nineteenth century, the issues of wage slavery, self-reliance, and autonomy were examined by perceptive observers such as Henry David Thoreau. In *Walden*, Thoreau describes the alternative economics of voluntary simplicity that liberated him from the tyranny of striving for wealth and security. He observed that "[t]he cost of a thing is the amount of what I call life which is required to be exchanged for it, immediately or in the long run."[39] Thoreau demonstrated that he could work a mere six weeks to fulfill his basic needs and be free the remainder of the year to develop his talents, capacities, and interests. Thoreau's willingness to examine the tensions between liberty and work has remarkable resonance with contemporary artisans, who often eschew predictable careers and live on minimal incomes to be free to explore their passions. Thoreau's examinations of the cost of convenience also have contemporary parallels. In *Walden*, Thoreau offers the example of a train trip he was contemplating. He calculates that he could walk the distance of the trip in a shorter time than it would take him to work for the price of the ticket. Similarly, today's cycling artisans argue that bicycle transportation is more cost-effective, healthy, and convenient when compared to the total cost of auto ownership and the average vehicle speed of autos in traffic.[40]

The voluntary simplicity movement is intellectually indebted to Thoreau, but also draws from a deep well of religious and philosophical traditions from Epicureans to Quakers. Advocates of simple living argue that "less is more" and that unlimited choice can be its own form of tyranny.

For them, consumerism is a diversion, an obstacle standing in the way of personal growth and living a life of balance. An important step for practitioners is to unlink the symbolic value of things from their functional value and perceived need from real need.[41]

Slow movement: The slow movement—a close relative of voluntary simplicity—began in resistance to fast food and the agro-industrial complex that supported it. Fast food represented all that was wrong with contemporary food systems: the loss of connection to local and seasonal foods and to an appreciation of the ecology, economy, and food preparation practices of the bioregion. From its initial critique of the food system, the slow movement has since expanded to slow cities, slow travel, and slow education. The essential critiques that join all these "slow" sectors are a resistance to standardization and speed-up in food, travel, and education; the deep appreciation of people, locality, and nature; and sensitivity to the natural rhythms of days and seasons.[42]

Rediscovering place and local knowledge: From the tyranny of work and consumption to what Jürgen Habermas has called "the colonization of the life world," scholars continue to be concerned with the expansion of the functional enactments of modernity into a dense web of mystified practices and tacit understandings that make up our everyday lives.[43] In *Seeing Like a State*, James C. Scott shows in fine detail how modern practices such as industrial forestry, cadastral maps, the urban grid, and standardized measurements undermined the legitimacy of local ways of knowing, interpreting, and acting.[44] They reduced a rich palette of local practices to the uniform simplifications of abstract systems. The many enactments of modernity that now populate our life world also served to redistribute power upward to the national state and to large-scale capitalist enterprises run by a professional managerial class. In his concluding chapters, Scott presents the rich possibilities of a return to what he calls "mētis," the practicality and particularity of knowledge of place and in place—knowledge and skill that are transmitted by culture and individually refined by repeated approximations.

Scott's description of historical conflict between local and abstract knowledge and his discourse on the richness of local knowledge is resonant with the work of preservationist organizations, such as Common Ground, that are attempting to find the balance between reclaiming lost cultural landscapes and the commodification of place. Common Ground has published a fine series of essays on local distinctiveness. Editors Sue Clifford and Angela King identify important characteristics of locality, such as *detail* and *particularity*: the small intricacies that create distinctiveness, like the particular drip tips of leaves that are suited to local climates; *authenticity*: the relationship of place, climate, and culture to a particular product; and *patina*: the wear and aging that produce a richness of surface and structure.[45] Clifford and King's sensitive parsing of the qualities of local distinctiveness is supported by a growing literature on the aesthetic, political, and communal qualities of place;[46] ecology of place;[47] place and sustainable design;[48] and the integration of culture, economy and place.[49]

Rediscovering craft and the integrity of work: The legacy of British essayist and critic John Ruskin—the intellectual founder of the Arts and Crafts Movement—infuses the sensibilities of contemporary artisans. Ruskin was deeply concerned with the dehumanizing effect of factory labor where the creativity and imagination of workers was disconnected from the process of production. He decried the Victorian obsession with uniformity and exactitude and the cold perfection of mass-produced goods. Inspired by Gothic architecture and the spiritual coherence of medieval work, Ruskin argued for a new aesthetic, one that honored the irregularities, eccentricity, and mistakes that were a natural part of human experimentation with material construction. He believed that perfect workmanship was unnatural and that the evidence of improvisation was a sign of humanity and humility. For Ruskin, the factory removed the worker from the creative process and from nature itself, but salvation could come from the redemptive reintegration of beauty, craftsmanship, and utility. Ruskin's work touched his generation and ignited the Arts and Crafts Movement that greatly influenced art, architecture, and design on both sides of the Atlantic, from the 1870s through the early decades of the twentieth century.[50]

William Morris, socialist and designer, implemented many of Ruskin's ideals. His design firm, Morris and Co., became a working model of Arts and Crafts ideals. Rejecting the elitist standard of his day that art was the exclusive domain of painters and sculptors, Morris focused on the design of everyday household objects such as furniture, wallpaper, glassware, and pottery. He believed that ordinary people would be lifted in spirit if the things they used were well designed and aesthetically pleasing. Morris practiced the principles of his democratic art in his workmanship and in the organization of his firm. A hands-on designer with a deep interest in and knowledge of the materials and the production process, Morris encouraged a type of labor democracy that allowed the workers considerable creative autonomy. Unlike other utopian experiments of his era, Morris's firm thrived while remaining true to its principles of integrating work, life, and art.[51]

The Arts and Crafts Movement is no longer the potent social force it once was, but the craft ideal is periodically revisited, most recently by urbanist and philosopher Richard Sennett. In craftwork, Sennett finds a way to heal the modernist rift between manual and mental labor. Craft joins the head, hands, and the material in a continuous process of resistance and response. The mental skills of playful experimentation, appreciation of ambiguity, and confidence that comes from mastery are particularly relevant to our current time. Working for the intrinsic reward of a job well done rather than its exchange value enables the work to transcend the maker. For Sennett, the larger claim for craftsmanship is its democratic promise. The craft approach of learning by doing is available to all, helps us become more fully human, and trains us in self-governance, the essential tool of good citizenship.[52]

Conclusion: The post-Fordist era created severe strains on central cities and urban economies. City leaders largely followed a growth agenda to attract mobile capital and creative class workers. The response from the grassroots was quite distinct. They rejected the neo-liberal model and opted for a model of local, small-scale, self-reliant, artisan-like enterprises that would not overwhelm the carrying capacity of the region and that could sustain themselves over the long term. In the next chapter, we synthesize what we have learned about working and living in the post-Fordist world. We describe this synthesis as the artisan economy.

Chapter 2
Characteristics of an Artisan Economy

Charles Heying

It is said that the laborer works with his hands, the craftworker with her hands and head, and the artisan with his hands, head, and heart. This homey maxim succinctly grounds the integrative principles of the new orientation to economic life that we are calling the artisan economy. The term artisan economy is our own, but it has some precedents. Scott uses the term "neo-artisan manufacturing" to refer to industrial firms that make special-order, short–run, high-design niche products.[1] The term artisan sector is more commonly used, but it is usually restricted to fine-art production, traditional crafts, and specialty foods. Our term, artisan economy, stretches the definition beyond art and craft to something broader, something grounded in the artisan approach that signifies a new orientation toward the making and use of goods; an economy that integrates the work of hands, head, and heart.

In the preceding chapter, we drew eclectically from traditions as diverse as nineteenth-century philosophy, contemporary economic geography, and the complex ecology of local production. In describing the *characteristics* of the artisan economy, the work of this chapter, we synthesize the lessons of these works, selecting ideas and concepts but recombining them into something distinct. We intentionally draw sharp distinctions between an artisan economy and a Fordist economy. We do this with a full understanding that contemporary economies are not one or the other but something of both. Similarly, we are aware that some of the sectors we include in our description of Portland's artisan economy do not perfectly fit our idealized model. We purposefully paint in high contrast in order to highlight the differences we observe.

This chapter serves two additional and possibly contradictory purposes. First, it is a manifesto for the artisan economy as a path of resistance in a globalizing world, a path that is immediately accessible to individuals and communities who are looking for alternative futures. Second, it is a statement of expectations in a rather conventional research project. The chapter authors who interviewed artisans for this book used concepts developed in this chapter to frame their interviews. In their chapters, they discuss the extent to which their respondents supported or contradicted our expectations of an artisan way of living and working.

QUALITIES OF ARTISAN PRODUCTS

Handmade: Artisan products are most often described as handmade and one of a kind, while modern industrial products are described as standardized and mass-produced. Fordist economies excel in producing uniform products in high volumes for low cost. The production process is organized intentionally to exclude producer-induced variation that might compromise uniformity, quality, and efficiency. Artifacts of the production process—like the break lines in molds, or accidental marks like thumb prints that would establish a connection between the product and its making—are removed, their appearance a sign of imperfection. The ideal is a product that is uniform in character, quality, and price.

The industrial product is once removed from the touch of the designer, whose creative work largely precedes the production process. The hegemony of mass-production techniques constrains the creative interventions of the designer and reinforces the anonymity and distance of the design touch. Materials in the mass-production process are likewise undervalued. The character of the material is manipulated to serve its mass-production and commodity purposes. The inherent integrity of the material is disguised by finishes to heighten product appeal or repositioned through faux design to seem to be something more precious than it is. The product is packaged in all of its aspects and meanings.

Artisan products integrate design and production, intentionally reveal the touch of the maker, and honor the inherent qualities of the material being shaped. While the artisan may employ a repeated set of skilled actions to

41

produce many items that are similar, variations in production are expected and valued rather than discarded. Obsessive uniformity is not the goal; the goal is to make a product where design incorporates and reveals the producer and her mastery of the process. A wheel-thrown pot reveals the slight indentations of the potter's fingers as she shapes the form and thickness of wall; it retains the slight asymmetry of line that results when the wet pot is moved from wheel to drying bat; it celebrates, as an element of design, the mark of the potter's thumb where she seals the handle to the body of the vase. These touches, adjustments, and adaptations are celebrated as artful elements of an integrated process of design and production. When they come together in the moment of creativity, the artisan work shows, in its total presence, how the touch of the artisan has shaped the medium in a way that reveals some wonderful aspect of its materiality.

Outside of the traditional crafts like pottery, the touch of the artisan is found in the unique problem-solving approach that results in an artful solution to a complex design challenge. For example, a design-build firm develops a reputation for skillful renovations of period housing; specialized manufacturers are sought out for their ability to repair or replace production equipment on a tight schedule; a house-moving firm develops a specialty in moving large commercial buildings. In these examples, the mark of the artisan is evident in the reputation of the firm for complex and rapid problem solving using an assortment of specialized tools and techniques honed over an extended period of experiential learning.

Authentic: While artisan products are often described as higher quality than standardized products, this sense of quality derives from a sense of integrity rather than the inherent functionality of the product. An inexpensive mass-produced dinner plate may be more durable, and perhaps even more serviceable, than a hand-thrown plate, but it is perceived as lower quality. Authenticity implies wholeness or oneness, parts wholly integrated, the whole, one with its purpose. Not only must the details be right, but they must be coherent and rightly situated. It is a kind of aliveness, not beauty in a universal sense, but truthfulness.

Designed to age: Mass-produced items are intended to wear out, become dated, and be replaced. This built-in disposability is part of the ever-new, spotless consumption ethic of modernity. In contrast, artisan products are enhanced by use and wear. Like Willie Nelson's guitar, artisan wares embody a narrative of use through the vital evidence of their slowly accumulating change. Patina is created slowly, imperceptibly, deeply. It is not about what's on the surface, but how age has gotten into the surface. It is the vitality that is produced as a material interacts with the atmosphere, or a surface gets reformed by constant wear, or a structure settles in on itself and into the land. It is also the accretion and accumulation of unplanned additions: the moss on the stonework, the worn paths to the outbuildings. Patina is not reproducible; it can't be sped up. This constraint makes it one of the most valuable clues to authenticity.

Locally distinct: The term *terroir* is often used to describe the qualities of taste, texture, and appearance of foods derived from the soils, climate, and traditional production practices of a specific locality. Those with a discerning palate will recognize the singular taste of a Wensleydale cheese or a Willamette Valley Pinot Noir. Clifford and King write passionately about the importance of recognizing and understanding the complexities of locally distinct practices, products, and traditions. They define local distinctiveness as "essentially about places and our relationships with them. It is as much about the commonplace as about the rare, about the everyday as much as the endangered, and about the ordinary, as much as the spectacular."[2] They emphasize the dynamic interrelationship of culture, landscape, process, and production. What is locally distinct is not necessarily indigenous or derivative of elements of the landscape (that would eliminate the possibility of change and evolution), but it must become a part of the landscape. In a sense it must make its place, and its place must make sense. As Clifford and King note, the cows that produce Wensleydale cheese were not indigenous to the area but, over time, they were found to be particularly adaptable and suited to the producers who co-evolved their production practices to suit the land and climate.

Appreciated: Artisan wares are appreciated rather than simply consumed. Consider two loaves of bread: one a product of a mass-production bakery and one a product of an artisan bakery. The former is consumed, it fills you up; hopefully it meets your nutritional needs and may be "fortified" to accomplish this. The taste and texture are predictable, designed to appeal to the typical consumer. The goal is broad appeal so that production capacity is efficiently utilized and profits are maximized. The narrow goal of profit maximization competes with quality concerns, leading to selection of inputs that only just meet consumer tastes. In contrast, a loaf of artisan bread is appreciated. Eating the bread engages the senses in an experience of delight. Each loaf has a signature aroma and texture recognizable for the bakery that produced it. These aromas and textures become embedded in memory and explode to the senses with the breaking of the loaf. The artisan baker creates a relationship with the patron, offering them a deeper knowledge of the qualities of the bread by building a narrative of the product, its origins and making. Unlike the instrumental relationship between mass producer and consumer, the relationship of the artisan and patron is one of trust and loyalty. The patron trusts the baker to use the best quality materials, and to create a satisfying experience of taste and association. The baker is rewarded with a loyal patron who does not simply buy and consume but appreciates the quality and uniqueness of the artisan bread. In the artisan economy, quality will undermine the tendency (encouraged and amplified in the Fordist economy) to over-consume or accumulate a hoard of things because patrons will learn that appreciation is enhanced by simplicity and moderation.

Egalitarian: In a Fordist economy, elites attempt to establish a boundary between fine arts for the few and popular culture for the masses. Access to the arts and to the appreciation of beauty is reserved for those who possess the cultural capital of refined tastes and the wealth to exercise discretion. In a Fordist economy, popular culture reinforces this distinction by subjecting all products to price competition that drives down quality, dumbs down taste, and engulfs ordinary people with faux materials intended to satisfy short-term impulses and ultimately be replaced by a continuing stream of poorly designed products. The everyday becomes a treadmill of searching, buying, breaking, and finally replacing the inferior product with an unworkable substitute. In the artisan economy, these artificial boundaries between the aesthetic and the everyday are transgressed. The material aspects of everyday life that are immediately accessible to the ordinary person—the food, music, films, household items, gardens, fashions, tools and conveyances—all become objects of care and beauty in a wonderful fusion of art and utility. This egalitarian ethic extends to public spaces like parks, streets, transit options, festivals, and even back to elite institutions, like art museums, that are infected with this new egalitarian ideal.

ARTISAN WORK

Work as improvisation: Artisan training is a combination of apprenticeship, learning by doing, and skill sharing among a community of practitioners. Artisan skill is the accumulation of a bag of tricks, of knowing how and when to apply rules in a concrete situation. The artisan exercises a practical improvisational knowledge, the trained hand and senses, rather than abstract reductive knowledge. This knowledge is the feel, the hang of it, the knack, not overly accurate but as accurate as it needs to be, accepting of variation and exhibiting a practiced and joyful imprecision. It is adaptive, local, and situated knowledge rather than universal abstract knowledge. It is about this material, this place, this tool. Mass-produced products are largely disconnected from their production histories; ideally, the first batch is identical to the last. As a result of successive approximations and practical experimentation over time, the artisan and their creations evolve in the making. Artisan products reveal their histories and the deepening skill and experimentations of their maker.

Work as vocation: The Fordist worker has a time and place of employment, a work day, a paycheck, an anonymous identity as one of a class called labor. Labor is regulated to make for a governable workforce that is marginally protected from the worst abuses. Workers in the artisan economy are always on task but seldom at work. Work times are not fixed, rather they follow the requirements of the material, the rhythms of the project, or the flow of the season. Work follows the artisan around; it's an identity and a vocation. Educator Parker Palmer describes vocation as a dialogue where the material calls out to the learner: "Geologists are people who hear rocks speak, historians are people who hear the voices of the long dead, writers are people who hear the music of words."[3] Artisan work is always being practiced, and the artisan is always open to connections and opportunities for enactment. Exploitation in the artisan economy is often a form of self-exploitation, an attempt to apply limited energy to the insurmountable opportunities of the craft.

Working and living: The separation of places of production and consumption from places of residence, a defining characteristic of the Fordist economy, reified in urban zoning codes, is being reconfigured in the artisan economy. Several factors are pushing the reintegration of live/work spaces, including lower combined rents and transportation costs, availability of small-scale spaces suitable for artisan production, twenty-four-hour work styles, and the desire for the creative ambience of communities where the boundaries between living, working, and socializing are intentionally and enjoyably blurred. Scholars such and Lloyd[4] and Zukin[5] have provided rich accounts of bohemian enclaves where these artisan lifestyles flourish, but artisan workers can be found even in the sedate homes of traditional residential neighborhoods. On the block where one of the authors of this book resides, a typical middle-class neighborhood with modest homes and no hint of edginess, numerous households have members who work from home and off the clock. They include a part-time designer of children's costumes, an environmental consultant, a lighting specialist for media shots, two authors, a sculptor, a craft furniture builder, an owner of a basement recording studio, a long-term care consultant, an in-home daycare manager, a support supervisor for turnkey management software who splits work between international sites and his home, a landscape contractor and rock wall builder, an academic with a home office, and a producer of radio playlists who works from home for an out-of-state client.

ORGANIZATION OF ARTISAN WORK

Small-scale, high-autonomy, flexible specialization: Fordist production is large scale, vertically integrated, and hierarchically managed. The historical advantages of this organizational structure are lower transaction costs, economies of scale, market dominance, and the ability to provide a structure in which those with specialized talent (design, engineering, management, finance, marketing) can develop and refine their skills in service to the firm's product line. Artisan economies organize work differently. They are generally small- and medium-sized firms, flatter and more horizontally organized, with higher levels of firm and individual worker autonomy. They are characterized by their responsiveness to new product needs. The particular advantage of artisan firms is their ability to assemble resources in a flexible way. The audacious artisan firm can scale up or down quickly to meet market demand and can adapt new market technologies. This new flexible specialization is made possible by a cluster of supportive firms that make capital and specialized resources more accessible. For example, an artisan bicycle firm that sees an unexploited local niche (perhaps a bicycle that combines kid and cargo capacity for trip chaining) can search for prototypes globally. With that knowledge now instantaneously available, the artisan can purchase fully assembled bicycles or buy parts from global suppliers and experiment with various models that will appeal to local needs. It is the particular ability to access resources through personal networks, trade groups, blogs, and web-accessible product suppliers—and to mobilize the capital and activate the supply chain nearly overnight—that makes local artisan production possible.

Art of assemblage: The ability to assemble human, financial, and physical capital is remarkably fluid in the artisan economy. The audacious artisan can literally start from nothing and, with pluck and luck, build a substantial organization that can survive at any niche or level personally suited to the artisan entrepreneur. The particular skill of the artisan is in understanding how to mobilize these resources. The artisan economy is not an organization of command and control, but an organization of coordination, cooperation, and assemblage. It depends on social networks, trust developed through repeated interaction, participation in learning communities such as conferences, blogs, trade groups, and advocacy organizations, and being recognized in the small world of specialized suppliers and producers. The importance of the global networks is the modeling of opportunity, the sharing of knowledge and information, and the access to resources.

The importance of the local networks is the specific knowledge of the local situation and the ability to physically collaborate on projects that require cooperation to scale up, share resources, or assemble a project team to take advantage of a particular opportunity. It is also the ability to cooperatively build the interest in an artisan product or service. The network of engaged artisans will, through their expansive energy and enthusiasm, create the "buzz" about their new product or service. In terms of support necessary for artisans to take risks, being embedded in local networks collectivizes the risk. Failure for a particular firm is not catastrophic, as the specialized skills and connections that are acquired as an artisan practitioner will be valued by other more successful artisan firms and will provide an alternative path of opportunity. The reduced sense of risk resulting from an artisan's understanding of the upside of failure—combined with the intuitive knowledge that the firm is only a provisional boundary that temporarily identifies the collective efforts of assembled actors—helps make the artisan economy flexible and adaptable.

Artisan clusters: It is in the nature of the artisan work to create clusters of firms that elaborate product niches of taste, quality, distinctiveness, and service. Because of the unique quality of each product, it is more productive to create cooperative networks rather than to consolidate. For artisan firms, economies of scale are less relevant than flexibility, autonomy, creativity, and collaboration. The context in which small artisan firms can survive is one in which services that were formerly handled in house by large-scale firms (and that gave them scale advantages) are now available as needed and in scale for the small firm. Artisan clusters depend on other diverse firms that serve small-scale entrepreneurs across multiple industries: logistical and support services such as packaging, shipping, marketing, printing, accounting, inventory, payroll, and budgeting. With the new communications technologies and the fluidity of capital, even access to specialty suppliers and to credit is increasingly available to the small-scale artisan firm.

In an artisan economy, microclusters in one industry seed clusters in other industries because they share cultural values, engage in cross-fertilizing social networks, use similar entrepreneurial techniques of collaboration and assemblage, and make use of common suppliers of contract services. Artisans support other artisans, encourage their work, buy or barter each other's wares, and participate in a similar social milieu of musicians, eateries, and living and working spaces. In essence, they create and share "the scene."

Soft infrastructure and learning communities: Fordist firms tend to limit the flow of information by creating proprietary barriers. While they are constantly engaged in a search for new ideas and new opportunities, they simultaneously attempt to guard against sharing of their ideas with potential competitors. Fordist firms use knowledge to create temporary monopoly positions in order to enhance their price position. Artisans tend to be more open about sharing information and learning from others. Since so much of the product quality is embedded in the skill and approach of the specific artisan, there is more to be gained through sharing of techniques and resources than by hiding them. Consequently, artisan work tends to generate a plethora of soft infrastructure of listservs, blogs, websites, newsletters, trade zines, trade fairs, training workshops, and special events, as well as academic certificates, institutes, and centers that quickly spring up to seed and support specific industry clusters. Other soft infrastructure develops to encourage entrepreneurship and the skills of business management and collaboration.

For artisans, the additional transaction costs for working in a learning community are offset by the constant skill enhancement, currency of knowledge, access to resources, and pure fun of mobilizing the assemblage networks.

Low barriers to entry: Artisan enterprises seem first to appear in sectors that can be learned by doing (self-teaching, peer sharing, and apprenticeships), do not require difficult-to-attain professional licensure, have accessible production technologies and low-tech resource inputs, depend more on skilled labor than capital, and initially have minimal space needs that can be met by a variety of configurations. The low-rent storefronts and living spaces in declining areas of cities have been an important precondition for the emergence of neo-bohemian districts where artisans have thrived. The internet, as well, has created a new space for artisans. With collaborative websites like Etsy and powerful search engines, even the smallest artisan enterprise has a prime location on Main Street.

While we think of the typical artisan enterprises as a craft shop, eatery, or garage band, new artisan firms can be spun out in any part of the economy by those who possess technological expertise and are already immersed in production networks that give them access to upstream resource providers and downstream markets. The history of Portland's New Seasons Market is an exemplar of this development cycle. Nature's Northwest, the precursor of New Seasons, was a product of three entrepreneurial partners who opened a small natural foods store in 1969, which eventually grew from one store to three before being sold to GNC in 1996. Four years later, Brian Rohter, one of the founders of Nature's, parlayed his experience, his network of former partners, and funds from ninety-nine of his closest friends to launch New Seasons. New Seasons is bringing local and organic foods to the mid-priced market dominated by huge national chains. Opening its first store in 2000, New Seasons now has nine stores in the metropolitan area and over 1,400 employees.[6]

COMPLEX MORAL ECONOMY

Less is more: The essential dilemma of the Fordist economy is its unquenchable drive for growth and expansion. In the bottom-line vernacular of business culture, if you are not growing, you are dying. Paradoxically, this structural imperative for overproduction drives down the price of mass outputs and deadens the appreciation of inherent product qualities. As a consequence, producers are driven toward ever more intense competition based on price and output or conversely toward ever more elaborate product differentiation. In either case, they must make more. In the context of an unregulated competitive economy, the imperative to grow or die demands that all available resources be recruited into the production process and all possible costs be externalized. And while an individual capitalist may be inclined to recognize the social and environmental consequences of this dynamic, the competitive impulse that drives the Fordist firm works against taking comprehensive action to mitigate its downsides. It is the tragedy of the commons writ large. Resources invested by individual firms to support regulation or mitigate social and environmental externalities will be expropriated by the free-riding, non-cooperative firms. This structural flaw forces capitalists to disassociate cause and effect and express unjustifiable optimism about the limitless compensatory and regenerative capacity of the environment and human social systems. In simple terms, more is always better; resources are always available for exploitation; substitutes will always be discovered.

In an artisan economy, less is more, and better is better. The artisan economy deepens in place and in the relationship of place and product. The artisan product is continually refined by the application of accumulated knowledge about the product, its use, and its relationship to its environment and its user. This deepening creates a space for resistance to the insistent drive for consumption for its own sake. It encourages the patron to develop an appreciation for the inherent quality of artisan products and to reconnect to the social and ecological implications of production technologies. The Fordist economy is designed to exploit nature and expand without limits. The artisan economy is designed to work with nature, within limits, and be sustainable.

Local production and self-reliance: Fordist economies are characterized by separations: creator from production process, management from labor, producer from consumer, place of industry and consumption from place of residence, the market from its communal and environmental consequences. Reconceptualizing economic relationships around locality introduces more complex systems for thinking about work, use, and waste. Thinking of products in a closed-loop, local ecology reintegrates waste into the cycle of energy and material inputs and makes both artisans and patrons more cognizant of the cost, reconstitution, and risks of product inputs. A closed-loop economy is also one that considers the social consequences of work relationships for individuals and communities. Thus, the ethic of "going local" is really about understanding the social and environmental footprint of the local economy. It is both a practical effort and a moral one.

Resisting the homogenizing tendencies of the global economy, local economies will arise from and be connected to a particular place. Local economies encourage small-scale, local production because they value the importance of shorter chains of accountability where artisans and patrons develop relationships of knowledge and trust. For example, institutions such as farmers' markets have become the exemplars of the "going-local" economy because they specifically emphasize dialogue and information sharing between growers and patrons and because they establish standards of reliability, such as defining and enforcing codes of localness or highlighting local grower certification programs. This recognizes that shorter chains of accountability developed through personal or local reputational information will be more complex and reliable. The implication is that growers will share an ethical concern for the impact of the production process on the ecology of the region and a concern for socially just relationships between workers, owners, and buyers. Shorter chains of accountability, therefore, will create a market that favors producers whose practices have minimal impact on the environment and who are socially and civically responsible.

Other aspects of sustainability are engendered in the preference for local products, specifically a more rigorous understanding of the embodied energy of products. Products that have substantial weight and volume, such as food, embody large amounts of transport energy as they travel the thousands of miles that are now typical for global supply chains. Those who favor "going local" argue that the current low prices of industrial agricultural products are underwritten by subsidized energy that does not account for the environmental and social costs of extracting, transporting, and burning mostly non-renewable energy sources. The low cost of products delivered through global supply and production chains does not reflect the true costs of degraded environments, exploited labor, declining social infrastructure, and an intergenerational debt of lost opportunity and abused resources.

It is also assumed that creating an economy of local suppliers will keep economic gains democratically circulating in the local economy of small producers rather than being filtered upward and outward to non-local megacorporations whose assets are owned by an increasingly smaller population of wealth holders. Thus, local economies will better be able to protect themselves from global exploitation. Organizations outside the domain of local systems are less likely to have a sense of shared space and responsibility and are more likely to exploit localities. This can come from disruption of corporate takeovers and layoffs, monopoly price-gouging, the expropriation of local resources and revenues to distant profit centers, the destruction of local production by the dumping of mass-produced products whose appeal is elevated through mass marketing, or the inability to retain wealth in local financial institutions that are responsive to local needs for funding for infrastructure or innovation.

In its totality, "going local" embodies a complex practical and ethical calculation that local production, monitored through shorter chains of accountability, will be more likely to produce socially just working conditions; environmentally responsible practices, including the reduction of the embodied energy; closed-systems thinking about waste and reuse; and democratically circulating wealth. Rather than the exploitation and disinvestment of distant corporations, locally self-reliant economies will be willing to reinvest in the social infrastructure of the locality—that is, the governments, schools, health systems, civic organizations, and family networks that protect individual dignity, ensure community stability, and facilitate a resilient economy.

Wealth creation: An enduring concept of Fordist economic thinking is that economic growth comes from expansion of the traded industries. Local wealth increases when specialized industrial products or services that possess a competitive advantage are traded to other regions. The non-traded sectors, which constitute up to two thirds of private employment, are not considered wealth generators because they chiefly meet the needs of the local population for personal services such as health care, retail, and so forth. Non-traded sectors have been dismissed as engines of economic vitality because, in the words of one economist, "no state or metropolitan area can reasonably expect to expand its economy by developing a higher than average concentration of grocery stores."[7]

The artisan economy challenges this economic truism. Farmers' markets and locally oriented neighborhood grocery stores like New Seasons grow an economy by changing how and what food markets do. New Seasons is proactive in developing relationships with local and organic producers. It has a "buy local first" vendor policy and a private label, Pacific Village, to actively promote its connection to Pacific Northwest family farms. 27 percent of its products carry its distinctive yellow tag indicating their Northwest origins. New Seasons emphasizes its responsibility to the community through its educational and local giving programs, and its employment policies that encourage worker autonomy and provide full benefits even for part-time employees.[8]

This seems to be something different from simple import substitution. Import substitution is about replacing a product sold to a region by an identical product made locally. It comes down to a basic accounting decision for a firm or region. All things considered, is it more cost efficient to make or buy? With alternatives like farmers' markets and firms such as New Seasons, we see something different from simple cost accounting; we see the invention of a new relationship and a new way of doing things. A patron may not eat more, but may eat something that is better in quality and more sustainably produced. When locality itself becomes an important signifier for the embedded practices of a local artisan cluster that utilizes resources more efficiently (for example, less embodied energy, better fit of variety to ecology), that offers shorter chains of accountability (therefore reduces transaction costs), and that exhibits unique qualities of taste and style, then the non-traded sector becomes something relevant to wealth creation for the community. This new orientation challenges the more narrowly conceived idea of creating wealth primarily by selling more of what you produce to other regions. In the systems approach of the artisan economy, wealth is created by enacting more comprehensively understood production and distribution efficiencies, as well as new product qualities associated with the appropriates of production to place. When a product becomes better because it embodies these complex qualities associated with locality, it creates wealth by replacing a lesser product. This is the genius of wealth creation in the artisan economy.

Summary of artisan economy characteristics: In Table 1, we summarize our discussion in the form of a simple matrix comparing the characteristics of artisan and Fordist economies.

TABLE 1: ARTISAN AND FORDIST ECONOMIES COMPARED

Artisan Economy	Fordist Economy
Product Qualities	
Handmade	Standardized
Similar but not uniform	Obsessive uniformity
Variation is appreciated	Low tolerance for variation
Design is adapted during the process of making	Design separated from production process
Indications of the interventions of the designer are considered a mark of craftsmanship	Indications of the designer touch or production process are concealed
Integration of tool, material, artisan skill valued	Function, marketability, production efficiency valued
Authentic	Faux
Designed to age gracefully	Designed to be become dated, be replaced
Locally distinct	Universal, generic
Artisan wares are appreciated	Mass-produced products consumed
Egalitarian access to objects of beauty and utility	Art for the cultured; degraded popular culture for the masses
Work Life	
Improvisational work	Routine work
Local situated knowledge	Abstract universalized knowledge
Increasing skill of artisan worker is rewarded	Role of designer obscured by product brand
Work as vocation	Work for pay

Work follows rhythms of season, project	Work times fixed and monitored
Integration of work, living, socializing spaces	Segregation of work, living, socializing spaces

Organizational Structure

Small and medium scale enterprise	Large scale enterprise
High worker autonomy	Low worker autonomy
Flexible specialization	Vertical integration
Clustered, collaborative firms	Hierarchically organized firm
Coordination, cooperation, assemblage	Command and control
On-demand producer services	In-house producer services
Low barriers to entry	Proprietary knowledge and market dominance exclude competitors
Innovation supported by soft infrastructure and learning communities	Innovation protected by proprietary knowledge

Moral Economy

Less is more	Structural imperative for growth
Price related to appreciation of inherent product quality	Price driven by competition and artificially constructed scarcity
Complex systems thinking about work, waste, and use	Focus on firm survival and short term competitive advantage
Local, self-reliant enterprise	Footloose, dependent enterprise
Democratically circulating wealth	Surplus wealth extracted by global capitalists
Reinvestment in social and ecological infrastructure	Exploitation of social and ecological infrastructure
Lower transaction costs through shorter chains of accountability, higher trust level between producer and patron	Increasing share of product costs relates to need for intense marketing
Wealth created by transforming the non-traded sector	Wealth created by trading for competitive advantage

In drawing the distinction between Fordist and post-Fordist economies, some scholars have suggested that the important change is one from production to consumption. They argue that post-Fordist economies have solved the production problem and that now the challenge is how to stimulate consumption. For us, this insight does not represent what we are seeing and serves only to direct attention to one or the other side of the production/consumption coin. We suggest that something different and more essential is changing in economic life, something we have called an artisan approach to making and using. In this chapter we have distilled what are its basic characteristics, including the qualities of artisan products: handmade, authentic, locally distinct, and appreciated rather than consumed. We have also directed attention to how artisan work is done, its improvisational and vocational aspects, and to how artisan work is organized into small-scale, autonomous enterprises that substitute assemblage and collaboration for hierarchy and control. Finally we have emphasized the complex moral economy of artisan work, where the focus is on local self-reliant communities that embody shorter chains of accountability and democratically circulating wealth. In the remainder of the book, we look at Portland's artisan sectors in order to determine whether these characteristics are evident in the narratives of the sectors and its artisans.

PORTLAND'S SIGNATURE SECTORS

CHAPTER 3
BREW

Laura Cesafsky

IT WAS NOT as though I was heading to Puerto Rico for the beer—nobody does. Sun, beaches, and San Juan top the typical tourist agenda, washed down with a rum punch or two in the home of Bacardi. It was March, and I had flown across the entire continent to join family and friends for the sun, leaving behind the massive gray cloud that envelops Portland from October to May. Ironically, considering this was a vacation, I was also leaving behind some of the best beer drinking in the world. Portland has been called Beer City, U.S.A.; Beervana; Beertopia,[1] a land so rich in handcrafted, artisan brews that beer lovers have been known to make pilgrimages to imbibe—except not usually in March. It rains then.

Sunny Puerto Rico, on the other hand, is the land of Medalla Light, the ubiquitous, mass-produced lager that could substitute easily for Miller Lite—might even be Miller Lite. But I had done my homework. There was one beacon of hope for the beer lover marooned on this otherwise enchanting island: Old Harbor Brewery, Puerto Rico's lone craft brewer. We stopped in on one of the last days of our trip to rest our feet and quench our palates after an afternoon touring Old San Juan. Arriving around 4 PM—"happy hour" in the beer drinker's vernacular—we were greeted by the comforting malty aroma of beer brewed on site, as well as a completely empty bar. Oh well, more for us. We bellied up to the bar, and, minutes later, a fresh lager, stout, and pale ale were nestled safely in our raised hands. *Ding!*

Before long we were joined in our revelry by a young couple. Brushing their dinner menus aside as they sat down, they went straight for the sampler,

59

a collection of eight-ounce "tasters" of each of the five beers on draft. And in a move that screamed, "Sharing is for the schoolyard, not the bar," suddenly another sampler was on order, one for each of them. We were going to like these folks. Misunderstanding my expression, a confused amalgam of envy ("Why didn't I go for the sampler?") and amusement, they felt compelled to explain: "Oh, we're from Portland. We need good beer." I was surprised by the coincidence, but certainly understood the sentiment.

Perhaps the most remarkable thing about Portland's craft-brew culture is not the ubiquity of microbreweries—and there are a lot, more than in any other U.S. city—but the degree to which Portlanders have been acculturated to craft brewing. A full 50 percent of the beer consumed on tap in Portland is brewed in Oregon, and no respectable pub or restaurant in the city is without a local brew on draft.[2] They are on order everywhere, from top eatery Higgins, where the beer list is as meticulously conceptualized as the wine selection, to the Rose Garden Arena, home of the NBA's Trail Blazers and Widmer's pilot ten-barrel brewery. The Portlander has come to expect—to need—freshly brewed beer, with locally sourced ingredients, in five styles, even if they have to pay more for it, even if they are in Puerto Rico, land of sun, beaches and Miller—er, Medalla—Light.

FROM LOCAL TO GLOBAL: BEER-MAKING IN THE UNITED STATES

HOW IS IT that beer in America has become synonymous with tasteless, mass-produced lagers? Why has a new culture of beer sprouted in places like Portland? To answer these questions, we have to take a swing through American epicurial history. A good place to start is to note that all early American brewers were craft brewers, though out of necessity rather than the aesthetic iconoclasm that typifies the modern craft brewer. Until the 1840s, English ales—darker, richer, more diverse, and more potent than the German lager—dominated the American market. These beers were brewed in small batches and consumed locally because, in the absence of modern storage techniques, they would go bad in a matter of days.[3]

Then, in 1840, the first lager beer was brewed in Philadelphia. This event opened the doors for the relentless consolidation that would come to define the American beer industry. Lager beer was more time-consuming to make because it required several months to age in a cool storage area, but it could be kept longer in cool storage and was more amenable to bottling and shipping, and therefore to larger scale production. The great German migrations to the industrial centers of the East and Midwest launched the era of lager. But this early preference was later enhanced when U.S. brewers adopted the bohemian-style brewing technique of adding a rice grain adjunct to the all-barley malts. Developed in cities such as Pils and Budweis, the technique created a sparkling translucent golden lager that made the term pilsner interchangeable with lager, and Budweiser the name of the most popular U.S. brand.[4]

Initially, though, lager brewers were craft brewers, too. Every city had its clutch of smaller breweries, and the early German brewer sold mostly to the growing German immigrant community, often within a mile of the brewery. Locals would bring a pail to the brewery or saloon and bring home their daily supply. Over the course of the 1840s, most of what became the major brewers—Blatz, Miller, Coors, Best, Anheuser, Busch, Pabst, Schlitz, Stroh, and others—got their start as local brewers, remaining family-owned through the 1950s. But the 1950s marked a watershed for American brewing, as the mass production of lagers out of Midwestern cities like St. Louis, Cincinnati, and Milwaukee began to pick up steam. These cities benefited originally from their strong immigrant markets and their ready access to winter ice and cold storage caves. Later, as pasteurization, new bottling technology, and refrigerated rail cars were introduced, these cities pressed their locational advantages as transport hubs to expand their markets in the South and West. Smaller breweries suffered, and from 1947 to 2000, the number of independent, commercial U.S. beer companies decreased from four hundred twenty-one to just twenty-four.[5]

A critical juncture in the transformation of the American beer industry— not to mention the American palate— took place in the 1970s, as the new beer oligarchs engaged in a scuffle for market dominance later termed the "beer wars." The 1970 Philip Morris purchase of Miller Brewing Company marked the opening salvo. With the deep pockets of Philip Morris behind it, Miller increased production capacity and advertising funds and, using a technique that had been successful in cigarette marketing, introduced four new brands pitched to different market segments. While three of the brands were marginally successful, the fourth, Miller Lite, changed the game for the brewing industry, establishing an entirely new beer category.[6] Designed to please the bland modern palate and to appeal to the broadest market segment, light beers were marketed for their cross-gender appeal ("great taste, less filling"), convenience (easy-open cans), and pale, dry taste, with a minimum of the bitter hop flavor.[7] Driven by the success of its Miller Lite, Miller moved from the eighth largest brewer in 1970 to second in 1977. The other major brewers responded with their own painstakingly advertised iterations on the theme, and Anheuser-Busch eventually won the beer wars with its top-selling brand, Bud Light. Since 1992, light beer has been the most popular market category, seemingly marking the final step in the journey of American beer from hearty, small-batch ales to bland, mass-produced lagers.

The consolidation of the beer-making industry was so sweeping that, by 2000, only four companies controlled 96 percent of the domestic beer market: Anheuser-Busch, 54 percent; Miller, 23 percent; Coors, 13 percent; and 6 percent for Pabst.[8] Unable to expand profits domestically, American brewers took a sharp turn outward, following the traditional path of con-solidation and new market expansion into the global arena.[9] There, however, they were no longer the biggest fish in the sea, and the major American brewers became victims of their own game. In 2002, South African brewer SAB bought U.S. giant Miller Brewing. Soon after, Molson, Canada's largest brewer, merged with Coors, and then SABMiller and Molson Coors merged their U.S. operations in an effort to shave off a corner of Budweiser's market share.[10] The watershed moment, however, came in 2008, when Anheuser-Busch, the market leader and an icon of American brewing—of American culture—sold to Belgian InBev. Suddenly, all but Pabst, the smallest of the American brewers, was foreign-owned.[11]

THE RISE OF CRAFT BREWING

BEHIND BIG BEER'S MOVE to the international market lay a stark reality: since the 1970s, in the United States and other developed countries, consumption of mass-market beers was stagnating. Suddenly market growth was occur-ring only in the specialty and import sectors, where the strengths of mass-market brewers—large advertising budgets, efficient production, low prices, extensive distribution networks, and standard taste and quality—were less critical factors.[12] In the shadow of the great consolidations, the beer wars, and the ascendance of light lagers, artisan brewers were quietly changing the rules of the game. Returning to the basics of beer making, small craft brewers were creating a new market among those interested in distinctive taste and local connections.

The rise of craft brewing has to be understood in the context of the larger cultural trends of the 1970s. The Vietnam War, Watergate, and severe recession had wrought widespread suspicion of the "establishment" in its public and private incarnations. At the same time, major revisions to the American diet, first emergent in the 1960s, also went mainstream, as people rediscovered small, pure, upscale, and delicious food. These new sensibilities produced a market for a different kind of beer. At first, while craft brewing was just getting off the ground, much of its future clientele had to turn to imports—in the first half of the 1970s, sales of foreign brews rose by 88 percent. Home brewing also became increasingly popular, as clubs popped up across the United States and instructional literatures flew off the shelves. Despite being illegal since the repeal of prohibition, home brewing was so mainstream by 1978 that Jimmy Carter simply legalized it.[13]

Though the revolution in food and drink took hold nationwide in the 1970s, the West Coast was its spiritual home. In Berkeley, Alice Waters launched Chez Panisse, an influential bistro devoted to serving fresh, seasonal foods. At the same time, the first Starbucks was opening in Seattle to indoctrinate patrons in the finer points of artisan coffee. Northern California, in particular, became the early centerpiece of the nascent craft-brew economy. Frederick Louis Maytag III was one pioneer. He purchased the struggling Steam Anchor Brewing in San Francisco, maker of Anchor Steam Beer, and turned it around by making quality beer that advertised its old-fashioned character. The West Coast was also a home-brewing hub, producing a generation of self-taught brewers that would go on to launch an armada of commercial microbreweries. Few were as successful as Ken Grossman, whose Chico, California-based Sierra Nevada Brewing Co. became the model for many ambitious upstarts. Craft brewing was suddenly a viable, if risky, career option.[14]

So what exactly is craft beer? The Brewers Association, a trade organization that represents most U.S. craft brewers, has a technical definition: "An American craft brewer is small, independent, and traditional." Small means that annual production must not exceed two million barrels for a regional craft brewer, or fifteen thousand barrels for a microbrewer. (A microbrewery may have a bar or restaurant attached, and it becomes a brewpub if sells more than 25 percent of its beer onsite.) To be independent, a larger alcoholic beverage consortium may not own more than 25 percent of a brewery (purists, of course, would prefer total independence from big business). Traditional means that beers are mostly malt-based, though experimentation with additional, flavor-enhancing ingredients is encouraged and increasingly common.[15]

Though the distinction between mass-market beers and craft beers depends on attributes like company size and independence, Chad Kennedy, the brewmaster at Laurelwood Brewing Co., an award-winning craft brewery in Portland, thinks it's about the beer: mass-market beers, he says, are dumbed down and stripped of character and uniqueness (and, of course, bitterness) so as to appeal—or, perhaps better, so as not to offend—the sensibilities of the greatest number of people.[16] Formerly in advertising, Kennedy finds it telling that, until just a few years ago, beer commercials talked about everything except the beer they were actually selling. That has changed, perhaps in response to the recent growth of the craft-beer market, but still the objective is to avoid giving the consumer tangible information about what differentiates their product. "'Great taste, less filling.' What the hell is that?" Kennedy wonders. He mentions a recent ad by Miller that boasts of "triple-hopping" their Lite beer. "I suspect it means that they add hops three times as opposed to once," Kennedy says sarcastically. "Well, most beers have more than one hop addition. That's sort of how you make beer."

Differentiating craft beer by quality rather than by production process makes sense in America, where the decades-long reign of the mass-market brewers has left many people believing that watered-down pilsner is beer, period. Beer that is made to taste good, taste interesting—beer that pairs with food rather than simply washes it down—is inherently artisanal when held up against a product that is created specifically so as not to bear the markings of human creativity. Much of the excitement around craft brewing has been that it brings innovation back to beer making. Craft brewers reintroduce historical styles to the American palate even as they reimagine them for a modern audience.

Traditional English styles have benefited most from the craft beer movement, as stouts, porters, pale ales—and their hoppier cousin, the India

Patrons enjoy the atmosphere and art at McMenamins Market Street Pub in southwest Portland. Mural by Lyle Hehn. Photo © Rachel Moore

pale—are increasingly recognized and enjoyed. Still, as Portlander Bill Schneller, an amateur beer historian and nationally certified beer judge notes, that does not mean that they are all that similar to their original incarnations. "Beer history is not an unbroken line. Everything gets reinterpreted."[17] Take porter. Invented in the eighteenth century in England, porter was in serious decline by World War I. Modern American craft brewers have resurrected it, but the dark, creamy, chocolaty brew we know as a porter today would hardly be recognizable to its English inventors. For one thing, porter and stout—what we think of as porter's bitter, coffee-flavored cousin—were interchangeable terms.

As styles have proliferated with the growth of the craft-beer movement, they have been subsequently parsed and subdivided, as the "style Nazis," as Schneller playfully calls them, scramble to impart a classifying order on a chaotic and expanding beer universe. For the Great American Beer Festival, the world's largest craft-brew party and tasting competition, held annually in Colorado, categories are updated annually—inevitably making more complex, rather than simplifying, the encyclopedia of beers. This year, there are seventy-eight recognized styles, many with several subcategories.[18] The style parameters include quantitative measures of bitterness, original and finishing gravity, color, alcohol content, and ingredients, as well as qualitative guidelines meant to capture the intangibles that lend overall character.

The rapid growth in recognized styles points to the fact that innovation in brewing is moving in several directions. For one thing, a perpetual game of one-upsmanship has led maverick craft brewers to go for maximum booziness and bite. "There's a lot of envelope-pushing," Schneller says, with mild disapproval. "Like 'if you can make a big beer, I can make a bigger beer. If you can make a hoppy beer, I can make a super-hoppy beer.'" At the same time, brewers are playing with new combinations of spices and yeasts. They make new tastes to match the changing seasons, hearty winter ales giving way to lighter and fruitier summer selections. And, as if in protest against this cult of radical innovation, the newest trend in brewing is to doggedly recreate obscure, often all-but-extinct styles. Ever the beer hipster, Schneller is already on board. He has been brewing saison at home, a historical Belgian farmhouse ale that he will identify, when pressured, as his favorite style ("My favorite beer is the one in my hand," he prefers to say.) Fruity and extremely dry, it was brewed to quench the thirst of Belgian farmworkers. Schneller has also been experimenting with traditional porters and stouts. "I like that you can't buy them anywhere."

Like Schneller, Kennedy, the Laurelwood brewmaster, finds the creative element one of the best parts of brewing. He likes dreaming up flavors, concepts, and names so that they come together neatly in new commercial products. Since consistency is important, Laurelwood's flagship beers, like the Mother Lode Golden Ale, rarely change. But Laurelwood also makes around fifty seasonal, short-run beers every year, ample outlet for the imagination. Inspiration can come from many sources, including what other craft brewers are doing. "If there's a buzz about a beer—pardon the pun—we try to check that out," Kennedy says. Some Fridays, all six Laurelwood brewers gather for blind tastings, where their own beers are placed on a panel with commercially available craft brews of the same style. The idea is to see where a beer stands within the ever-shifting brew landscape. At the same time, something as silly as a clever name can launch a beer. In the lead-up to the 2008 presidential election, Laurelwood offered a super-hoppy seasonal called the Audacity of Hops, a riff on the title of Barack Obama's best-selling book. Such innovation has made craft brews increasingly popular. Craft brewing grew by 5.9 percent in 2008, while imports lost 3.4 percent and non-craft domestic grew just 0.6 percent.[19]

CRAFT BREWING IN PORTLAND

IF ANECDOTAL EVIDENCE isn't convincing enough, the numbers say it all for craft beer in Oregon: There are currently seventy-three brewing companies in Oregon, operating ninety-six brewing facilities. Even smaller cities like Ashland, Bend, and Hood River have their own breweries. What is more, the Oregon market is the largest for every craft brewer in Oregon. Another way of saying it is to point out that Oregon boasts the highest percentage of local craft beer consumption in the country, at 12 percent of beer consumed (compared with a 4 percent national average). A more impressive 37 percent of draft beer is Oregon-brewed, which adds up to a lot, because Oregon has the fourth-highest percentage of draft beer sales in the United States. This is a phenomenon unimaginable in, say, Mississippi, the least microbrewed state; Mississippi has just one microbrewery for a population of nearly three million.[20]

At the epicenter of this craft brew mania is Portland itself, the largest craft-brewing market in the United States. The Portland metro area has thirty-eight breweries—thirty in Portland proper—more than any other metro area in the United States. As Schneller says with pride, "Beer gets a tremendous amount of respect in Portland, much more so than it does nationally." That was not the case just twenty-five years ago, when Portland was slugging Budweiser in lockstep with the rest of America. The watershed year for craft brew was 1983, when a new law passed allowing beer sales at the site of production. The law paved the way for the now-ubiquitous brewpub. Almost overnight, what Schneller dubs the first generation of Portland breweries sprang up. Widmer, BridgePort, and Portland Brewing began commercial operations in 1984, and McMenamins opened its first brewpub location, the Hillsdale Brewery & Public House, in southwest Portland in 1985.

The legal change amounts to an enabling factor, but falls short of causal explanation. Why did craft brewing become so mainstream in Portland rather than, say, San Francisco, where it got its start? Culture matters, of course. Portland is proudly DIY and iconoclastic, but making these traits prime movers can be tautological; it is easy to say that DIY bike, music, and beer scenes developed because other things were already DIY, but what was DIY first? Certainly people like to support local businesses, an intuitive affinity for the underdog being something of a shared Portland trait. Lately, shopping local has been subsumed under the umbrella term "urban sustainability," the twenty-first century Portland brand, and it certainly helps to make micro-brewing a viable profession.

Schneller points to environmental factors. The Pacific Northwest is the nation's dominant hops grower. If nothing else, this has produced a distinctive regional terroir, as Cascadia brews bitterer beers than most any-where else. The fermentation science program at Oregon State University provides technical support with its cutting-edge hops research, working to isolate various aromatic compounds and determine what gives them the smell and taste that they have. The local water is soft and perfect for brewing, "probably softer than Pilsen in Bohemia, which is probably the softest of all the traditional European brewing centers," says Schneller. Larger dynamics in urbanization and the built environment probably matter as well. Deindustrialization made factory spaces obsolete and available to start-up brewers on the cheap, while gentrification brought a wealthy clientele back to the city to make the new downtown brewpubs into neighborhood watering holes.

Once craft brewing started in Portland, however, it was easy to trace its proliferation. The first generation of Portland brewers, like the McMenamin brothers and the Widmer brothers, were self-taught home brewers. Later generations have been the beneficiaries of these organic intellectuals, as their breweries have served as training grounds for the second and third generation of Portland brewmasters. When brewers finally strike out on their own, precious jobs open up in a very competitive industry, and the local brewing family tree grows. Chad Kennedy, the brewmaster at Laurelhurst, began as a home brewer. As he became more and more interested in the history and technical aspects of the craft, he decided to pursue it as a vocation. Kennedy started out with a small beer distributor to get his foot in the door, not long before they started selling product for a new brewery, Laurelhurst. Kennedy made a point of getting to know the owners and slowly worked his way in, first part-time, then full-time. When brew master Christian Ettinger left Laurelwood in 2006 to create Hopworks Urban Brewery, Kennedy was offered the open position.

Hopworks is a part of the third generation of Portland breweries, established around twenty-five years after the first craft breweries opened. Like many newer Portland businesses, this generation is embracing sustainability explicitly as a business ethic and marketing tool. Craft brewing lends itself naturally to sustainability, in that producing in small batches for local consumers from locally sourced products has always been a viable and attractive business model. In 2002, Laurelhurst became the first local craft brewer to produce a certified organic beer, and it continues to brew organics alongside conventional varieties, usually at a slightly higher price point.[21]

Hopworks, however, has taken sustainability to the next level—Portland's first all-encompassing "eco-brewpub." Hopworks has been well received in an increasingly crowded field; one year after it opened in March 2008, it was already brewing at a brisk pace of 3,200 barrels a year. "The whole point behind Hopworks," Ettinger says, "was to bring together as many thoughtful, green, and ecological aspects into one project as we possibly could."[22] All Hopworks beers are organic, and its pizza, the heart of the Hopworks menu, is sustainably produced. Formerly an office space for an oil company, the Hopworks building and grounds were completely deconstructed and remodeled, outfitted with new energy-efficient appliances, reflective roofing and skylights, permeable pavement in the parking lot, and native flora in the landscaping. Waste pizza-oven heat is captured to heat the brewing water. Beneath a decorative awning of thirty or so bicycle frames that covers the length of the bar, local cyclists gather regularly for happy hour organic brews. Though an upstart will no doubt rise up to topple him, Ettinger, for now, is king of artisan brewing in this hotbed of beer innovation.

IS CONSOLIDATION A FOUR-LETTER WORD?

IF HOPWORKS IS THE FUTURE of the Portland brewpub, Widmer might be the future of the Portland microbrewery. All the first generation craft brewers—BridgePort, McMenamins, Portland Brewing, and Widmer—have grown substantially over twenty-five years, but they have taken very different paths. BridgePort and McMenamins have remained independent. BridgePort now does a brisk business at the regional craft-brewing level and McMenamins took its innovative brewpub concept to the masses, and now operates fifty-five locations in Oregon and Washington. Portland Brewing and Widmer went the way of consolidation. Pyramid Breweries acquired Portland Brewing in 2004, making it the third largest of the West Coast craft breweries. Widmer joined with Redhook, Kona, and Goose Island to become the Craft Brewers Alliance. Ironically, this production and distribution conglomerate is no longer technically a craft brewery, having sold partial ownership to Anheuser-Busch, now InBev.

The net decentralization of the beer industry in recent years masks a continuing tendency toward growth and consolidation among top brewers. This should not be surprising, since regional breweries have been the most successful of the craft brewers of late, with sales up 12.5 percent by volume in 2008 alone.[23] The regional brewery model is attractive, marrying quality, artisan beer making with powerful distribution channels that can tackle the commercial microbrewer's greatest challenge: accessing and maintaining retail shelf space. But scaling up has met with inevitable brio from the craft-beer purists. Regional brewers are criticized for "selling out," even if they brew the same product in essentially the same way, only in larger batches for wider audiences.

The ethical uncertainty surrounding large-scale artisan brewing derives from the fact that craft brewing drew on two cultural critiques that are ultimately distinct, one of big business, the other of American epicurean sensibilities. For a time in beer making, they were aligned: big beer was the only game in town, and big beer tasted terrible. But choosing not to make interesting beer as a business strategy is not the same as being unable to make interesting beer. Today, good-tasting, hearty English ales can be, and are, made in large batches and sold over great distances. Craft brewing has in some sense stumbled over its own success, moving the market to the extent that Budweiser looks like a global beer while regional breweries like Widmer's Craft Brewers Alliance start to look like national ones. Take the analogy far enough and Portland is your twenty-first-century Milwaukee. For craft-beer aficionados, the question becomes, does big have to be bad? "I would rather drink a good beer from a huge brewery than a crappy beer from a small one," Schneller says. Kennedy concurs. Though both delight in the arcane and inventive, they concede that the difficulties of distribution make scaling up attractive and reasonable. "I don't think you

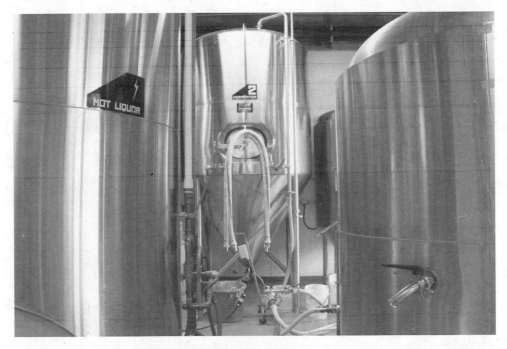

The glass-lined brewing tanks at Hopworks Urban Brewery. Photo © Whitney Gayer

Christian Ettinger, owner of Hopworks Urban Brewery, shows off his custom "beer bike"—complete with pizza rack and built-in stereo system. Photo © Whitney Gayer

have to be a teeny company to stay true to your core values. If you have a cool message it's nice to be able to take it to more people," Kennedy says.

The Widmer brothers started out as their only employees, working dusk-till-dawn brewing, bottling, and distributing their product. Widmer is now approaching 250,000 barrels a year, most of it their flagship *Hefeweizen*. The much-maligned Craft Brewers Alliance-InBev deal puts further growth within easy reach. In crucial ways, though, Widmer has remained grounded. At the Gasthaus, the Widmer brewpub located just across the street from the brewery, small-batch, experimental brewing is still the order of the day. "If you haven't been to the Gasthaus, you haven't had Widmer beer," Schneller says. Widmer stays in touch with the local brew community through efforts such as their Collaborator line, for which home-brewers' concoctions are selected on a competitive basis, brewed by Widmer brewers, and sold commercially in the Gasthaus. Schneller is evidently proud that two of his home brews have been selected. With efforts like Collaborator, Widmer's success morphs from hipster liability into precious asset.

As the heart of the craft-beer movement with a populace well versed in the finer points of good beer, Portland has been able to make room for multiple viable models of beer-making. Could this truly be beer nirvana, not just for the beer lover, but in terms of industry structure as well? In this system, the regional brewer corners the volume market, making good tasting, seasonal, even regionally specific brews while taking advantage of economies of scale. The upstart brewer and brewpub, on the other hand, fill in at the seams, keeping the beer hipster, microbrew purist, and happy hour reveler well supplied, all while putting pressure on the bigger brewers to keep innovating. Given that the new regional brewers compete in part by making different styles of beer, rather than by trying to make the same product more efficiently, a Beer Wars II among them seems unlikely. But even if Widmer somehow becomes the next Budweiser, raining from every tap from Connecticut to California, at least a new generation of Americans would grow up believing that "beer" is synonymous with a pretty good tasting *Hefeweizen*, rather than a watery pilsner. Perhaps not the moral economy of the artisan, but still something like progress.

CHAPTER 4
FOOD

Talia Jacobson
Tracy Braden
Lauren Larin

IN JUNE 2007, the Grand Central Baking Company opened its sixth and largest location in a warehouse in the industrial district, beyond the trendier neighborhoods of northwest Portland. It's now the heart of the company's operations, housing the central offices, all artisan bread production, and a skylit café where customers who nab the good seats get an unobstructed view of the bakers at work. With its bright new facade and well-tended landscaping, the Sawtooth location stands out among its faded utilitarian neighbors.

Grand Central's co-owner, co-founder, and president, Ben Davis, blends right in.

On the day of our interview, he's wearing old Carhartts powdered over with flour. He's obliging and unpretentious, answering questions without jargon or spin. When we get onto the topic of what defines artisan baking, his eyes sharpen, and he shifts forward in his chair.

"Some people define artisan baking on size, some people define it as hand-forming, and some people define it as no equipment besides a mixer," Davis explains.[1] "How I define it is by the method—however you're doing it, it doesn't really matter. It's about mixing the dough properly. We can mix great dough in any kind of mixer, I don't care what it is, we can probably get a decent dough out of it, and if we can't,…then I can get the character

I want out of it by how I fold it, by how I ferment it, how I hydrate it, and what temperature I ferment it at." As he talks, his hands sketch through the steps he describes, working their way through the tasks as though the table in front of him holds mixers, pans, and bowls of dough.

When Grand Central opened its first bakery café on Southeast Hawthorne in 1993, Davis was the head baker. Sixteen years later, he oversees bread production for six retail locations and dozens of restaurants, stores, and markets. He's up to his elbows in everything from product R&D, purchasing (they're switching to Shepherd's Grain flour, a no-till farm cooperative), to planning and designing the new locations and helping maintain the hearths. He's hired and trained hundreds of employees—promoted them when he could; fired them when he needed to.

It's been a long time since it was his job to form the day's loaves, but his hands still remember the bread.

TERROIR

THERE'S NO SHORTAGE of artisan food in Portland; what draws eyes is how much of it is grown or made locally. There are seven Portland chocolatiers, more than a dozen artisan bakeries, ten meat producers, and at least fifteen Oregon-based cheese-makers selling their wares in town.[2] The Oregon Farmers' Markets Association lists thirty-four markets in the region. Portland homebodies can buy subscriptions to any of three dozen community-supported agriculture projects (CSAs), while the more industrious can drive out to one of the 106 U-Pick farms located in Multnomah, Washington, and Clackamas counties. For people who want grocery store convenience, New Seasons Markets are attempting to bridge the price/quality gap between Safeway and Whole Foods.

As for the Portland restaurant scene, so many reviews have sung its praises that it sometimes feels like the nation's food journalists are trying to bring back the genre of epistolary romance. Idle googling will get you half a dozen *Sunset Magazine* articles extolling the virtues of Portland restaurants (plus more than twice that many highlighting the region's recipes or ingredients), thirteen more from *Gourmet*, and a handful of scene-surveying articles and favorable restaurant reviews from the *New York Times*. There are odes to Portland waffles, desserts, and food carts. If you take the hype as fact, then this city is the place to go to get a meal made with skill, artistry, quirk, sensitivity to season, and a side order of education.

It's easy for longtime residents to take the diversity and quality of Portland food for granted, but after a while you start asking, *why here?* Pose the question to the people who make up the chain that gets Portland's food from ground to plate, and you get several answers, all interconnected.

Let's start with geography. The Portland region is located in a narrow strip of land that runs from Mexico through Washington, where the Coast and Interior Ranges cradle 10 percent of the world's most fertile agricultural land.[3] As Wildwood restaurant founder and Oregon Farm to School's Food Coordinator Cory Schreiber points out, "This area was self-sufficient long ago. People would come here and be amazed at the agricultural resources— the salmon and tuna, the abundance of things. People talk about the cuisine here being a recent phenomenon, but before there was transportation, or other modern infrastructure, Portland had a food economy."[4]

The value of these agricultural assets has not escaped Oregon's lawmakers, who have created political structures to protect them. Since 1973, Oregon's land-use laws have preserved and maintained agricultural lands for farm, forest, and open-space uses, buffering these lands from encroaching urban growth and zoning out uses that adversely affect farming.[5] This stewardship has kept the Portland region agriculturally active while other West Coast cities paved over nearby farms. Today, the bounty available here ranges from "vegetables to local fisheries and small beef, lamb and pork producers. Not far away is the Hood River Valley, with its myriad fruit growers who supply glistening fragile berries and stonefruits of every stripe and color. World class wine is produced in the Willamette Valley…just a half hour's drive away."[6]

For decades, this wealth of ingredients has influenced the ethics of nativeborn food artisans and drawn gifted transplants seeking a place to put localism into practice. James Beard, Portland-born father of the American culinary movement, spent childhood summers at the Oregon coast helping his family gather and catch food for their table.[7] These experiences formed his stance as an "early champion of local products and local markets,"[8] which influenced the chefs who later followed in his footsteps.[9] Starting in the 1970s, Portland benefited from the shifts in culinary and agricultural philosophy also seen in the Bay Area, where Alice Waters founded Chez Panisse.[10] The rise of

The expert staff at Grand Central Bakery rolls and proofs the day's yield. Photo ©
Rachel Moore

People's Food Co-op, founded in 1970, and Food Front Cooperative Grocery, founded in 1972, gave Portland customers an opportunity to support local businesses and growers. Nearby family farms formed a trade group in 1977 (now called the Tri-County Farms) to print a guide advertising directly to consumers. In the mid-1980s, the region's winemakers received French recognition for their pinot noir, and the wine industry got the boost it had been looking for.[11] In the mid-1990s, locally minded fine dining restaurants like Wildwood, Paley's Place, and Higgins opened their doors, and the acclaim and awards that followed raised the profile of Portland's food scene. The Food Alliance, the Western Culinary Institute, and the Portland Chapter of the Chefs Collaborative all got going around the same time. The momentum kept building.

Portland's unique culture and socioeconomic characteristics are part of what makes the current food economy so vital. Portland enjoys a lower cost of living compared to other West Coast cities, which creates opportunities for chefs who might lack the financial resources to make a go of it elsewhere. Chef Andy Ricker of standout Thai restaurant Pok Pok translates this into local vernacular: "There are a ton of people here who are going at it in sort of an indie rock way, mostly because they can."[12] Portland is also increasingly wealthy in what Richard Florida terms the "creative class"—people who make their living in the realm of ideas, information, and technology, who play an increasingly large role in the national economy, and who tend to seek out cities that offer amenities beyond just good jobs.[13] Portland's reputation as funky, livable, and green-minded draws educated young people looking to get their start.

"There's an ethic in Portland that's different than anywhere else that I've been," says Brian Rohter, CEO of New Seasons Market.[14] "The people are very interested in supporting local business, they're interested in supporting progressive and sustainable businesses, they're interested in knowing where their food came from and how it's grown. Businesses like New Seasons Market or Powell's, the Bike Gallery, Kitchen Kaboodle, Rejuvenation, they also *attract* people to Portland. People come here for all sorts of reasons, but one of the reasons is the environment that's been created by these sorts of businesses. It's a cyclical process. People come, they support the businesses, the businesses get stronger and get more of a national reputation, so more people come. It builds on itself." In other words, as more local and artisan businesses spring up to take advantage of the region's resources, the market for those businesses gets more fertile.

CULTIVATION

ASK HOW AN ARTISAN food economy forms, and you get complex, multidisciplinary answers. Ask how any given food business gets started, and you're likely to get an answer that's much simpler. Take Rohter's history of New Seasons: "Many of the folks who work in New Seasons were also involved in Nature's, which was a predecessor company. Nature's was purchased by General Nutrition Company in 1997.... Then in 1999, General Nutrition sold Nature's to a company called Wild Oats. Many of us who worked at Nature's didn't have the same view of the world that Wild Oats had, and so a few of us got together and decided to start New Seasons. That was in 2000, and over the course of the last nine years, we've opened nine stores in and around the Portland area."

There's more to the story than that. In between the lines of Rohter's diplomatic explanation, lives intersected and changed course, people took huge risks, hopes lived and maybe died. Still, even that stripped-down account contains the common themes we heard in our interviews: these businesses begin at a human scale, often with modest resources. They grow in increments. And ultimately, they move forward because of relationships.

Grand Central Bakery came into the world when Ben Davis and a college buddy got a family friend to loan them the start-up cash, licensed the name from a bakery Davis's mother owned in Seattle, and moved to Portland to open their first store. "We started with eleven employees and really not knowing what we were doing," Davis recalls. He could bake, but none of them knew how to run a business. They figured it out as they went.

Rebecca Larson,[15] an herb and flower grower, started out through a similar combination of drive, friendly support, and naiveté. A friend who owned a large amount of farmland offered to let her start growing there for free. "I had no choice! It was a dream come true," Larson says. But she had next to no experience to guide her. Her first efforts at farming involved going out to the land and just throwing seeds into the ground.

The artisans we talked with said their businesses grew the same way they started: with a lot of improvisation. After a couple of years, Grand Central's Hawthorne location was pulling in a million dollars in sales annually. Davis and his partners had money saved and a strong, youthful, ambitious team. They used these resources to open a second location on Southwest Multnomah. Four years after that, they opened a third location on Northeast Weidler. "It's just been that same leapfrogging—get the cash, get the people, and then make the move. So a lot of it's come out of, you know"—Davis laughs—"boredom, to tell you the truth."

This is a striking difference between artisan food businesses and their mainstream counterparts: quality, not maximized profit, is their indicator of success. They can grow and adapt without the rigid by-the-numbers approach that limits corporate decisions. As Davis explains, "We're organized, but it's more intuitive, gut, horse sense. I mean, that's how we run this place. No one has business degrees, and we're not analyzing a bunch of charts and making a bunch of business plans and predicting the future, because I've found that that's just a waste of time." When sales drive a business, he says, it's easy

Ben Davis, founder of Grand Central Baking Company. Photo © Rachel Moore

to lose efficiency, and quality suffers as a result. Davis and the other people behind Portland's artisan foods want their businesses to succeed, and they define success broadly enough to understand that market analysis alone won't get them there.

TOOLS

TRYING TO RECONCILE "artisan" and "business" can get a little sticky. There's a danger of falling for a romantic idea of artisan work as a timeless calling, practiced without the taint of modern business practices or modern equipment. Introducing contemporary technology or efficiency improvements would seem to dilute the purity of that vision, removing it from the platonic ideal.

Ben Davis is quick to dismiss the idea that artisan bread loses authenticity when machines or structured production procedures are involved. "No one can deny that a cabinet-maker is probably an artisan," he points out. "He doesn't make cabinets with his bare hands, he uses tools, but they're thoughtfully used, they're used with skill…. It's the same with us. But within the baking community there are some sacred cows that some people won't let go of."

At New Seasons, Brian Rohter blends both sides of the table, comparing artisan and Fordist economies (Chapter 2), calling into question our dichotomy between artisan and mainstream business practices. "We're trying to mainstream the idea that people would buy locally grown food and buy high-quality food," he says. "So we would pick from both categories [artisan and modern] to try and accomplish our goals." For example: fixed procedures and set shift times, however unexciting, are a necessary condition for the company to succeed. They're part of what Davis describes as "thoughtful mechanization."

Davis brings up another unapologetically modern term: *quality control*. A sandwich, for example, has to be built in the right order: "Employees want to put on what they like and how they would build it, but they're not making a sandwich for them. We're making it to what our specs need to be." Such strict procedures don't fit with the idealized version of an artisan business, but quality control has always been an intrinsic part of traditional artisan work. Artistry wasn't the only thing that made artisan goods superior—their creators were trained to consider everything they made with a critical eye for flaws in the workmanship, and they held their assistants and employees to equally rigorous standards.

One of the differences between artisan and industrialized businesses is that artisan businesses control quality without mistaking their employees for mechanisms themselves. Davis and Rohter see their employees as people whose lives outside of work are important business considerations. Both New Seasons and Grand Central are committed to providing health insurance to their employees. Both expanded their operations to create opportunities for advancement. Both pay significantly above the state's minimum wage.

There's a careful balance to be maintained between ethics and practicality. The "parental function" Davis says Grand Central fills for its relatively young work force is authoritative, not permissive. The company holds employees to high expectations and keeps things running smoothly with training, regular performance reviews, and management visits. Still, he and Rohter try to focus on the aspects of employee performance that really matter—competence, reliability, commitment—and dispense with what Rohter calls "lots of stupid rules that people have to follow." At both Grand Central and New Seasons, you meet employees with tattoos or mobility devices, with dreadlocks or fauxhawks, or who are visibly queer or genderqueer. No one's told them to break out the black and khaki, or to break off conversations when customers are in earshot, or that they're not allowed to lean. They're laughing, they're talking—more often than not, they seem to be having a genuinely good time.

"We've tried to create a really progressive workplace where people get to be themselves," says Rohter. "Our people are definitely working for pay, and we hope that we've created a situation where they can figure out that there's knowledge involved. Then it's a vocation also."

AT THE MARKETPLACE

THERE'S A WEB of close connections among Portland's artisan food businesses. Grand Central writes most of its checks to cover direct farm purchasing, and the bakery frequently sets up wholesale contracts with new high-end restaurants not yet out of construction. The New Seasons website highlights hundreds of "home grown" producers shelved in their stores. Herb grower Rebecca Larson swaps a goat farmer's herbs to flavor his cheeses for manure to fertilize her plants. David Yudkin of local chain HOTLIPS Pizza offers a line of all-natural sodas made from local ingredients, and he gets the most support from small markets, sole proprietors, farm stands, and local mom-and-pop establishments.[16] Chef Greg Higgins works with over forty suppliers, many of them small-scale growers, to get the ingredients that lavish the tables at his eponymous restaurant and bar.[17]

The fates of these artisan businesses are deliberately intertwined. Part of it is the ethical commitments the people at the helm feel to promoting bioregionalism and shortened supply chains. Part of it is their understanding that, when it comes to the market share won by local businesses, they are literally all in this together. It's part of the cycle Rohter described earlier: the higher the profile of the "buy local" movement, the wider the range and better the quality of the local products available, the more consumers choose local businesses over global chains. By supporting each other's businesses, they're supporting their own.

HOTLIPS Pizza's electric delivery vehicle, parked outside their Hawthorne Boulevard location. Photo © Rachel Moore

The businesses at the top of the local food chain the restaurants—the bakery cafés, the markets—understand this symbiosis, and they go out of their way to negotiate contracts that support their suppliers long-term stability. Getting the lowest price isn't their primary goal; they're opting out of what Davis calls "the race to the bottom line."

While New Seasons doesn't eschew modern business practices, their relationships with local and artisan suppliers stray pretty far from the strategies used in the modern economy. The New Seasons produce merchandiser meets with growers in late fall to commit to a price and volume for the next season, so the farmers can have clear expectations of what their revenues will be. The company has also been known to advance money to help growers through the months between harvests. Along with directly recruiting new vendors from farmers' markets, New Seasons puts new products on their shelves through joint sponsorship of a program at the Food Innovation Center, where emerging food entrepreneurs learn how to package their products. Some New Seasons employees make artisan foods of their own, and if their results are good, then New Seasons will stock those too.

Regarding their choice to nurture small growers and new products, Rohter explains that New Seasons' status as a private company gives them the freedom that publicly-owned national grocery chains lack. With no obligation to report quarterly earnings to stockholders, the company can make long-range decisions without being undercut by impacts to short-term profits. As Davis points out, diversifying your contracts—especially in terms of sales—also increases financial stability. One partner can go under and the bulk of your business remains untouched. It's one of the many areas in the artisan food economy where ethics and pragmatism go hand-in-hand.

BRINGING MOUTHS TO THE TABLE

FOR SOME PEOPLE, the word *artisan* invokes a favorable set of concepts: *quality, artistry, craft.* For others, it calls up a more loaded set of descriptors: *luxury, elite.* The people in Portland's artisan food economy are well aware of the equity issues at play in the marketplace. For Grand Central and New Seasons, selling good food that's affordable across a range of income brackets is a priority. "I see people of all economic backgrounds who enjoy our food, from college kids with a baguette in their backpack to your West Hills housewife," says Davis. "Our average retail sale is six bucks—there's a lot of college kids who can still afford six bucks. They can treat themselves to a good latte and a great scone or a turnover or a sandwich. It's all pretty approachable."

New Seasons, like Grand Central, checks its prices against its competitors in town. Average the variation between the national grocery chains, and there's essentially no difference between their prices and what New Seasons charges for comparable products. "Milk, butter, bread, eggs, tuna fish, Campbell's soup, cereal, all that stuff—it'll cost about the same," Rohter says. "Our price of organic milk, to the best of my knowledge, is fifty to seventy-five cents cheaper for a half-gallon than anywhere else you can buy it in Portland."

New Seasons has gone a step further in its efforts to make good food accessible by opening stores in sites the national chains had abandoned years earlier. These locations include some of Portland's most ethnically and economically mixed neighborhoods, some of them struggling with crime and economic difficulties. "When we went to open our Concordia store in northeast Portland, we couldn't get funding for it because the banks thought that the demographics of the neighborhood did not match with their view of our store," Rohter recalls. When asked about the decision to serve communities that national chains had dismissed as too much of a risk, his response is nonchalant. "We were thinking that if you open a store that is fairly priced with staff that are treated well, so they're in a good mood and consequently they treat the customers well and respectfully, then regardless of the type of community where you open those stores, the neighbors will respond positively and shop there." Nine years after it opened, the Concordia location is a bustling success.

It's hard to quantify the accessibility and quality of food options. Some research suggests that the Portland region's residents benefit from the richness of the local food scene without suffering increased costs. One study found that Portland-Vancouver consumers don't dedicate more of their annual income or expenditures to food than national consumers do, but a greater share of their food budget goes to fruits, vegetables, and meals eaten outside the home—all arenas where local and artisan producers are well-represented.[18] But while some businesses may offer affordable access to artisan and local foods, other artisan producers say they're serving a more limited clientele. Herb grower Larson has found her niche serving what she describes as an elite market. Chef Berkeley Braden[19] says he owes some of his professional success to word-of-mouth referrals from high-end private clients, who enjoy spending money to have someone create varied menus with high-quality ingredients. "People are paying more for this than they have to just to get fed," Braden says.[20]

Cory Schreiber knows different levels of the artisan and local food economy. In 2007, he left Wildwood Restaurant to coordinate the Oregon Department of Agriculture's Farm to School Programs, which puts Oregon produce in K–12 cafeterias. He sees the region's food costs climbing and notes that immigrant communities participate unequally. (They garden, he says, but aren't part of the restaurant scene.) He thinks we're creating an affluent food culture here in the Portland area. "We sort of romanticize this notion of a local food economy, but the moderate-income family may not be able to afford it," he observes. "The system is sustainable only when you can pay a premium."

With the wide range in price between different kinds of artisan foods—$1 for a dinner roll at an artisan bakery, over $50 a head for dinner and drinks at some of the city's best-praised restaurants—it's obvious that affluence makes a big difference in access. On balance, is Portland's artisan food economy inclusionary or exclusionary? Economists have yet to run the numbers, but on an experiential level there's no single answer. It's neither, and it's both.

BOUNTY

DESPITE THE INEQUITIES of access afforded to individuals, the artisan food economy enriches the region as a whole. The Institute of Portland Metropolitan Studies identifies nine key resources in the food system: land, water, energy, labor and talent, capital, technology and knowledge, consumer choice and spending power, political influence, and social capital.[21] But the industrial and community-based food systems value and utilize these resources in quite different ways. A decade-old report for the USDA lays the differences out on the table. For the industrial food system, it's about maximizing profit and minimizing consumer costs, chasing the inflection point on the marginal cost curve: "Profitability is achieved by replacing labor with capital; maximizing throughput; controlling nature with technology, fossil fuel and chemicals; and by specializing and routinizing tasks. Conversely, sustainable community food systems operate at a human scale with strong attention to environmental integrity, economic self-reliance and social well being."[22]

While *local* has become a fully-fledged buzzword, proponents insist that it is because there is tremendous value in keeping food resources and their outputs close to home. As Chef Greg Higgins puts it, "local and seasonal foods...are consumed while they're still fresh, while they're still high in nutrient value, and they also nourish the community of people who are growing them, preparing them, and vending them."

In Cory Schreiber's view, creating a sustainable food system will require "changing the fabric of everyday awareness," so that consumers know what local options are out there. To build this kind of consumer knowledge—and prompt the change in purchasing behavior Schreiber and others hope will follow—artisan food businesses need to help their customers understand where their food comes from. At Wildwood, Schreiber prided himself on the ability to look patrons in the eye and truthfully explain that 80 percent of what they were eating came from within 150 miles. "You can't just do that anywhere," says Schreiber. "There is something different and special about what we have here." Higgins likewise sees the meals his restaurant serves as an opportunity to draw attention to all the people and environmental influences that bridge the gap between land and table.

These local narratives aren't just a sidebar—the story is what sells. More than half of the consumers surveyed by market researchers agreed that it was important to them to learn about the story behind a local product, with images of the people and production site increasing local products' credibility.[23] "Showing people the connection between themselves and the land, between the food and where it comes from, elevates the importance of food beyond sustenance or even the pleasure of a good meal," Schreiber says. These stories create a relationship between the origins of food and the people who eat it that's been largely absent from the mass-market food economy for decades.

In addition to the tabletop education offered by the people who sell artisan foods to consumers, Portlanders benefit from the presence of a variety of research, educational, and social change organizations which offer much-needed institutional support. We've already mentioned the Food Innovation

Center, the Western Culinary Institute, and the Farm to School Programs. There's also Ecotrust, which engages in policy work, research, and economic activities to promote environmental sustainability and social equity. They run programs that support coastal fishing communities and link up small farmers, ranchers, and fishers to food buyers.[24] Oregon Tilth provides organic education and certification to growers of all sizes, and the Food Alliance offers an alternative certification for foods produced through environmentally and socially responsible practices.[25] Portland State University houses the Food Industry Leadership Center and the largest farmers' market in the city, as well as several research centers tackling topics related to food-shed sustainability. New Seasons and People's Food Co-op both offer free educational classes on nutrition, homeopathy, healthy diabetic eating—even how to keep chickens. For those who prefer to get their food-for-thought in a more celebratory form, there's the Muddy Boot Organic Festival, the Northwest Chocolate Festival, the Bite of Oregon, the Oregon Brewers Festival, the Portland Indie Wine Festival, the Portland Seafood and Wine Festival, and at least a dozen others. On weekends and holidays in the warm months, you can stuff yourself on local cuisine without ever leaving the vendor tents.

The currents of food education and activism run so strongly through the region that some foodies wonder if we haven't gotten too far from the original motive for seeking out artisan foods: the pursuit of a really good meal. In 1991, Portlanders started the nation's first chapter of Slow Food, an international organization promoting the fundamental right to pleasure in food. In recent years, the chapter has shifted to a more political stance, planning tours of farm-worker housing and sponsoring anti-hunger activists to the biannual worldwide food congress Terra Madre.[26] Other chapters around the nation have taken a similar turn, and Slow Food USA's redrafted mission statement now describes the hope of inspiring "a transformation in food policy, production practices and market forces so that they ensure equity, sustainability and pleasure in the food we eat."[27] When asked about the changed manifesto, Slow Food Corvallis founder Ann Shriver was conflicted, "What they've done is wrung out all the pleasure aspects from the statement."[28]

Despite skepticism, Portland's food artisans continue to build their businesses on the assumptions that good eating and good works really can go hand in hand.

Fermentation

It's hard to say what's on the horizon for Portland's artisan and local food economy. The breadth of its offerings has blossomed in the past decade, and no one we talked to saw signs that consumer interest was leveling off. As *New York Times* reporter Eric Asimov observes, "Every little neighborhood in this city of funky neighborhoods now seems to be exploding with restaurants, food shops and markets all benefiting from a critical mass of passion, skill and experience and all constructed according to the gospel of locally grown ingredients."[29] While inflation-adjusted earnings for most Oregon food system sectors remained stable between 1990 and 2006, earnings for food services and drinking places increased by more than a billion dollars, near doubling.[30] Portland's five farmers' markets draw up to twenty-two thousand shoppers a week.[31] Meanwhile, media surveys show national interest in eating local continuing its upward swing.[32]

For individual businesses, though, it's clear there are limits to scaling up, even if they can't be sure where those limits lie. Davis wants to make sure that Grand Central doesn't overreach: "You can only get so many people through the door. All our places, we try to keep them small—we've learned that we have a nice little model." When pressed, he thinks there might be two or three more neighborhoods in Portland that could support a new Grand Central location, but that's it.

As for moving outside the city, Davis is absolutely opposed. The company runs on an intricate system of internal transfers, with different locations housing different functions, and it wouldn't be possible to provide the same quality and support to a location even forty-five minutes away. "I truly believe that we need to stay where we are, and we need to stay tight and small," he says. "That's why I believe that Eugene needs their own artisan bakery that's doing it to supply Eugene. Bend needs Bend's. Portland needs Grand Central…. It should be unique to the town."

The artisan model is seductive to producers and consumers, but it can also be unstable and susceptible to co-option. "As a term, [*artisan*] could get hijacked by Sara Lee and all these other places—all they have to do is stick it on their label," Davis warns. He watched the same process when Washington agro-businesses fought to loosen the meaning of *organic*. Chef Greg Higgins has concerns about efforts to interest companies like Walmart and McDonald's in sustainability, because of the threats to smaller companies if the thousand-pound gorillas vie for a share of the green market. Some corporate practices might change for the better, but many structural problems—the small growers and retailers out-competed, the consumer capital funneled out of local economies—will remain.

There are a whole host of questions no one can answer yet. If Portland's local foods economy becomes larger and more successful, will the artisan ideal begin to erode? How will the economic downturn, rising costs of living, and changing real estate prices affect small artisan businesses? Will the sustainability movement result in more resilient food sheds, or just greenwash the problem out of sight? Are we just watching the same old economic processes at work and calling them by a different name? What do the regional trends of population growth, increased precipitation, decreased snowpacks, increased reliance on groundwater for irrigation, and rising energy costs mean for the Portland metropolitan area's food shed?[33] Are we asking these questions at the expense of paying attention to more pressing community needs: costly housing, struggling schools, working class neighborhoods waiting decades for their streets to be repaved?

We're not sure. Like a lot of people who believe in this new return to an older way of eating, we've got hopes and fears. We've got guesses, some educated, some just conjecture. None of them are solid enough to commit to paper. But if you're curious, come meet us at Grand Central on Southeast Hawthorne and 23rd Avenue. You can get the Columbia Gorge organic apple cider and the basil egg salad sandwich—one author's favorites—or stick with Stumptown coffee and a raisin-walnut panini if you just want a snack. If the weather's nice and there's an open outdoor table, we'll smuggle in a box of Sauvie Island berries from Uncle Paul's Produce Market on the next block up.

We can all talk it over while we eat.

CHAPTER 5
FASHION

Laura Cesafsky
Marianne Ryder
Shanna Eller

"FASHION IN PORTLAND? Like, other than flannel shirts and Birkenstocks?"[1]
With an acerbic tone and a slight roll of the eyes, Adam Arnold dismisses this
bottom-shelf journalistic trope, one that has framed so many stories about
the recent flourishing of a local fashion economy in Portland. "Everyone
thinks they have to say that." A successful Portland clothier who creates
higher-end, made-to-measure fashions for men and women out of his spar-
tan southeast Portland studio, Arnold is incredulous of the safe and well
trodden, in words or in work. "If something feels right to me, I do it. That's
always been my business plan."

Arnold is something of the consummate artisan. Trained in the finer
points of apparel design and construction at the Fashion Institute of Design
& Merchandising in San Francisco, he is known in Portland's design community as a talented and meticulous crafter. He left a promising career in
corporate fashion for the lure of creative freedom (and the reality of relative
penury). While contracting out even the most monotonous of his measuring,
snipping, and sewing tasks could free up more time for design, Arnold does
not believe in this division of labor, so basic to the (in)famously globalized
apparel industry. "How can you design something that you don't know how
to make?" he asks. Though he works from his own drawings, he finds further
inspiration during the construction process itself.

It is quite easy to see that Portland's days as a fashion backwater steeped in tie-dye, sawdust, and grunge are long gone—if they ever existed at all. Simply notice the spate of funky little clothing shops that have popped up like so many dandelions, stocking limited-edition—often one-of-a-kind— creations that you will not find on the racks of the big-name department stores, though they compete in price and quality. These clothes tend to be handmade, often locally produced, and quite distinctive, if not always "affordable" in the way that the cultural economy of globalized apparel has led us to expect. It is, after all, the contradiction between the cost of American labor and the middle-class expectation of a walk-in closet full of up-to-date fashions that necessitates the contemporary (and near universal) outsourcing of production to distant shores.

So the question becomes, what is it about Portland that makes it possible for artisan clothing designers and crafters to defy this logic and survive, if not necessarily thrive, while doing what they love?

It is a sometime joke among restaurant professionals—servers and bar- tenders in particular—that the industry is self-sustaining: no strangers to the nightlife and typically zealous over-tippers, money simply circulates among them. Musicians work at small-time coffee roasters to fund the purchase of locally crafted happy hour beers; bicycle mechanics and tattoo artists trade services. But mutual support only goes so far. A relatively extensive local clothing economy depends on the participation of a class more flush than that of the typical independent artisan. Some designers admit that they could never afford the things they make. While one of Arnold's best customers is a record store clerk—"I don't know how he does it, but he does it"—he also caters to medical professionals and businesspeople.

The story of the local fashion economy must account for the motivations of both parties, the makers and the buyers. The story outlines a particular constellation of economic forces, embedded values, and soft infrastructure that create the conditions for certain ways of creating, producing, distribut- ing, and consuming fashion, while placing limits on other possibilities.

OUT OF NOWHERE

BY MOST ACCOUNTS, the artisan fashion scene in Portland got off the ground with the launch of Seaplane by designers Kathryn Towers and Holly Stalder in 2000. The clothing boutique emerged, says Arnold, "out of nowhere, out of nothing," the only retail space in the city where one could buy and sell locally made indie fashions. Returning a generous portion of each sale back to the creator (50 percent), it became something of a home base for a burgeoning collective of local designers with similar aesthetic sensibilities. The collection was organized around "deconstructed" clothing, a look that defined (and, to some people, still defines) what "Portland fashion" means.

Deconstruction involves taking apart or modifying vintage garments, sometimes combining them with elements from other garments, to create wholly unique and irreproducible pieces. It is a design ethic that preferences the use of what already exists before reaching for something new, as well as a practical solution to the problem of gaining access to exotic and expensive fabrics on a limited budget. Local designer Emily Katz, who for a long time made deconstructed clothing, described the process: "I would be inspired by the shape of a garment or a color or the era that it was from; sometimes the drawings that would go on would be inspired by it in that way."[2] The found materials very much dictate what can be made, and the designer's work is to create an artful dialogue among them that maximizes their latent potentialities. In creating a deconstructed garment, then, the division between design and construction—between the conceptual realm and the physical realm—is pushed toward negation, much more so than even in Adam Arnold's work. Those familiar with postmodern lines of thinking may recognize the resultant garments as embodiments of pastiche—amalgamations of design elements that reference different modern periods but are liberated of their historical context and content.

Having a reliable place to sell such garments locally helped immensely to grow the local fashion economy, but it didn't make anyone rich. The ability to get by on an artisan income in Portland speaks to the fabric of the city itself. As almost any young creative will avow, the draw of the place comes down to the combination of low rents, compact geography, walk- and bikeability, good public transportation, and overall livability that Arnold sums up as "people-centered"—as opposed to the "business-centered" atmosphere of fashion capitals like New York and Los Angeles. Affordable studio space, a prized asset in any city, can readily (or at least more readily) be found. Some designers work out of spaces in their—or even their parents'—homes, while artist loft living is a viable option for others. Arnold has a good-sized,

Fashion designer Adam Arnold relaxes for a moment in his southeast studio. Photo ©
Whitney Gayer 2010.

street-level studio near the city center, and he is aware of the luxury of his situation. Musing about a dream move to a European city, he suggests jokingly that he'd have to learn to get by with "about one-sixteenth" of his present space.

While this basic feature—the ability to get by on less—serves in Portland as a steady and beneficent tailwind that can push an artisan designer toward economic viability, a healthy dose of soft infrastructure provides further monetary, informational, and social resources. Among the most important of these, indeed vital for the deconstruction set, has been Portland's veritable wealth of vintage outlets. Anna Cohen, a local designer and fashionista who grew up in Portland, is a longtime patron of these establishments. She is hard-pressed to explain why the city should be so well endowed.

But if this resource was once a well-kept secret, the word is getting out—reaching even the rarified air of high fashion. Designer clothing has selectively incorporated elements of indie and alternative fashion in recent years, bringing in vintage references in a highbrow iteration on pastiche. Cohen,

Hundreds of pattern designs line the walls of Adam Arnold's studio. Photo © Whitney Gayer

who reveres Balenciaga, used to raid local vintage shops on trips home and bring her most interesting and inspirational finds back to the fashion houses in Italy where she was working.

The PDX Fashion Incubator was another resource for the local fashion economy, though it lasted just three years. About the same time that Seaplane was taking off, Stella Farina was concentrating on putting together the non-profit incubator to nurture and support fashion entrepreneurs. It was instrumental in bringing designers together as a community; sparking interest in the business aspects of fashion at the local design schools; planting the seeds to revive technical training in pattern-making and sewing at community colleges; and establishing Portland Fashion Week, an event that stages the freshest local designers' upcoming collections in a series of high-production runway shows. On that note, fashion shows in general have been instrumental in increasing awareness and excitement around artisanal design in Portland since Seaplane provided the model early on, holding in-store soirees nearly from the first.

Portland's muscular DIY collectivities were also, for some artisans, vital learning communities—particularly deconstructionists who often begin with no technical training. The combination of such factors has made Portland rich soil for a budding crop of diverse independent clothing and accessories makers.

But success in making requires finding a community of buyers who share the values and sensibilities of local designers. Buoyed by the migration of sustainably minded, creative, independent thinkers from across America over the last decade, Portland has coalesced as community around the realization that a dollar spent locally is often worth more socially and environmentally. Portland's creative professional community is undergirded by the city's original "fashion" industry, the cluster of activewear designers (Nike, Adidas, and Columbia Sportswear, among several others) that have made the metropolitan area their corporate home base. This professional community creates a strong market for the work of local designers and for one-of-a-kind pieces, reflecting the contemporary tendency among young creatives to assert individuality through unique consumption. This class, in this place, will open the door to creations that speak to locality, reuse, sustainability, and a DIY spirit.

Somewhat removed from the media-driven hubbub of New York or Los Angeles, Portland's moral economy is complemented by a studied indifference to labels and the hierarchies of taste that define such places. In this vein, and with characteristic sass, Adam Arnold insists that he "hates fashion," by which he means he could do without the spectacle of it. He purposely avoids looking at fashion magazines, preferring to draw from the lived experience of the senses and the muddy waters of memory. His goal is to make clothes that are modern, timeless, natural, and wearable—"familiar but not"—for him, the distillation of what Portland is. Indeed it's hard not to experience the city as fundamentally relaxed, a place where the boundaries between chic and casual, fun and fiscal, feel blurred. "The cool thing about Portland," he says, "is that you can do whatever you want. It's an independent place. The Portland spirit is very stubborn, very independent.... The whole Northwest is like that."

Emily Katz agrees: "I definitely use that as a marketing tool. I'm not from LA; I'm not from NY; I'm doing something a little different."

Dressed in dapper gray slacks, worn brown boots, a fitted black sweater atop an equally fitted—and quite striking—printed navy blue button-down shirt, Arnold embodies the Portland aesthetic he describes: simple, modern, "familiar but not." And why wouldn't he? After all, he designed the outfit himself. Unable to afford the labels his junior-high sensibility yearned for, Arnold starting clothing himself as a young teenager (though he insists he no longer wears his own creations exclusively). As it turns out, the fabric for the navy blue button-down, covered in small white hexagons with angular designs inside, was a gift a friend brought back from Japan. Always into geometry, Arnold found that the fabric sparked an interest in hexagons that then translated into the creation of a dress, engineered from black, fist-sized hexagons, assembled in a feat of mathematics so that the dress curves according to the contours of the female figure. He turns over the bottom of the dress to reveal a brightly colored silk lining. "Like nature," he laughs. "Think of a kiwi. The outside looks like a monkey's ball, but inside it's sizzling."

DOING THE NUMBERS

SO HOW MANY independent fashion designers are there in Portland, who are they, and how well do they know each other? How many local boutique outlets exist to sell their work? In 2006, when this project began, we put a serious effort into answering these questions. Indeed this book started with a more narrow ambition, to chronicle and account for the improbably large community of independent fashion designers and boutiques that had emerged in Portland in recent years. With this limited scope came the luxury of understanding the fashion sector in greater depth than any of the other sectors discussed in this book. We completed interviews and surveys with fourteen individuals, including eleven designers, a designer/retailer, a fabric boutique owner, and Farina, the developer of the PDX Fashion Incubator. From these it became possible not only to gain a solid grounding in the local fashion "scene," but also to draw some preliminary conclusions about the demographic attributes of Portland designers as a whole. With the caveat that fashion designers in Portland are mostly women, the data may also provide some insight into the characteristic of other artisan sectors in Portland.

A majority of all the designers we talked with are women (78 percent). The average age is thirty-one, less than half are married, and only two of fourteen have children. (This ran contrary to our expectation that the flexibility of the artisan lifestyle would operate as a benefit to young mothers.) Most (71 percent) moved to Portland from somewhere else, while Cohen, Katz, and Arnold, among the few area natives, have gone away and returned. On average the designers have lived in Portland for about eight years, but designing clothing has only provided a significant portion of their income for three years—a testament to the strength of Portland's soft infrastructure for developing new design professionals organically. Two are high school graduates, three have some college, seven have college degrees, and two have advanced degrees. Half have undergraduate or advanced training in the arts; the others have a variety of liberal arts and technical backgrounds. Most (69 percent) make $20,000 or less, four (15 percent) make from $20–40,000, and just one (8 percent) earns $40–60,000 (We received only thirteen responses to this question.). Half of the designers have or have had part-time employees.

In 2006 we found ninety artisan designers working in Portland. There are almost certainly more now. What's more, there is tremendous difference among them. Frocky Jack Morgan specializes in deconstructed dresses for weddings and special events. Pen Felt is an accessories maker: flower pins, hair clips, and scarves. Queen Bee makes higher-price-point, whimsical bags and wallets out of a southeast studio/shop, now employing eleven workers.

And Arnold, of course, produces biannual lines of men and women's fashions that are reproducible and, for customers that come to his shop, customizable. Despite such differences, local designers were cognizant of the creative sharing of ideas and general cohesiveness of the local design community—though a healthy dose of competition among them was likewise reported. A survey of network connections given to twelve designers found that on average they knew 54 percent of the ninety local designers personally, and knew 74 percent of the designers professionally.

With so many local designers pumping out fashions, it shouldn't be surprising that a wealth of boutiques have sprouted up to distribute them. When Seaplane opened in 2000, it had no competitors. By 2006, twenty shops were in operation. Some have closed, but more new ones have opened, again elevating the total after three years. Many of these operations have connections to Seaplane. The studio that Adam Arnold (a former Seaplane consigner) occupies is an example of one type of space, where only the designer-owner's creations are sold. Elizabeth Dye (another former Seaplane consigner) operates The English Dept., a space in which she works and sells her own designs, but also the designs of others, local and international. A third model, typified by sustainable design boutique Olio United, sells local and non-local designs but is not designer-operated.

The designers we spoke with sold 80 percent of their clothes through retail outlets either in Portland our in boutiques in other cities. Of the 20 percent that were direct sales, several had significant online sales, but on average this accounted for only 15 percent of all sales. The remainder (5 percent) were sold directly to friends or personal customers or as a result of fashion shows. Half of all their sales (retail and direct combined) were local and half occurred outside of the metropolitan Portland area; those with the highest percentage of local sales were the fashion designers who had their own retail outlets. Portland's relatively small size operates as a limiting factor on the number of items that can be sold by a given designer. Each retailer is selective in whose designs they display because they do not want to stock the same designers as other local retailers. This forces them to seek markets elsewhere. On the other hand, this lowers the barrier to entry for new designers since it limits the number of shops a single designer can consign to. The web pages of designers interviewed show a diverse set of boutiques across the nation and internationally that handle their designs.

Unlike Manhattan's concentrated "garment district," Portland's fashion economy is scattered geographically among nearly every retail business district in the city. Would-be boutique owners have benefited from the city's attention to the needs of small businesses. Target area grants have been issued to improve retail business districts in nearly every corner of Portland, helping to maintain a quality stock of commercial storefronts. Artisans from hairstylists to chefs to clothing designers have benefited from these constantly evolving, appealing, and well-trafficked retail spaces. What's more, because the supply is good, rental costs have remained low. This makes it more likely that the retail market for clothing can expand and become more diverse. Compared to high rent and concentrated, big-city districts, the geographic diversity and relatively low cost of Portland's design retail sector have operated to the benefit of new entrants.

HIGH DIY TO HIGH FASHION

"DO WE TAKE it for granted? No! Do we know how good we have it? Yes!" So declares the Fashion page on Ultrapdx.com, a top website for style, fashion, design, art, and culture in Portland. "Something's happening here as the scene moves from high DIY to high fashion." Such an evolution—from the production of sometimes amateurish, if inventive, deconstructed garments to more professional, seasonal collections from new fabrics—is something Adam Arnold has witnessed with obvious approval. In the early years of the decade, he says (with a healthy dose of bravado), a lot of people "said they were designers" but they would "just take a bunch of t-shirts and rip them up and put glue and glitter on them and call it fashion." Returning to Portland from Seattle in 2002, Arnold brought some clothing into Seaplane for the first time, and the owners, he says, were taken aback that he had produced a proper line. "You mean you have more than one size?" they asked him with surprise.

In the years after, everyone has upped the ante. Healthy competition has allowed Seaplane (and the other new shops that opened their doors) to be choosier about the apparel that will grace their racks, and local designers have grown and improved.

The story of Emily Katz's career in fashion is a case in point. An art school graduate with no formal training in clothing design or construction, she and her boyfriend, Shaun Deller, started messing around, "drawing on used shirts" with a sewing machine. They were in Baltimore at the time, living in Deller's parents' house. He had graduated and was working; she was also staying there "with nothing to do." Some time later, they decided to move to Portland—Katz because she wanted to return home to where family was still living, Deller because he was attracted to the area's natural amenities. But when they arrived, they had frustratingly little success finding jobs (Katz thinks an art school education can be a hindrance in a town already overrun by creative types). Katz's father, an entrepreneur himself, suggested they make clothing embroidery their full-time business.

They dubbed themselves Bonnie Heart Clyde and set to work amassing a stock of uniquely embroidered t-shirts and sweatshirts. The design process was organic, says Katz. "I would just put the needle down and start moving the fabric and there would be this shape, and then all of a sudden it would be a figure, and then there would be a couple and they were dancing, and then there would be music notes." Bonnie Heart Clyde made their debut in July 2003 at Last Thursday on Alberta Street, a monthly street festival where local artisans of all stripes are free to set up a table and hawk their wares. "We just hit it off. We were on the streets selling our designs.… We had made eighty pieces and sold about sixty of them. They flew off the rack."

Within the first two hours at Last Thursday, a passerby stopped to suggest that their designs would sell well in the Japanese market. He had a friend who was a distributor for Japanese stores, who just so happened to be coming to Portland to check out some designers two weeks later. Soon Bonnie Heart Clyde was gracing the shelves of large, well-known department stores, "like Barney's in New York, only the Japanese version." After the Last Thursday experience they moved their operation into the Everett Station Lofts, where Katz's stepmother had an art studio that she no longer used. They began to travel intermittently across the country to sell their work. "We did our own repping.… We went to New York; we went to Philadelphia; we got stores in Portland that wanted to sell the line. So, from the very beginning we were self-sustaining; we didn't have other jobs, we had a little bit of money saved up from before, but mostly the business from the beginning was taking care of us."

Soon Katz was moving away from embroidery and found garments, toward planned lines of women's fashions from new fabrics. "It's a year in advance now, whereas before it would not even be a second in advance." She started going to trade shows across the country, which proved to be important not only as spaces to market her work as a "really serious designer," but also as fantastic learning communities for her increasingly chancy entrepreneurial endeavor. Deller, her boyfriend, dropped out of Bonnie Heart Clyde, not because of conflicts with design but because the trade shows, at thousands of dollars per season, were so costly—"not a risk he wanted to take." Today Katz has dropped the Bonnie Heart Clyde label in favor of working under her own name, and Deller has developed his own business designing bike apparel. Katz has found success while associating herself with the newest trend in Portland fashion—an explicit attention to sustainability in the design and construction of garments. Her website now reads: "Emily Katz: Sustainable Contemporary Fashions."

SCALING UP?

ADAM ARNOLD REACHES for an organic metaphor to describe how he approaches one of the most challenging issues facing all successful artisans: how fast to grow, and when to stop. "Your business or career is your baby. It grows at a biological pace." Arnold chose to build slowly and naturally, eschewing loans in favor of sustainable growth. Indeed, he gets a bit philosophical about business economics, refusing to take credit cards not because of the fees, but because they "upset the balance." He continues: "When someone throws down a credit card, it's more than just a credit card. They are paying you with time that they haven't spent, and you're supposed to spend time working on stuff that doesn't exist.… It screws everything up. All of a sudden I have more work than is possible for me, and I have to hire someone." Arnold has a mysterious faith in the beneficence of the market that prevents him from worrying about money, even when times are tough. "I know that when I need it, someone will always walk through the door and order something."

Arnold's business has already achieved a state of homeostasis at what, for him, is the ideal size. The only man on the payroll, he prefers to complete every aspect of the garment-construction process himself. For other designers who would like to contract out parts of production to free up time for the more imaginative aspects, difficulties often arise, particularly in Portland. Whether or not they align themselves officially with sustainability, artisan designers here tend to be cognizant of the problems of exploitative labor that undergird the globalized fashion industry. Even production facilities on American soil, concentrated in Los Angeles and New York, are not guaranteed to treat their employees fairly. Despite greater expense, sourcing production locally would offer the twin benefits of supporting the Portland economy while permitting designers to personally monitor the social conditions of production.

But production capability in Portland is still quite underdeveloped. As Katz's business has expanded, she has had difficulty with the production aspect. "I would really, really love to have my entire line made of organic materials and made in the U.S., and ideally made in Portland… but there are still things that are holding this city back from that. Like, there isn't a big manufacturing infrastructure here for apparel, and so a lot of the designers that started in Portland did use, and continue to use, recycled garments." This is another angle from which deconstruction becomes so emblematic of Portland: It is not only the materials, but also the production facilities themselves that are rare, pushing designers toward alternative options. This is not to say that local production cannot be done. Queen Bee, for example, has assembled a small in-house manufacturing facility using local labor. But its viability depends on a model of year-round production of a relatively stable line of bag and accessories designs, not the on-again-off-again production needs of fashion designers who put out suites of annual or biennial fashions. Katz ended up working with a woman in Los Angeles who does "full-service," including screen-printing and computerized embroidery.

The lack of reliable productive capacity in Portland can operate as something of a limiting factor on business models. In a place with low barriers to market entry, a collaborative spirit among producers, and a moral economy that favors the underdog, this lack becomes yet another factor that dictates a certain form for players in the local fashion world. As one designer told us, "There are a lot of fish in the pond in Portland, but they are mostly the same size."[3] Fashion entrepreneurs in New York or Los Angeles would have trouble staying afloat on so little, but they have a wealth of production options in their fashion economies that make scaling up much easier.

While production has proven a limitation for ambitious designers who want to expand in a socially responsible way, it became near crippling for a local designer whose skyrocketing popularity was based explicitly on the message of sustainability. Anna Cohen, the New York- and Italy-trained fashion designer, found immediate, unexpected success in Portland in 2005 when she launched an eponymous line of women's fashion that married a commitment to sustainability with cutting-edge Italian design. She had worked in Italy for several years, a carnival for the senses that drew her in aesthetically but turned her away ethically. "The industry there is not based on integrity," Cohen explained.[4] A Portland native, she yearned for its healthier relationship to nature and returned home in 2004. After a short stint at Adidas, she launched her line with an ambitious commitment to socially and environmentally responsible production and organic, alternative fabrics.

Though each line that Cohen produced over the three years that she operated would total a maximum of five hundred or so constructed garments, the press and attention she received far outstripped the numbers. She almost single-handedly put Portland on the map for a new type of clothing, adding sustainable high fashion to its established prowess in high DIY. Cohen earned two covers of *Women's Wear Daily*, the trade magazine that all fashion insiders take care to read. Interns came from across the country, and the world, to work essentially as volunteers and were rewarded with goodies such as trips to Paris—where Cohen was invited to do a show for free. Sales inquiries poured in, even a year after the unexpected success essentially overwhelmed Cohen's production and organizational capacities. "Next time I would build a relationship [with a producer] before starting a line. I didn't know what I was getting into." To find such instant success as an independent designer, Cohen explained, is almost unheard of. She was certainly among the most successful to come out of Portland.

So why the astronomical success? Cohen sums it up succinctly: "It was the right time, right product, right message. Nobody was doing sustainability in a way that was fashionable." Right product meant a design that spoke to people. Though Cohen keeps her eye trained on international developments in fashion, elements of place, of Portland, emerged in her work. "I'm influenced locally by nature.... It comes through in a very intangible way. It's the simplicity and the perfect asymmetrical balance of nature as an underlying theme." Indeed, Portland is increasingly branded in conjunction with those themes—nature, livability, simplicity, and especially sustainability—as it moves from a regional metropolis to one that is on the radar of consumers both nationally and internationally.

Sustainable design

Anna Cohen represents the fashion incarnation of a sustainable approach to business that now operates across all sectors in Portland, essentially forming an economic cluster united not by type of product or service, as is traditional, but by process. More than with other fashion designers, Cohen has found a supportive learning community among a diverse group of entrepreneurs united by an advertised commitment to sustainable production, some of whom are involved in Portland's Sustainable Design Alliance, which she helped found. Such communities are helpful in overcoming the unique challenges that sustainable businesses face, primarily a steep learning curve and substantial information costs. It's simple to buy the cheapest product or service available, but when you throw ethical factors into the decision-making mix, every choice becomes an attempt to reconcile the "triple bottom line," essentially finding that precarious balance among financial, ecological, and social priorities.

Small-scale artisan designers like Arnold, or those doing deconstruction work, operate sustainably in their own ways. But this can be something of an inadvertent sustainability, since it is difficult to do much harm when you are doing something so small. Arnold doesn't label himself a "sustainable designer" in the way that Cohen and, now, Katz do. He doesn't use organic fabrics, but, on the other hand, he has never owned a car. During a break on a rainy day, you can catch him riding his bicycle on the streets of southeast Portland with a bolt of fabric strapped onto his back. For Arnold's customers, such details can be important; they can be woven into the story of a product that consumers of artisan wares value. The experience of having clothes created in a studio for you, Arnold says, is addictive, and keeps customers coming back.

The "sustainability" label is likewise intended to communicate a story of product, operating as shorthand for environmental and social responsibility—things conscious consumers increasingly care about. It trades specificity for ease of recognition; buyers can see the word and act quickly, without needing to investigate the details of production—the story—themselves. So "sustainable production" exists in a complex relationship to the artisan economy. The artisan economy tends to operate according to the tenets of sustainability more than conventional production simply because artisans are interested in things other than making money, but the sustainability-as-business-label system ultimately operates in the service of more efficient (if responsible) consumption.

Cohen's success demonstrates, in part, the marketability of the term. From a strategic perspective, then, the more Portland can make itself synonymous with sustainability, all the better. The mayor's office, aware of this, has been busy for years pursuing a variety of sustainable development initiatives. To the extent that the local fashion economy has marketed itself as green, the city has shown signs of responsiveness. Mayor Sam Adams, then a city commissioner, was involved in the 2008 Portland Fashion Week, three years after it made a move to align itself explicitly with the term sustainability (Cohen is now on the board). The press attention it received, particularly outside of Portland, increased in kind. Several of the new boutiques market only sustainable designers, from Portland and elsewhere. Chances seem good, in light of all this, that high sustainable fashion will replace high DIY as the essence of Portland clothing design in the future, provided production difficulties can be overcome.

Sounds like a winning situation all around, right? Arnold begs to differ. He is worried that, just as tie-dye and Birkenstocks came to define (and thus limit) the old Portland in the collective imagination, sustainability is stifling and girdling future possibilities. What's more, he worries that it will be a gimmick that detracts from real design innovation and quality. Arnold is clearly irritated when we broach the subject: "I could totally strangle people with a sustainable rope!" he cries. He believes that what he calls "the glory days of Portland fashion," from around 2004 to 2005, are dead. "Nobody knew what was going on, and it was total magic. There was every possibility." Ultimately it is difficult to agree with Arnold. Not because it is false to think that certain possibilities have inevitably been foreclosed, but because one person's glory days are always another's dark days, as each person struggles to shape a different reality. The present is the visible moment in a long story that unravels in unpredictable directions. A rainy Northwest metropolis emerges, somehow, as a case study in the dynamics of an artisan economics, with a fashion cluster leading the charge.

CHAPTER 6
BIKES

Oliver Smith
Bridger Wineman

ALL EYES IN THE CYCLING INDUSTRY turned to Portland in February 2008, when the North American Handmade Bicycle Show (NAHBS) was held at the Oregon Convention Center. That the convention would be held in Portland was no surprise. Just a few months before, the *New York Times* described Portland as "Bike City, USA," a recognition that derived from the city's deep cycling culture, but also from the reputation of Portland's burgeoning cluster of bike builders.[1] At the 2007 NAHBS, Portland builders had taken home awards for "Best City Bike" and "Best New Builder."

A year before the show, product designer Aaron Hayes was burned out. Ready for a change, he listened intently to a friend describe his visit to the shop of a Portland bike builder. He was intrigued, and in researching what it would take to get started, Aaron discovered the United Bicycle Institute, a school for bike builders in Ashland, Oregon. Quickly completing the school's two-week crash course, Aaron jumped into Portland's expanding local industry of handmade bike construction. He was determined to make a splash at NAHBS, establish a new business, and redefine his career. "I had six months, basically, to get started, create a shop, start making bikes, build a brand, and put four bikes in the show…. It was a very fixed time line."[2]Aaron had two goals for the show: to win "Best New Builder," and to sell a bike. He did both.

Like other Portland bike builders, Aaron's brand, Courage Bicycle, capitalizes on a combination of factors converging in the city: bike-friendly initiatives by government agencies, an increasingly pervasive local cycling scene, renewed interest in the traditional roots of bicycle construction, the special place in the national and global market being etched out by Portland frame builders, and low- or no-cost marketing available through the internet. Portland bike journalist Jonathon Maus describes current trends as "the simultaneous flowering of many different aspects of the bike culture—frame builders, shops, racing, nonprofits, fun rides, the political scene; everything seems to be hitting on all cylinders."[3]

Portland has become the place for bikes. For his part, Aaron is already looking towards next year's show. "I'm going to redouble my efforts," he says of preparing again for the show that launched his new business. "I have blocked out three months just to work on it. I'm going to come to NAHBS with really cool stuff."

PORTLAND'S BIKE ECONOMY

BICYCLE ARTISANS—THOSE WHO BUILD BIKES and their components, accessories, and apparel largely by hand—form part of a large and growing local bike economy reinforced by the thousands of Portlanders taking up biking. According to a 2008 study by consultants Alta Planning + Design, Portland's bicycle-related industries were estimated to contribute $90 million to the city's economy, an increase of 38 percent since 2006. The study also found that the total number of companies in the bike sector increased 50 percent, to 143 over the same period, and that collectively, bike-related businesses provide up to 1,150 local jobs.[4] The recent growth of Portland's overall cycling economy is mirrored by a sharply increasing number of cyclists on the city's roads and trails, both overall and relative to auto traffic. Traffic counts compiled in 2007 by the Portland Department of Transportation (PDOT) at locations throughout Portland show an 18 percent increase over the previous year. PDOT also found the proportion of bikes relative to motor vehicles crossing the Willamette River has more than doubled since the decade's beginning.[5]

CAR-FREE CULTURE

PORTLAND'S ENCOURAGEMENT OF ALTERNATIVES to auto transportation goes back to 1971, when effective advocacy by a nascent bike lobby and the Oregon Environmental Council led to the passage of the Oregon Bicycle Bill. This path-breaking bill was the first in the country to mandate that 1 percent of the transportation funds going to Oregon cities and counties be used for construction of bike and pedestrian pathways. These funds had the effect of pulling bike advocates into Portland's transportation planning infrastructure and helped seed Portland's wide-ranging bike culture.[6] Efforts beginning in the 1990s by city planners provided numerous improvements to the city's bicycle infrastructure, including the designation and signing of bicycle boulevards, striping of roads with bike lanes, and the creation of several off-street paths. Such efforts helped create an increasingly comprehensive regional bicycle transportation network. These infrastructure improvements, together with maps and other public education and outreach by government and advocacy organizations, have helped make bicycling safer and more

The mark of a maker: Courage Bicycles. Photo © Whitney Gayer

accessible. A flood of new and more frequent bike riders—ranks bolstered by transplants drawn from less bike-conscious reaches of the country—is evidence of the success of these measures. The result is obvious during a morning commute on one of the four bicycle-friendly bridges crossing the Willamette River, which carried an average of more than 14,000 cyclists each day in 2007. Interestingly, this dramatic increase in bicycle use is greater among women, who now account for 31 percent of all cyclists in counts conducted by PDOT.[7] These successful efforts at increasing cycling paid off with national recognition in 2008 when Portland became the first large city to earn the League of American Bicyclists designation of "platinum-level Bicycle Friendly Community."[8]

Although car ownership in Portland is relatively inexpensive and convenient compared to large cities, such as New York and Washington DC, a "car-free" lifestyle has blossomed. This development was recognized in 2008 when Portland hosted the World Carfree Network conference, the first such conference held in the U.S.[9] The bike network, combined with the city's transit system and planners' focus on developing amenities in neighborhoods, allows people to access work, shopping, and social and recreation destinations without a car. Portland's emerging reputation for a car-free lifestyle is a significant draw for a new creative class, especially bike-related artisans. Natalie Ramsland of Sweetpea Bicycles notes that, after college, she wanted to move somewhere that she could bike. Ramsland moved to Portland and became a bike messenger before turning to bike building (after a stint in graduate school for architecture).[10] Bike builder Joseph Ahearne relates a similar story. After traveling through the states and living out of the country for several years, he finally settled in Portland. "[T]his was the only town I wanted to be in because…I didn't want to live in a place where I had to drive everywhere. I came just because I could ride my bike wherever I needed to go."[11]

Other bike artisans cite intangibles: the attitude of the community, the proximity of services, and the ease and life in Portland that make it a compelling place to take root and start a business. Sean Chaney, a new frame-builder who recently moved his family from the Washington DC area, says, "Just the vibe of Portland is really a major thing that helped us make a decision to move here. It's a bonus that it's such a great bike city."[12] Ahearne, now an established frame builder of over five years, describes the ease of doing business in Portland, "I have it pretty easy, I mean, I know a good portion of the bike shop workers on a first name basis. I incorporate wood into some of my racks, and the guy who does my wood is right around the corner; I've got a hardware store down the road; there's a bike shop two blocks away. I mean, it's all very, very easy for me."

A system of connected bikeways, distinct neighborhoods, vibrant commercial districts, and relatively flat topography make the east side of Portland an especially compelling micro-environment for bike artisans, where it is practical, convenient, and pleasant to live a cycling lifestyle. Local framebuilder Jordan Hufnagel describes the setting: "This is a city designed to support local businesses and develop self-supporting neighborhoods. To find a big-box store you have to go well out of the city center, and there is no reason to. You can find most things you desire within twenty blocks."[13]

"For the most part I bike everywhere and use my trailer to haul the stuff," explains Shaun Deller, formerly of Bonnie Heart Clyde fashion designs, and now a maker of biking hats. "It's really convenient to have a post office down the street, my [seamstress] is down the street, most of the bike shops in town just down the street. So I can get to everything within five or ten minutes and do all my business by bike. Even riding out to the Goodwill [where Deller acquires bulk used fabric for his hats] I can ride on the Springwater Corridor the whole way there and have a nice leisurely ride through the park. I feel like location is really important."[14]

Portland's (and Oregon's) bicycle racing scene has also helped lay groundwork for the artisan bike builders, many of whom were racers themselves. Several road and mountain bike races are held each week, and hundreds flock to view and participate in cyclo-cross races in the fall. Tony Pereira writes on his website: "After doing just a few 'cross races, I was hooked. The scene is the biggest in the country, and the vibe is a lot like the early days of mountain bike racing—laid-back, beer-flowing good fun."[15] The city also annually hosts a criterion race through downtown streets. In total, races—together with rides, events, and tours—are estimated to contribute over $9 million to the Portland economy.[16] These races allow local bike builders to show off their creations to other racers and spectators, a potentially large market for handmade bikes.

Aaron Hayes, owner of Courage Bicycles, outside his northeast workshop. Photo ©
Whitney Gayer

THE FRAME BUILDERS

THE HEART OF PORTLAND'S artisan bicycle economy, the frame build-ers—men and women whose livelihood is the design and construction of entire bicycles in shops and garages—represent a tiny and specific occupa-tion, but anchor an intrinsically local artisan cluster of increasing national fame. The recent industry survey sponsored by the Portland Department of Transportation found that the number of handmade bike manufacturers more than tripled between 2006 and 2008, to a total of seventeen.[17] Local bike journalist Jonathon Maus notes that a new builder comes on the scene "every month or so."[18] The characteristics of the custom bikes they create are as individual as the builders themselves. While there is great variety in their individual products, a shared ethic binds them as a group of innovators and collaborators. Their work centers the artisan bike sector.

The first of Portland's bike builders was Andy Newlands, who began constructing his steel-framed bikes over thirty years ago under the brand Strawberry. Andy continues building bikes to this day, and his shop is a fix-ture of Portland's Goose Hollow neighborhood. Other relatively well-known handmade-bike manufacturers include Ira Ryan, who constructs bikes of the same name, Joseph Ahearne of Ahearne Cycles, Natalie Ramsland of Sweetpea, Sacha White of Vanilla Bicycles, and Tony Pereira of Pereira Cycles. Other small builders have emerged in recent years with names like Signal Cycles, Courage, and MAP, the classic material used to construct frames, is used most often, but more exotic materials such as titanium and wood are used by builders like Sean Chaney of Vertigo Cycles and Ken Wheeler of Renovo Hardwood Bicycles.

An imperative of continual refinement and the search for perfection informs the craft of these frame builders. Tony Pereira insists, "My goal is just to have the most perfect finished product as possible. You're always trying to make it better. And if there's something wrong with it, then that's going to lead to it being better the next time." Aaron Hayes, the product designer turned bike-maker, cites constant innovation as the calling card of a new generation of Portland bike builders. "That's one thing too that I don't think most people realize: that if you're in consumer products you have to be constantly evolving and changing and coming out with new stuff." While much of the "new stuff" has been done by builders of past generations, the current generation of builders uses new techniques, materials, and applications of different concepts that result in bikes that are part original and part classic.

Cooperation and collaboration

Collaboration, both formal and informal, has been crucial for many of the frame builders trying to break into the trade. Formal apprenticeships, roundtable discussions focused on business issues, and regular get-togethers at local brewpubs each play a role in fostering the development of the Portland bicycle-building niche. Tony Pereira describes the ease in which he was introduced to the city's bicycle builders upon moving to Portland. "The other frame builders were very warm.... Within a few days of moving here, I was at [Andy Newlands'] shop, hanging out, talking shop." Andy Newlands also served as a mentor for Natalie Ramsland, teaching her key frame-building skills. Ramsland credits Newlands for being "incredibly generous with his time" and offering knowledge from his thirty-plus years of experience that she will carry on. Several mentorships such as this have occurred or are currently underway that provide new entrants to the market.

One of the most significant partnerships has been spearheaded by a public agency, the Portland Development Commission (PDC), a semi-autonomous agency tasked with aligning development efforts with public goals and effectively applying public funds to such efforts. In 2006, the PDC gathered frame builders together for pizza and asked them to describe their business problems. Several sessions were held in which PDC personnel and business-persons from the wider bike industry mentored builders about issues such as marketing, bookkeeping, and taxes. More importantly, the meetings helped provide builders a stronger sense of purpose and opportunity. "I think we began to take ourselves more seriously as a group," says Ramsland. "I think they've done an excellent job in creating an atmosphere where you feel like you're part of the city and they really want you here," adds Hayes.

The meetings helped Portland's artisan bike industry coalesce. Capitalizing on the collective energy developing at the time of the PDC meetings, several of the frame builders recently organized the Oregon Bicycle Constructors Association (OBCA). Tony Pereira, the ad hoc president, notes that the OBCA was modeled after the Oregon Brewers Guild. Goals of the association currently include trying to obtain group liability and health insurance, as well as pooling for buying power.

Most collaboration between the builders, however, is informal and spontaneous. The nature of the business presents problems that can only be solved by others in the industry. For example, Pereira notes that "often you'll run out of something, and it'll just grind everything to a halt, and you'll just call up another builder down the street and say 'do you have such and such?'" Ramsland describes how when she needed help learning how to do a certain technique called fillet brazing, Pereira invited her to his shop and provided "an amazing stream of consciousness talking me through what it was that he saw as metal melted in front of him."

Of course, there is some competition among the builders, given that many produce overlapping types of bikes. "It's crowded with builders," says Ahearne. Yet, the competition is not too oppressive, because the demand is currently steady and the market is expanding, largely due to effective low-cost marketing, such as word of mouth and the internet. Ahearne identifies an international market for handmade bikes that is still being developed, "I don't really feel the heat from that because we're all doing our thing, and I think we're all pretty busy. There's enough room for all of us. At least 50–75 percent of my market is outside of Portland." Most of the full-time builders in operation for more than a year have waiting lists. Builders respect the work of others, each of whom have a distinctive style that differentiates them from others. According to Ramsland, "it's not the cutthroat, survival-level competition; it's more the kind of competition where you spur each other on to the next level." With a rising number of frame builders attempting to make it their full-time work, it is uncertain how competitiveness in this sector will change in the future.

CHALLENGES OF RUNNING A BUSINESS AND SCALING UP

BICYCLE-RELATED BUSINESSES IN PORTLAND encounter both opportunity provided by an open, collaborative culture and an expanding interest in cycling, and challenges associated with economic realities of starting a small business and growing it to a comfortable size. "Rent is fairly cheap here. That's something that makes it easier to start a small business," explains

Shaun Deller. "Portland's been the reason I've been able to do this really.... I feel like moving to Portland was just the right thing for me because of the bike culture here, the do-it-yourself kind of craft culture of people starting their own small businesses. And people are really receptive to that. I don't really know of any other place where I could have made that happen."

Currently, most of the bicycle artisans work by themselves. There are exceptions (e.g., Vanilla has a staff of six), but most are entirely run by one person. As a result, the artisans must deal with a host of business issues in addition to creating their products. Pereira looks back on how his expectations for his company have evolved, saying "You get into it because of your passion, and then you realize you have to run a business. Goals and planning and things like that, for most frame builders that I know, came later." Most of the frame builders started building for reasons other than creating wealth. But in order for the artisans to sustain themselves, they have to generate some money.

That many of the frame builders have one-year or longer wait lists would indicate to most business-inclined people that the builders should hire more people and expand their operations. In fact, however, several of the frame builders are clearly hesitant to hire anyone else. For one, the artisans do not want to lose any creative control. "The more you expand, the less of an artisan product it really is," says Pereira. "Where is the artisan if you've got eight people touching the thing?" Aaron Hayes agrees, "There's definitely a cult of personality that exists around a lot of the builders. How much can you have someone else do and still have someone want to buy your bike because you built it?" Ahearne agrees that maintaining artistic control is absolutely crucial to his business: "I wouldn't mind having someone to help with some of the smaller things, but as far as the detail work it's got to be me. It's my name on the bike, so I've got to have control of that."

Another reason for hesitancy in scaling is that profit margins are currently thin. Many of the well-known frame builders still earn a net profit of less than twenty thousand dollars annually despite their reputation. Aaron Hayes describes the financial reality faced by many builders, unable to scale up their businesses without losing the artistic control that makes them unique. For new builders like Hayes and Chaney, both of whom opened shops in 2008, the initial investment in equipment has been a challenge. "I put in a ton of money and sixty-plus hours of work a week," says Hayes.

"I'm really busting my butt trying to start this small business…. I feel like it's working so far; it's just going to take a few years to become profitable. So the question is, 'Can I stick it out that long?'" Finally, some artisans may neither want to work for, nor manage, others. Negative past experiences working for others helped lead some to a vocation in which they have more flexibility and command of their work.

Nonetheless, several of the frame builders see paths for expanding production. One is through simply making the operation more efficient—builders are constantly looking for ways of reducing the amount of time it takes to do various tasks. Even the most efficient builders make a maximum of just forty bikes per year. Other builders pay assistants to help with bookkeeping, taxes, and other tasks separate from designing and building bikes. Some, such as Ramsland, envision working closely with customers on fitting and designing bikes, but not actually building each frame. A few builders express similar ideas about increasing production while maintaining control over design. Sacha White's company, Vanilla Bicycles, introduced a line of bikes in 2007 under the name Speedvagen, all of which had the same basic paint job, materials, and purpose (cyclo-cross), but were custom fit for customers. Other builders have expressed a desire to have one or more "custom stock" models.[19] While builders currently have wide-ranging opinions regarding scaling up, the industry is still young, and it is hard for builders to predict how their goals and expectations will evolve as time goes on.

PORTLAND AS A BRAND, INTERNET AS A VEHICLE

TWO KEY TOOLS help market Portland's artisan bike goods: One is the internet, which allows people from around the country and the world to gain knowledge about the products. The other is Portland itself: the association of products with Portland, the "platinum" bike city, makes builders more attractive to bike-savvy individuals beyond the region.

The growth of the internet has undoubtedly facilitated the artisan bike industry. The current wave of Portland's bike artisans has followed saturation of the internet in American households. Customers use the internet to easily get a sense for the products, the potential of the artisans to create what they desire, the process, and the costs. The artisans themselves often blog about, and post photos of, their latest builds, which are widely circulated via blogs and internet forums. Before a phone call is made or an email sent, interested customers can pore over the builders' work from home or the office. As a result, many of the bikes produced in Portland are sold to customers living elsewhere. Indeed, several of the builders estimate that only 10 percent of sales are within Portland.

Nevertheless, the city's many bicyclists and the work of the frame builders have developed Portland itself as a marketing feature. According to one bike apparel maker, "Portland has the potential (and may be well on its way) to become like a brand of its own within the industry, representing authenticity and quality within the international industry."[20] Many builders specify phrases such as "handcrafted in Portland" or "handmade with love and fury in Portland, Oregon." The explosion of bicycle builders in the city and media coverage of it has given "made in Portland" a new and strongly positive meaning that bicycle enthusiasts around the country increasingly recognize. Pereira envisions that eventually, "people will come to Portland for a bicycle, much like they would go to Switzerland for a watch or to Milan

Tony Pereira proudly displays one of his handmade bicycles. Photo © Whitney Gayer

for a suit," and hopes that the OBCA will help further this vision. Ramsland agrees, and would like customers to visit Portland and experience the city by bicycle when buying a Sweetpea bike.

While the place of origin for conventional bikes (usually Taiwan or China) is rarely a selling point, handmade bikes are deeply place oriented. The internet offers clear details about the handmade bikes as well as a view of the places from where they came. In essence, Portland has become a brand, and the internet has become the vehicle for selling this brand. Ahearne describes the impact this way: "Because Portland is such a big bike town it lends validity to what I'm doing…. Even if I were [somewhere else] doing what I'm doing exactly the same way, I think it would be a little bit different for outsiders because they would be like, 'Oh he lives in wherever, and what can those people possibly know about bikes?'"

ACCESSORIES AND COMPONENTS

MANY ACCESSORY AND COMPONENT MAKERS, ranging from creative craftspersons working from home to multimillion-dollar parts makers, also call Portland home. Portland-made accessories include handcrafted wooden fenders by Sykes, recumbent bike machined parts by TerraCycle, even woolen "smittens" made of recycled materials and "beer-view mirrors" made from spokes and bottle caps. At the other end of the scale is Chris King Precision Components, an internationally distributed maker of bicycle headsets (a component that connects the handlebar stem and fork to the bike frame) and wheel hubs. The company positions itself in the market with a characteristically Portland mix of innovation, quality, and social and environmental consciousness. Distinguished by a reputation for quality and durability, Chris King products and processes express the business' social and environmental consciousness. Part of the sales revenues from Chris King's distinctive pink Pretty and Strong series components, for example, is donated to breast cancer advocacy. In addition, the usually dirty industrial process of anodizing was taken in-house with state-of-the-art facilities that eliminate waste-water discharge. Used oil and metal chips, byproducts of the manufacturing process, are recovered and recycled. Even an ongoing shop renovation is guided by imperatives for energy conservation, use of "green" materials, the recycling of waste, and engineering a clean manufacturing process.[21]

CROSSOVER ARTISANS

COLLABORATIONS AND CROSSOVERS between cycling and other artisan sectors inevitably result from the spirit of innovation and openness that characterizes Portlanders. Local cycling-bag manufacturer Elias Grey describes it this way: "The more you are [rooted in the community], the more you keep seeing the same people and meeting new people that all know each other and all do similar things."[22] Bicyclists involved in business, recreation, and advocacy interact with each other in a dense and overlapping network of social connections where people share support, information, and even passions about politics, social initiatives, and the environment.

The flow of ideas between the cycling community and other artisan sectors goes both ways. While builder Tony Pereira reports he frequently discusses his creative process, problems, and sources of inspiration with nearby metal artists, painters, and a guitar maker, other craft enterprises look to bike culture for their inspiration. Local craft breweries often hold cycling events and style pubs and products with cycling themes. The Lucky Labrador Beer Hall hosts biannual "Hottest" and "Worst Day of the Year" rides benefiting the Community Cycling Center, a local bike education, service, and advocacy nonprofit. Cyclists can use an indoor bike rack in the former Freightliner garage, which now houses the beer hall, to keep their bikes safe while quaffing a pint of the brewery's "Bike Route Rye" ale. At Hopworks Urban Brewery in southeast Portland, owner Christian Ettinger has installed many bike-themed elements, including a spectacular scrap bike-frame sculpture above the bar and banana-seat headrests above urinals in the men's restroom. Hopworks also boasts parking facilities for up to fifty bikes out front. Other crossovers include Joel Domreis of Courier Coffee Roasters, who delivers hand-roasted coffee beans by bike to homes, restaurants, and offices. A partnership called Gracie's Wrench provides bike-commuting consulting with a female focus to individuals and businesses. Ellee's Yoga even offers yoga classes specifically geared toward the needs of cyclists.

Many Portland bike-apparel artisans share a signature ethos of quality, authenticity, local sourcing, and environmental and social consciousness. Shaun Deller recycles thrift store materials to create his unique hats in a production process out of his basement, relying nearly exclusively on two-wheeled transportation. Elias Grey looks for new waterproof materials for his cycling bags and backpacks, rather than the traditional petroleum-based fabrics used in most commercial bags. He finds his niche in the market with customers who value a local product, designed and put together in Portland by a local artisan. Both of these makers conduct routine business processes by bike, from picking up raw materials to delivering finished products for sale.

These crossover bike enterprises attest to the maturing of cycling as a cultural force in Portland. They are signs of exuberance from a local culture that is growing and deepening. New types of bike-related media that document and celebrate this energy often exhibit artisan traits and demonstrate the extent of cycling's impact on the local economy. Filmed by Bike is an annual film festival held in Portland that helps raise money for the Multnomah County Bike Fair. The creators of the festival of short films celebrating biking describe the motivation behind it in terms of cultural progress: "An advanced and mature society is one that recognizes, nurtures, revels in and celebrates its creative class, its art and culture. Here in Portland, our bike culture is beyond the basics, and we are wholly embracing our place in society as more than just bikers."[23] Similar sentiments are reflected in other Portland-based cycling media like BikePortland.org, the quintessential bike news source maintained by Jonathan Maus; Microcosm Publishing, an alternative media publisher behind *Bicycle!: A Repair and Maintenance Manifesto* and other "bikey" works; the KBOO *Bike Show* on community radio; *Cycle Seen*, a local bike photography exhibition; even *Pornography of the Bicycle*, a traveling compilation of short films celebrating cycling's alternative edges.

CONCLUSION

THE BICYCLE REVOLUTION has a history with deep roots but is still unfolding in Portland and elsewhere. Each day brings new and surprising developments to the bike economy. The current success of Portland's bike artisans can be attributed to the city's culture and public policy—it capitalizes on a setting that includes prized neighborhoods, parks, and parkways that provide interest, inspiration, and proximity of services. Portland's hard infrastructure (an extensive bicycle transportation network, materials suppliers, and warehouse space) and soft infrastructure (a thriving culture of diverse,

enthusiastic bicyclists and supportive city leaders) give artisan bike builders a foundation for their businesses. Artisans also receive assistance and
inspiration from other Portland artisans. Formal and informal associations
have allowed many of the artisans to simultaneously unite and expand their
visions. These artisans often share similar ethics about lifestyle and how they
relate to their customers, the broader civic community, and the environment.
They also share common opportunities and difficulties in managing businesses and employees, integrating personal values in their business, balanc-
ing product differentiation with efficient production, and collaborating to
grow the sector. Artisans also take advantage of increasing recognition of
Portland as a brand for bicycle innovation and the internet as a wide-reach-
ing, low-cost marketing vehicle. Every indication suggests the artisan bike
economy in Portland will continue to develop, tapping growing national
and international interest in authentic, custom goods and a renaissance of
cycling in general. With recognition of Portland's bicycle culture and builders
still growing, Portland's cachet as a brand will increase. As these builders
receive international recognition, the artisan bike industry will become more
varied. Some will expand their companies, and others will continue to build
each frame with their own hands. In any case, Portland will continue to be a
center of innovation for bicycle-related products as well as for cultural activities related to bikes. From child-carrying bakfiets to flask-holster-equipped
bikes to cold, mud-soaked cyclo-cross races, the revolution will be diverse.

ARTISANS ABOUND

CHAPTER 7
PORTLAND'S COFFEE CULTURE

Rebecca Ragin

IN PORTLAND, WHERE HUNDREDS of coffee shops dot the urban landscape, it's easy to take high-quality coffee for granted. Many residents don't realize that Portland is a mecca for the artisan coffee industry and the envy of coffee fanatics all over the country—even the world.

One indicator of Portland's importance is the fact that three coffee industry publications are based here. *Fresh Cup*, a magazine for specialty coffee and tea professionals, was founded in 1992. *Roast*, for the specialty coffee roaster, began in 2004. Four years ago, a magazine appeared for baristas, naturally dubbed *Barista Magazine*.

Another indicator is that students come to Portland from all over the world, including Europe, where coffee culture is hundreds of years old, to learn about coffee at the American Barista & Coffee School. "Portland is truly what I'd call the epicenter of independent specialty coffee," says Matt Milletto, director of the Portland-based school.[1] "Specialty coffee" is the industry term, coined in 1974, for what most would consider artisan coffee. The Specialty Coffee Association of America defines specialty coffee as "the highest quality green coffee beans roasted to their greatest flavor potential by true craftspeople and then properly brewed to well-established standards."[2] In other words, producing a cup of coffee that inspires the savoring of every sip takes careful work, from crop to cup.

Specialty coffees are, by definition, made from exceptional beans with distinctive flavors. Those flavors are partially a result of the location where the coffee is grown, similar to the concept of terroir for wine. To safeguard these special beans, harvesting and processing must be handled with great care, and the coffee must also be exported in a timely manner.

Once the coffee arrives in the United States, two groups honor the careful work of the farmers and processors in the country where the coffee originated: roasters, who transform green coffee into the chocolate-colored beans we all recognize as coffee, and coffee shop baristas, who grind and brew the beans, and finally serve the aromatic drink. In both areas, Portland's talent is unmatched.

The art of roasting: Stumptown sets the bar

It's hard for coffee lovers to imagine a Portland without Stumptown Coffee Roasters. Yet it was just over a decade ago that Duane Sorenson opened his first café on Southeast Division Street—the café that Stumptown's website describes as "the store that started a coffee revolution in Portland."[3] Although the description reads like marketing hype or arrogance, it is neither.

When Sorenson opened that first café in 1999, he brought the quality of the coffee front and center—and created a unique experience for the consumer—by combining roasting and retail in one location. As residents of the Pacific Northwest, where specialty coffee was born, Portlanders were familiar with espresso by the late 1990s. But according to Matt Lounsbury, director of operations for Stumptown, the independent coffee shop scene that is now so integral to the Portland experience simply didn't exist at the time.[4]

It was Stumptown that "really put a sparkle in people's eyes about coffee," says Julie Beals, editor of *Fresh Cup*. "For the longest time, it was really just Stumptown educating people as to what was outside the Starbucks experience. Even though Starbucks deserves credit for educating the consumer initially as to what a latte is and an espresso, Duane made it a hometown thing."[5]

From 2000 to 2006, the specialty coffee industry as a whole grew by half, from $8 billion to $12 billion. But it didn't grow equally in all parts of the country. Brent Fortune, owner of Crema Coffee & Bakery, relocated from San Diego to Portland largely because of the Rose City's burgeoning coffee scene. Fortune says, "When I came to Portland five years ago, coffee was still sort of exploding or evolving. Stumptown was this small, Portland-based company that was just starting to get some recognition in other parts of the country and the world."[6]

Stumptown doesn't qualify as small today. The company employs 120 people and has five locations in Portland, plus two in Seattle. In early 2009, Sorenson was at work opening a roastery in New York City. Despite the popularity of its cafés, Stumptown remains focused on roasting. "We'll continue to do what we're really good at, which is roasting coffee for people and getting it to them within a day," says Lounsbury. Continued respect within the industry for Stumptown's coffees demonstrates that it is possible for an artisan coffee company to grow significantly and still maintain quality. Sarah Allen, editor of *Barista Magazine*, says that Stumptown has "earned a reputation of consistent excellence and successful risk-taking in coffee buying."[7]

Stumptown typically pays at least 30 percent above fair trade price and has been known to fork over as much as one hundred dollars per pound for exclusive, small-batch coffees. "We're prepared to pay a lot of money because these are just beautiful coffees, and they're fun to share with the world," says Lounsbury.

To maintain close relationships with coffee growers, Sorenson and his employees travel regularly to the countries of origin to visit the farms. They also host the farmers' visits to Portland, opening their homes to the growers. Lounsbury says that as these relationships strengthen, so does the quality of the coffee.

BRANCHING OUT:
A DIVERSITY OF LOCAL MICRO-ROASTERS

AS STUMPTOWN HAS GROWN from a boutique roaster to a nationally and internationally recognized company, other roasters have sprouted in the space under its canopy, filling the micro-roasting niche.

In 2005, Din Johnson turned his roasting hobby of many years into a business, Ristretto Roasters, by opening a six-hundred-square-foot retail location in the Beaumont-Wilshire neighborhood. At the time, there weren't

The Division Street Stumptown roaster that started Portland's coffee revolution. Photo © Whitney Gayer

many small roasters in town. Johnson says, "Stumptown was the only kind of smaller, really super-specialty kind of roaster, but at that point they were edging toward bigger. There wasn't a whole lot [else], especially anything that was a roaster-café."[8]

In fact, Stumptown had such loyal followers that people frequently asked Johnson how he expected to compete. Did Portland really need another coffee roaster?

Several years later, the answer is clearly yes. Portland is home to nearly twenty different roasters. They run the gamut from larger operations like Kobos Coffee, with its 42,000-square-foot headquarters, and Boyd Coffee Company, which uses computerized roasters, to small-scale endeavors like Courier Coffee Roasters, whose coffee is served at about a dozen local markets and cafés.

Ristretto has done well for Johnson, who now employs seventeen. In 2008, he opened a second shop in north Portland, nearly double the size of the original Ristretto café. The new space includes a cupping room, where customers can sip samples of different coffees side by side to compare their individual tastes. Specific growing conditions make enough of a difference that specialty coffees have begun to be labeled not only with the region and country they come from, but also with the farm on which they were grown.

Although there are professional rating scales for grading coffee according to quality, small-scale roasting is—like winemaking—a largely subjective process. Johnson says, "Everybody's going to have their own unique signature on it. Even if you gave the same coffee to four or five different roasters, there'd definitely be a noticeable difference in how it tastes."

The first step, and one of the most important, is to choose which coffee to roast. Jeremy Adams of Cellar Door Coffee Roasters says, "In choosing beans, you're saying a lot about what you like, what you think is good."[9]

When deciding which coffees to buy, over the last decade local roasters have been taking an increased interest in social and environmental sustainability factors, such as the way the coffee is grown (shade grown or organic, for example) and the way the farm workers are treated.[10] In some cases, roasters create special programs to benefit the farmers who grow their coffee. Stumptown started Bikes to Rwanda, a nonprofit organization that provides cargo bicycles and a bike workshop and maintenance program to cooperative coffee farmers in Rwanda. In a similar vein, when Johnson traveled to a small village in Brazil to purchase coffee, he learned about a music program for at-risk village youth. For every pound that Ristretto has sold of coffee purchased in that village, Johnson has donated a dollar to the music program.

Once the roaster has chosen the coffee, he or she has to decide how to roast it to bring out the best qualities inherent in that particular coffee. Just a few extra seconds in the roaster can make a huge difference in how light or dark the coffee turns out, and by extension, how it tastes. Johnson says, "That's where the craft is: it's a few seconds here or there, or it's how you ramp the temperature up. You can sculpt it to [bring out] what you think are the optimal qualities in the coffee."

In the end, the consumer has the final say about how good a coffee is— also a subjective decision. Andrea Pastor, co-owner of Cellar Door, says that if ten Cellar Door customers were asked to name their favorite coffee, they might well name ten different coffees. "It's like with any sort of food: you have to agree with the palate of the person who is producing it," says Pastor.[11]

Like Johnson, Pastor and Adams first got hooked by roasting coffee at home. They used everything from a popcorn popper to a cast-iron pan until they learned how to roast coffee well enough to share it with friends. In October 2006, the couple bought their first roaster, which roasted five pounds of coffee at a time. After a successful season of selling their product at farmers' markets, they opened a coffee shop in February 2008.

By spring 2009, Cellar Door was roasting 200–250 pounds of coffee per week. Thirty percent is either used or sold at their café; the rest is sold to wholesale accounts—grocery stores, restaurants, and other coffee shops. By comparison, during their farmers' market days they went through about fifty pounds per week. To accommodate this growth, Cellar Door purchased a new roaster in 2008, which roasts four times as much coffee as their original Diedrich three-kilo machine, which they purchased on Craigslist.com. This upgrade should allow Pastor to spend less time roasting the eight or so varieties of coffee Cellar Door offers.

Part of the reason that many local roasters have learned the trade at home, through trial and error, is that coffee roasters tend to keep their secrets to themselves. Although an organization called Northwest Roaster's Group did form in 2006, Portland's roasters still have some work to do before they can be considered a cohesive community.

When they were getting started, Pastor and Adams found certain roasters to be helpful and willing to share knowledge and experience. One of these was Stanley Zemble of ZBEANZ, who has been in the roasting business for six years. "We really took our cue from him," says Pastor. Not everyone was as forthcoming, according to Pastor: "Other people definitely gave the impression that, unless you were apprenticing yourself to a master roaster for several years, you had no business even trying."

Roasters, however, do seem to be moving toward a more open exchange of information.[12] Johnson thinks that, as more small roasters set up shop in Portland, it's likely that a collaborative community will coalesce. "Portland has the potential to have a very open coffee community," he says.

THE SCIENCE OF SERVING

ONCE THE COFFEE LEAVES the roastery, it becomes the responsibility of the coffeehouse to provide the customer with an end product that represents the work put in by everyone else in the supply chain: the farmer, the harvester, the processor, the importer, and the roaster. The finest coffee, roasted with the utmost care, can be relegated to a mediocre or even bad beverage by the miscalculation of brewing factors such as grind, temperature, and time.

Naturally, proper brewing is emphasized in cafés run by roasters, like Stumptown, Ristretto, Extracto Coffeehouse, and Cellar Door, because these locations exist to showcase the roasters' coffees. Stand-alone coffee shops can be a different matter. It's all too easy for the quality of the coffee to slip when owners and staff split their focus between many tasks, from answering phones to grilling panini, from trouble-shooting problems with wireless internet access to organizing readings and music events.

To make sure vendors do its coffee justice, Stumptown employs four full-time espresso trainers who visit the cafés that serve its coffee. These trainers instruct the baristas in the finer details of espresso making and teach them how to bring out the best qualities inherent in each coffee.

Portland coffeehouses do better than most in terms of keeping coffee quality high. Kevin Fuller, owner of Albina Press coffee shops, says that there are dozens of people in Portland who make good coffee and that "even bad coffee in Portland is better than what you'll find in most cities."[13]

Then there are the coffee shops where the owners are committed to selling the highest-quality coffee. They invest in the best beans and top-of-the-line equipment—and put them into the hands of dedicated baristas. "When you try to pin down what separates us from someone else who has the exact same equipment and is using the exact same coffee, it would be the employees I have who are making it," says Fuller.

These are the places where, if the barista makes—or "pulls," in industry jargon—a shot of espresso that isn't up to their standards, they'll dump it and start over. Baristas like these are not dabblers. Most are professionals on a career track in the coffee industry, which could entail managing, opening a coffeehouse, or moving into roasting. Many have relocated to Portland from other cities for the express purpose of furthering their coffee careers.

At Albina Press, Fuller expects each and every one of his baristas to go on to other roles in the coffee business. He helps them prepare for that eventuality by investing time and money in training. For example, Fuller's employees compete in regional, national, and international barista competitions.

Portland is typically well represented in these competitions. In addition to Fuller, baristas from Blend Coffee Lounge, Coffee Bean International, Barista, and Coffeehouse-Five competed in the 2009 U.S. Barista Championship.

Over the past several years, as baristas have grown more and more focused and knowledgeable, the specialty coffee industry has struggled to fend off a perception of elitism. Ordering coffee from a barista who has such an intense interest in the nuances of artisan coffee can be off-putting to consumers who are not equally well informed. Fortune, who is a judge for the World Barista Championship competitions, in addition to owning Crema, says, "It's a fine line. It's really difficult to be knowledgeable about your product and share that in a way that doesn't come across as condescending and full of attitude."

In addition to consciously avoiding an air of superiority, gently educating customers is important to bridging that gap. Adam McGovern, owner of Coffeehouse Northwest, has honed his delivery of information on a number of topics, from brewing methods to different coffee regions. McGovern says, "You have a certain amount of time to communicate essential differences to people. Sometimes it's fifteen seconds, sometimes it's half an hour. You need to be able to judge that and deliver that in such a way that they aren't ever bored or confused, but they also are able to make an informed decision."[14]

Often it's a matter of retraining the customer's palate. Much of the coffee drinking population is accustomed to consuming large portions of heavily sweetened coffee beverages. Coffee shops that serve artisan coffee want customers to taste the flavors inherent in the coffee, not the syrups added to it.

So, when a customer asks for whipped cream on a latte, Fuller takes it as an opportunity to explain why Albina Press doesn't carry whipped cream: "We're trying to get them to taste the espresso and understand that everyone has these perceptions that they've created over time, like that if you drink straight espresso or have something small, it is going to be really bitter and really strong and really awful. Maybe in years past it was. But we've figured out how to make these drinks so it's almost like drinking a glass of wine or anything else: it's complex and beautiful."

Explaining something as ephemeral as flavor can only go so far. The next step, for some coffee shops, is to let customers taste the differences for themselves. Stumptown Annex has daily cuppings, where baristas serve a

Stumptown baristas prepare for the morning rush. Photo © Whitney Gayer

variety of coffees side by side so that customers can compare and contrast the nuances of each one, similar in concept to a wine tasting. Ristretto also schedules cuppings regularly.

Such exercises serve to bring the focus back to the coffee, instead of the barista. As McGovern puts it, "What's artisanal is being able to do something to the same degree that everyone else who makes coffee also does it and being able to represent clearly those qualities that are in the coffee—not something that you bring to it."

WHY PORTLAND?

THE COFFEE INDUSTRY often describes its evolution in waves. The first wave was "the coffee our parents drank," as thirty-eight-year-old Fuller puts it: coffee like Folgers and Maxwell House. The second wave was Starbucks, which created the U.S. market for espresso drinks like lattes and cappuccinos. The third wave is still developing, but no one doubts that Portland is on the leading edge of it. "Portland is the coffee community that has its finger on the pulse of what's happening in the industry," says Milletto.

What is it about Portland that nurtures this new coffee movement?

Portland's proximity to Seattle, where Starbucks was born in 1971, doesn't hurt, as *Fresh Cup*'s editor points out. Nor does the fact that the Rose City is still a relatively inexpensive place to live and do business when compared to cities like New York or Los Angeles—places where artisan coffee is just beginning to get a toehold. Those who want to start a shop in Portland can invest in an inexpensive space and work their way up.

McGovern, age twenty-six, believes that affordability is a major reason that Portland has so many young entrepreneurs. "Because rents are low, because start-up is lower, you don't have to work four other jobs just to support your hobby," he says.

Young, passionate entrepreneurs from different fields often grow their businesses in tandem. Cellar Door coffee is sold at a restaurant called Gravy. Adams tells his coffee shop customers about Gravy, and Gravy's staff tells their guests about Cellar Door. He believes that both businesses have grown as a result of these referrals.

Some of the best coffee in town is not served from a storefront at all. Café Vélo is a bike-powered coffee cart from which Rick Wilson makes made-to-order coffee for farmers' market customers.[15] Spella Caffe serves coffee roasted by its owner, Andrea Spella, from a street cart downtown.

All of these artisan businesses benefit from Portland's population of people who appreciate—and are willing to pay more for—handcrafted, unique goods and services. Beals says, "People here, more than in a lot of other cities, are willing to drive a fifteen-year-old car but drink really good wine and coffee, eat good cheese, and treat themselves to nice meals out."

McGovern agrees that Portland's demand for artisan coffee is unusually high: "Unfortunately, it's not national…. Portland is essential to this industry because there's already such an amazingly educated population."

Portlanders, especially, do seem to love having "their own special source for whatever they buy, whether it be a restaurant or a microbrew beer," says Milletto.

It's not a coincidence that local coffee industry insiders often mention fine restaurants and consumers who appreciate high quality coffee in the same breath—they credit Portland's active culinary community for residents' sophisticated palates. When the U.S. Barista Championship came to Portland in 2009, Fortune says that visiting baristas were "very envious of our whole food culture, our barista culture, and how those things fit together."

Between the city's affordability and a customer base that's willing to pay for a quality product, local coffee industry people who are at the top of their game can make a good income from their chosen profession.

Albina Press, Ristretto, and Stumptown all pay baristas more than minimum wage; Ristretto and Stumptown also provide health insurance. In addition, a professional barista can make as much in tips as a bartender or waitperson—sometimes more than 20 percent of a shop's daily sales. That kind of tip money is unique to independent coffee shops, according to Fuller, and perhaps even unique to Portland: "I think probably in other cities across the country there's still not that perception that people have, that customers of ours have, who come in and buy a dollar coffee and leave a dollar in the tip jar."

Specialty coffee companies also look after their own in non-financial ways. It's not at all unusual for an employee to start as a barista and work his or her way up to management. Even loyal customers are often brought into the fold, like Lounsbury was.

Coffee shops tend to be particularly supportive of artists. Many display employee-created art on café walls. Stumptown allows the musicians it has on staff to go on tour with their bands—and still have a job when they get back. "We want to have a place where we have those kinds of employees that are able to make a living but also have that other outlet.... Most of our employees are artists of one kind or another, whether they're in a band, a full-time painter, or they make clothes," says Lounsbury.

Hiring well-rounded people is important, because Stumptown employees end up spending time together outside the workplace. That tends to be the rule, not the exception, within both the local and national artisan coffee scene, which Beals describes as "a familial group."

Milletto says: "In the coffee industry, unlike some, people are so passionate. That's what makes it so great: the people. They're people I like to hang out with anyway, even if it's just drinking beers or coffee."

McGovern, too, finds that the separation between his work and "not work" life has disappeared: "The distinction is eroded as your profession becomes your life—and you're happy with that. It's totally fulfilling. There's nothing I'd rather be doing."

Room to grow

PEOPLE IN THE LOCAL COFFEE INDUSTRY are optimistic about the future of artisan coffee in Portland. Beals feels that Portland's market is just now becoming mature, catching up to Seattle, which boasts a number of excellent roasters. This kind of diversity is possible because a roaster doesn't have to capture the entire Portland metro region in order to be successful.

The owners of Cellar Door aren't aiming to corner the Portland roasting market. Their aspiration is to grow just enough to reach "a point where we're comfortable and providing a reasonable livelihood for ourselves and our employees," says Pastor. They see no need to distribute Cellar Door coffee outside Portland, instead believing that consumers should patronize roasters in their own metro regions or neighborhoods.

On the retail side, a proliferation of coffee shops means that only the ones that are doing everything right will thrive. The bar has been set high in Portland. Milletto says, "The days of someone throwing up an espresso sign and selling espresso are a little more limited. We're seeing that the retailers that are not completely focused on quality are struggling."

Those that do maintain a focus on quality seem to be doing just fine. Albina Press, which started in north Portland in a refurbished artists' gallery, has expanded to two locations in less than five years. Fuller, who expects to open a third shop in 2009 and has long-range goals to operate at least five locations, describes his business's mission as being "as much about coffee and espresso as we possibly can." Coffeehouse Northwest nearly quadrupled its gross income from January through September 2008; by mid 2009, McGovern was in the midst of opening a satellite kiosk.

There appears to be enough demand for multiple shops to prosper. Fortune says, "We've reached a point where consumers are interested enough in coffee and information that they are willing to pay a higher price for more quality in their specialty coffee and that they appreciate having options."

Case in point is Barista, a coffeehouse that former Albina Press barista Billy Wilson opened in early 2009. Within a few weeks of its opening, local coffee mavens were flocking to the Pearl District shop, drawn by Wilson's reputation and the fact that Barista is doing something that few, if any, other shops have done: serving coffee from different roasters. *Barista Magazine*'s editor calls the concept "no less than groundbreaking."[16] Milletto, who compares going to a coffee shop that serves only one roaster's coffee to visiting a wine bar that pours wine from only one vineyard, says that Wilson is "setting a great example and providing a unique experience."

Further experiments in artisan coffee may very well be in Portland's future. Lounsbury says: "There's still room for so many things in Portland. People think it's so small and that it's saturated—I hear that word a lot—but the reality is, it's just getting started. I think it's only going to become more interesting."

CHAPTER 8
DISTILLED SPIRITS

Moriah McSharry McGrath

ON BALMY SUMMER NIGHTS, twenty- and thirty-somethings stream into Rontoms, a lounge that eschews a sign in favor of a subtle silhouette painted on its façade. A certain disheveled chic predominates, with arriving patrons draping their tattoo-banded arms over the handlebars of sleek bikes as they glide up to the curb. Heading indoors after parking their rides, these artfully scruffy arbiters of taste traverse a polished concrete floor to join friends lounging on ersatz Eames furnishings and wearing skinny pants and vintage T-shirts with ironic slogans.

A self-conscious visitor might be tempted to seek refuge in the bathrooms, but with bespoke mirrored wallpaper, the space might not provide the desired respite from insecurities about one's design sense or sartorial prowess. Even alcohol might fail to provide an easy escape: instead of the standard European brands, the top shelf of the bar gleams with strictly local fare. Those scanning for the familiar blocky font of Absolut vodka or the jewel green of Tanqueray gin are out of luck. But those in the know recognize the contours of a local span on 12 Bridges Gin and the stalwart red M of Medoyeff Vodka. Both are distilled within a mile of the bar.

The manufacturers of these liquors—Integrity Spirits and House Spirits Distillery—are just two of Oregon's thirty-six distilleries, a number that has more than doubled since 2002. Only California, a much wealthier and more populous state, can claim more small distilleries. The concentration is particularly striking in southeast Portland, on the edge of which Rontoms is located: seven distilleries can be found in Portland's Central Eastside Industrial District.

THE CRAFT-DISTILLING BUZZ

THERE IS NO DOUBT that local spirits are hot in Oregon, with the state visitors' bureau having sponsored a "Create the Oregon Bounty Cocktail" contest in the lead-up to Portland's fourth Annual Great American Distillers Festival in 2008 and the recent formation of the Oregon Distillers Guild (underwritten by the city's development commission). This comes hot on the heels of the creation of the Oregon Bartender's Guild in 2007 and the 2006 founding of *Imbibe*, "the magazine of liquid culture," based in Portland but aimed at a national audience.[1] Portland is also the physical home for the recently founded online microdistilling community, Burning Still.[2] Upscale establishments like the Teardrop Lounge (established in 2007) and Ten 01 (established in 2006) have become important sites for the local cocktail scene, whose influence has diffused to neighborhood beer bars that now have cocktail menus featuring fruity drinks made with local spirits.

PLACE AND TIME

OF THE ELEVEN DISTILLERIES in the Portland metropolitan area, eight have been founded since 2003. As could be asked of any of the artisan sectors in this book, observers of this burgeoning industry wonder, "Why Portland?" Given its incredibly rapid expansion, craft distilling in Portland also suggests the question, "Why now?"

There are some structural reasons. In Oregon, a distilling permit costs just one hundred dollars, compared to several thousand in other states. In 1987, alcohol manufacturers gained the right to sell directly to customers (instead of through the Oregon Liquor Control Commission), enabling distilleries to sell their products on their premises. In 1998, another change ended the prohibition of businesses simultaneously owning both a brewery and a distillery.[3] Partially due to advocacy efforts by some of the early craft distillers in Oregon, distilleries can also have tasting rooms on the premises (still not permitted in California) and recently became able to serve cocktails

Barrels of liquor in various stages of the fermentation process line the walls of Clear Creek Distillery in northwest Portland. Photo © Whitney Gayer

and food.[4] Some distillers also point to the relatively low cost of real estate in Portland as a factor facilitating the launch of new businesses and the viability of continuing enterprises.[5] Another legal support is the state liquor control commission's preferential stocking policies for local products.[6]

The model reflects Oregon's well-entrenched brewpub tradition, which was also nurtured by activist brewers and distillers and helped to drive the nationwide craft-brewing trend.[7] As is the case with wineries, on-site tasting rooms can form an important sales base for distilleries. At Clear Creek Distillery in the northwest industrial neighborhood of Portland, forklifts, stills, and truck bays are tucked behind a reception office and tasting room decorated with wool rugs; this modest but cozy spot is on some days the site of several thousand dollars of spirits sales.[8] Breweries, wineries, and distilleries have become tourist attractions in Oregon, receiving copious national and even international press.[9] The Edgefield Distillery, run by the local McMenamins hospitality chain, is part of a resort with a hotel, golf course, spa, brewery, winery, vineyard, bars, and restaurants.

The timing of Oregon's distillery boom is influenced by a nationwide increase in spirits consumption. In the 1980s, public concern and increasingly stringent legislation about driving under the influence led to a decline in spirits consumption, and the market didn't begin to expand again until the late 1990s. Renewed interest in cocktails, aided by the introduction of many brands of flavored vodkas, has spurred growing liquor sales. In Oregon, spirits sales grew 8.5 percent in 2007 to nearly $400 million, after a 9 percent increase the previous year.[10] About $3.5 million of this was for products made in Oregon.[11]

Other states are taking notice of Oregon's distilling frenzy. In July 2008, the Washington legislature decreased its permit fee from two thousand dollars to one hundred for small distilleries using local agricultural products.[12] In the wake of this victory, the Northwest Agriculture Business Center continues to advocate further legislation to "support a renaissance of handcrafted, artisanal American spirits in Washington State and provide Washington's growers with a new value-added product opportunity."[13] Similarly, Washington and Idaho have tried to boost their wine industries, with Washington's Walla Walla Valley being one of the most successful. While strict controls on distilling and alcohol distribution were initially implemented out of concern for the character of communities, policymakers are realizing that alcoholic beverage industries may be an important avenue for community development in regions with a large agricultural base. This has been the case in Bend, Oregon, where Deschutes Brewery is considered a valued contributor to the city's unprecedented revival, and Bendistillery has forged a martini bar model that has been getting a lot of attention.[14]

Agriculture and distilling:
from field to bottle

A white-haired sixty-something, Steve McCarthy speaks eloquently to the cause of connecting farmers and distillers. His impetus for starting Clear Creek, which is named for a stream that flows through a family pear orchard in the foothills near Mount Hood, was to find a more reliable way to earn a living off the fruit that grows in the Hood River Valley. Though the rich soil and mild climate produce succulent pears, apples, peaches, and grapes, the vagaries of working the land and navigating the volatile wholesale market make for a precarious livelihood. Recalling years when his family didn't have enough money to pay the pickers that worked their land, McCarthy is passionate about the ways that distillers can build the market for local produce by selling luxury items with a much higher sticker price than supermarket pears. Recounting the history of eaux de vie (or traditional European fruit brandies), he explains, "These products were developed by starving farmers who knew they had to use every little bit of their produce or die."[15]

Local agriculture is an important touchstone for many distillers. Oregon's landscape and culture come through in the ingredients and flavors, from Hood River pears to Douglas fir buds to grapes from the Willamette Valley. Clear Creek is the most striking example, growing their own apples and pears and getting virtually all of their other fruit from Oregon farms (some of the Bing cherries for the *kirschwasser* come from Washington). One of Indio Spirits' flavored vodkas uses marionberries, a hybrid blackberry species developed at Oregon State University's agricultural school. Integrity Spirits offers their Lovejoy Vodka—which carries the whimsical name of city founder Asa Lovejoy—in hazelnut flavor, an homage to Oregon's robust filbert industry.

Some ingredients bear a direct lineage to Oregon's other craft beverage industries: House Spirits uses beer from the nearby Roots Organic Brewery to start the process of distilling their whiskey, and pomace (leftover grape-skins) from Oregon wineries is the basis for Clear Creek Distillery's grappas. At the McMenamin brothers' Edgefield property in suburban Troutdale, Hammerhead Ale and Edgefield Chardonnay—made on the premises— serve as the base for some spirits, and grapes grown in the Edgefield vineyard are used for their brandy.[16] McCarthy emphasizes that his use of winery byproducts means that grapes are being used twice to create "value-added" products: wine and then grappa.[17] On a local radio broadcast, he explained, "We create jobs out of what was compost, basically."[18]

THE DISTILLER'S CRAFT

NOT ONLY ARE MICRODISTILLERS making small batches, they are using different methods than larger distilleries. Most of Portland's distillers use pot stills, contraptions of shiny metal tanks and valves that suggest an old-time spaceship, with funnel-shaped tops evoking the onion domes of Eastern European architecture. Other equipment is adapted from wineries and breweries, or made by distillers to fit their personal needs. Housed in small, light industrial spaces (think garages) near residential neighborhoods, these distilleries bear little resemblance to the massive plants filled with huge column stills used by the "big guys."

Their ingredients and relationship to the product are also radically different. Pear brandy was Clear Creek's first product and remains its most popular; in 2007, they used five hundred thousand pounds of pears. As a comparison, the sum total used in mass-marketed pear vodkas—whose volume dwarfs that of all Oregon distillers combined—is zero pounds, ever. Each bottle of Clear Creek's brandy uses thirty pounds of pears and sells for about forty dollars. For twice the price, customers can get the iconic "pear-in-the-bottle" version: McCarthy has adopted the traditional Alsatian practice of growing pears inside bottles on the family orchard and filling them with eau de vie after the pear has grown for three months. A true artisan product, pear-in-the-bottle's preparation includes cleaning the bottles by hand with the pears inside, and it is only available in years when the necessary forces of the universe cooperate with the Clear Creek staff. Such painstaking methods take time to develop and deploy. Only after many seasons of experimentation did McCarthy create a raspberry eau de vie, which takes up to eighty pounds of berries per bottle—and doesn't always come out right.[19] His Douglas fir recipe took ten years to develop, the plum recipe twelve.[20] Clear Creek is currently working on apple-in-the-bottle, but only a quarter of the four thousand buds they covered with bottles grew into suitable fruit.[21]

Even the flagship pear eau de vie remains a challenge: "The Bartlett is like the pinot noir grape, fussy and finicky." McCarthy explains, "The most important thing is the ripeness of the Bartlett. You have to pick it at the right time, and then you have to ripen them—you can't tree-ripen a Bartlett. You have to store them at just the right temperature and humidity." It's still complicated once the ripe, fermented pears are in the still: "You can't just press a button and walk away. If you wait too long you lose pronounced aromatics. Too soon, and it's nasty."[22] Such patience—and tolerance for risk—would never be welcome on a factory floor.

Steve McCarthy, founder and owner of Clear Creek Distillery. Photo © Whitney Gayer

Clear Creek's German-built stills use thirty pounds of pears to create a single bottle of their signature pear brandy. Photo © Whitney Gayer

Many distillers come to the craft curious after working with beer and wine. Mike Sherwood—who has worked at both breweries and wineries—developed Sub Rosa Spirit's herb-infused vodkas by playing mad scientist in his family's kitchen. In the batches that go to market, customers taste the tinkering both he and Mother Nature do. Liz Crain of the *Portland Tribune* described the process this way: "Sometimes the tarragon throws off a little more chlorophyll than usual, making the vodka brighter and more vegetal. Other times, Sherwood chops cumin in addition to toasting it to extract more flavor."[23] The project is nothing if not labor intensive: "It takes about an hour and a half per pound to strip the tarragon leaves off of the plant. I tried just throwing the whole leaf and stem in there before, but it comes off as very vegetal and stemmy. You have to catch everything at its peak flavor," Sherwood says, echoing McCarthy's mantra.[24]

Ty Reeder, a distiller at the McMenamins Edgefield property, reports with awe: "I can look out my window and see the vineyard where my grapes are grown."[25] The opportunity to see grapes through harvest, fermentation into wine, and then distillation into brandy is quite rare. Craft-distilling aficionados believe that following the product every step of the way cultivates unique insights into how flavor is affected by the subtleties of ingredients and the influence of climate, barrel material, and aging time. For many craft distillers, this is a profoundly fulfilling—even spiritual—experience. Their lingo even has a touch of the celestial: the portion of alcohol that evaporates during barrel aging is called "the angel's share."

McMenamins, the regional hospitality chain started by brothers Mike and Brian McMenamin in the early 1980s, serves as a veritable incubator for local distillers. Christian Krogstad and Lee Medoff, co-owners of House Spirits, worked together as McMenamins brewers, and John Ufford of Indio Spirits was a corporate beverage manager. An enthusiastic and voluble Portland native, Medoff got a chance to help start the Edgefield distillery after cutting his teeth distilling at a French vineyard. He describes working at McMenamins in the 1990s as a "really hands-on education" and credits the brothers with inspiring creativity by giving their employees "carte blanche" to explore recipes.

Rogue is another regional brewer that has gotten into the distilling game, making vodka and the only Oregon rum. Their distilleries in Portland and Newberg (in the far reaches of the metropolitan area) have trained people like Mike Sherwood of Sub Rosa and Kieran Sienkiewicz of Integrity Spirits.

Blog entries by Sienkiewicz and his partner Rich Phillips offer an illuminating portrait of the beginnings of a craft distillery.[26] Frantically working day jobs, the men scramble around their newly-rented space trying to build, paint, and receive deliveries—all while trying to navigate the baroque paperwork the federal government requires of new spirits producers. Their approval finally arrives with a timeframe so tight that they must stay up all night to bottle, stopping only for an unplanned but desperately needed nap, during which their dinner burns on the stove. Holidays with families are spent using the extra manpower to bottle more. Marketing is far back in their minds, and they are blown away by presentations about the "branding" proposed by a local agency, barely believing that someone could take a look at them and come up with such a slick campaign. They select Sienkiewicz's dog Jackson—a surly drooling boxer—as their trusty mascot, and he promptly dies less than a year into the business' existence. The only connection between this labor of love and what happens at major distilleries is the science behind distillation itself.

DEBATE WITHIN THE DISTILLING COMMUNITY

THOUGH ALL THESE ENTREPRENEURS are deeply committed to their business, effusive discussions of the craft distilling scene can get snagged by an undercurrent of dissension. While some distillers start from raw ingredients, others start with base spirits that they season, infuse, and filter. When so many of the products are marketed on the basis of their artisan pedigree, the distinction becomes more than philosophical. Though some are less concerned, others are adamant that there are major differences between distillers (who start from scratch), redistillers (who start from spirits that have been purchased), and bottlers (who simply repackage spirits bought in bulk). Steve McCarthy is among those who see big differences:

> They buy it in bulk and they put it in a bottle with a pretty label and they call themselves artisan distillers, which I think is really questionable. But more important than that, my perspective, motivation, our whole mindset here is actually about making things.... Our joy, our job here is to find fruit in Oregon that we

can make wonderful things out of from scratch. With hardly any exceptions, everything we make here begins as a piece of fruit, and it's crushed and fermented and distilled and maybe barrel-aged or not depending on what it is, and then eventually bottled.

A Portland journalist describes the debate from the consumer end:

> The argument here is that if you do not have your hand in the process from beginning to end, you don't have enough control over your product. The idea being that not all base grain alcohols are created equal. Or rather, imported base grain alcohols are too equal to create a truly "craft" product.[27]

Yet Lee Medoff—whose House Spirits purchases most of its base spirits—maintains, "It's a petty argument; in the end it all comes down to the taste of the finished product and what you enjoy."[28] House Spirits currently produces spirits based on grain (e.g., vodka, gin), which may account for some difference of opinion from McCarthy, who makes fruit-based eaux de vie and brandies.

Portland distilling in the world context

Though local pride is strong, Portland's spirits scene draws heavily on other regional cultures. Lee Medoff fell in love with distilling during a stint at a French winery, and Medoyeff vodka was influenced by his travels to northern and eastern Europe[29] as well as his Russian heritage (the vodka brand employs the traditional spelling of his family's name). Travels through Europe also had a huge impact on Steve McCarthy's ideas about fruit cultivation and spirit consumption. Poire William eau de vie, a delicacy native to France, Germany, and Switzerland, was the inspiration for the Clear Creek enterprise. The pot stills used by Portland distillers are by and large purchased from European companies that have been crafting them for centuries. Steve McCarthy laughs when he recounts his experience receiving his equipment: "When my first still came in from Germany, it was in a big box with no assembly instructions! Because the stillmaker, Mr. Holsteiner, had never sold one before to somebody who was not already making eau de vie."

Portland distillers have been well-received by the city's local bars and restaurants, but some of their most important contacts are chefs and restaurants in larger cities like New York, Los Angeles, and Washington DC. Getting these tastemakers to put their products on the menu or in the kitchen is critical to establishing the distillery's reputation. Having one's product included in a drink at New York's Pegu Club or Death & Co., the *ne plus ultra* of cocktail bars, has become a dream come true for some Oregon distillers.

Important meetings with key figures in the hospitality industry are unfamiliar terrain for upstart distillers—most of whom have no formal credentials in the culinary or business arts—and it can be challenging for a scrappy do-it-yourselfer to get a foot in the door. But craft distillers benefit from the path-breaking Oregon wine and beer scenes. Steve McCarthy now realizes how utterly amateur he was on his first trip to New York, yet he managed to make several contacts because his home state's name served as something of a magic word. Gourmets who had experienced the unexpected success of Oregon Pinot Noir were willing to meet with a visitor who suggested that something equally interesting might happen in distilling.[30] A generation later, Medoff hears the buzz about Oregon in his travels around the world. Whether it's "the pioneer spirit or what," says Medoff:

> I think a Northwest stamp is doing something that doesn't fit any mold at all. I mean, there was no category for a big, hoppy pale ale until everybody started making it here. And now, it's this internationally recognized style of beer! And before that it didn't even exist. I think that's a sense of terroir.

Portland distillers are proud to have earned copious national and international awards, and while interstate distribution of spirits can be a complicated regulatory adventure, several businesses have managed to ship their products around the United States. The coup de grâce is having spirits imported to the nations that innovated the original recipes, as is the case with the sales of House Spirits' Aviation Gin in England and the success of Clear Creek's eau de vie in France.

DOING THINGS DIFFERENTLY: MORAL ECONOMY

DESPITE THIS WORLDWIDE REACH, Portland's craft distillers position themselves in opposition to the mass market for spirits. Though New Deal Distillery's website jokes that they "plan to rule the world," their philosophy makes it clear that this ambition would be achieved in a rather unconventional manner. From their homespun manifesto:

> Think global, act local means different things to different people, but at New Deal Distillery it means that we support local organic farmers, promote the Slow Food Movement, champion Farm-to-Table partnerships, source parts and equipment from local distributors, strive to be environmentally sustainable and socially responsible, and believe that "coopertition" should define business relationships. We think that the rapid growth and measured successes of the craft-distilling industry in Portland is proof that craft-distilleries will continue to offer locally-made, high-quality alternatives to the products of corporate conglomerates that dominate the alcohol beverage industry…changing humanity for the better along the way.[31]

For Medoff of House Spirits, being locally orientated has enabled their phenomenal success: "Our scale of economy, we don't have to be like the big guys. We don't have to sell a million cases to make the whole thing work." After only a few years in business, they have far exceeded their original goal of selling one hundred cases a year. To illustrate this issue of scale, House Spirits sold about fifteen thousand units in Oregon in 2008; the Jack Daniels brand of whiskey sold four hundred thousand.[32] For further contrast, House Spirits has started producing whiskey one barrel (about one hundred bottles) at a time.[33] Though their success has brought them distribution in fourteen states and three countries,[34] House Spirits intends to remain a local or regional distiller. They are less interested in expansion than in helping to build Oregon's regional distilling identity. Eyes gleaming, Medoff imagines a day when people "think of Oregon the way you think of Kentucky" and its heritage of fine bourbon production.

All of Portland's small distilleries struggle with the challenges of developing their products and managing their businesses. Virtually all of their staff members are driven by an abiding zeal for their work that doesn't necessarily make economic sense. Mike Sherwood, a jack-of-all-trades who still works a day job at a winery, describes his experience starting up Sub Rosa Spirits:

> You have to have passion. You really have to be driven and have a vision. It takes so much work to get out there and sell it. You still have to knock someone off the shelf or bar, so it has to be unique. I really like what I've done because I made things for myself first. You make something for you and if someone else likes it, great. That people like it is both gratifying and surprising.[35]

Twenty-five years into his career as a distiller, Steve McCarthy can see this spirit, and a reflection of his younger self, in Portland's emerging fashion industry: "There's no reason to do it, it's a total long shot...it's so improbable. And you look at these young women who are doing it, and they must be speaking to God every night and getting their marching orders," he says only partly in jest, because "it seems to me such an incredibly difficult thing to do." Whether it is foolishness or brilliance, this impulse is at the heart of many Portland distilleries and artisan businesses.

Also in the category of "no reason to do it" (following traditional economic logic) are the environmental practices of some distilleries. To these entrepreneurs, however, the purchasing, packaging, and waste disposal practices of larger distilleries are unconscionable. One of the products that runs counter to these wasteful practices is Highball Distillery's new Elemental Vodka, whose base spirit is made from organic wheat processed at the nearby Bob's Red Mill Farm, and whose production is enabled by electricity from wind turbines.[36] New Deal Distillery is collaborating with a Bay Area firm to make the first organic liqueurs in the United States. This line, LOFT Liqueurs, is free of "additives, preservatives, artificial coloring or flavorings, chemical pesticides, synthetic fertilizers, sewage sludge, bio-engineering, or ionizing radiation."[37] The California partners in the LOFT project boast of the liqueurs' natural sweeteners (agave syrup, as opposed to refined sugar), bamboo-paper labels, biodegradable inks, recycled cardboard cases, and kosher certification, in addition to the company's bamboo-floored offices.[38] Michael Klinglesmith of Highball explains why his company makes choices like these:

> Every bottle of vodka contains more then [sic] 2 lbs of grain. When you purchase a macro-distilled commercial vodka, you are supporting industrial agriculture (ADM, Cargill, etc). Our product provides an option for consumers who demand the highest quality product and want to support business that is striving to find a better way.[39]

This was a carefully considered choice for Highball, which "wanted to build a company that operated in a responsible way, a business that participated in and supported the local economy."[40]

Lee Medoff can relate. Born and raised in Portland, he bubbles with amazement over the transformation of the city's reputation from "the end of the earth" to a hipster mecca known for its "ethos to keep the city alive and vibrant." He hopes that his distilling business can forestall the negative impacts of gentrification by maintaining close ties between restaurants, bars, artisan food producers, and other small businesses.

Steve McCarthy, who has participated in civic leadership since the 1970s, sees the relationship between craft industries and things like Portland's metropolitan governance structure, transportation system, and land use legislation. Sound development controls and attention to providing public amenities have made Portland an appealing place to live, which draws a certain segment of the population:

> People with a choice—which typically means young. They typically have a relatively high level of education and typically have some financial cushion—not always a lot. And so they show up and they sleep on a friend's couch and usually go to work in bicycle repair places or pizza places or coffee places."

This description will sound familiar to most Portlanders, who are accustomed to handing over their money to cashiers with facial piercings, extensive tattoos, master's degrees in literature, and nonprofit collectives starting up in their garden sheds. McCarthy continues, connecting the dots to artisan work, "You have young people with brains and not enough to do: that's the magic ingredient. They've got a lot of energy, they've got a lot of brains, they've got money, no kids…and they start thinking about what they could do." He even includes the growth of cocktails in this realm, saying that inventing drinks offers a chance for creativity (and more tips) in unstimulating bar jobs.[41] In this way, a different kind of city and a different kind of business work symbiotically to foster artisan entrepreneurship in distilling and other sectors.

CONCLUSION

IF IT SEEMS LIKE there are another ten hipsters arriving at Rontom's for every ten who leave, it is because Portland is home to a critical mass (and then some) of people who put a premium on small-scale local production of everything from their bikes to their messenger bags to their cocktails. Their momentum has been building for many years, as Medoff explains: "the same demographic that drove the craft-brewing industry is driving this industry; they want something that's local, that has a story, that has something not being mass-marketed to them."

While there are people like this all over the country, their strong representation in Portland is part and parcel of a larger livability movement in the city and state as a whole. According to Steve McCarthy of Clear Creek, Portland's concentration of young people and artisan industries is not unique. He cites Austin, Texas, and Madison, Wisconsin, as other cities with a positive reputation for livability and a healthy helping of "bright young people not quite sure what they're going to do." Thus, things like public transportation and bike trails, parks and recreation opportunities, flexible and low-cost housing stock, and maybe even limited opportunity in lucrative industries may do more to spur craft industries than any business development plan.

CHAPTER 9
INDIE MUSIC: BANDS AND BREAKOUTS

Laura Cesafsky

IT'S A SOGGY NOVEMBER EVENING, and I'm huddled away in the cozy confines of the Aalto Lounge, a hip little spot on Belmont Street in the heart of Portland's eastside. The place is half empty on this Monday night, but a DJ behind the narrow bar still labors over his next selection. As if his job weren't enviable enough, I suddenly realize he is flanked by none other than three reigning doyens of indie-rock cool: Stephen Malkmus, Britt Daniel, and Janet Weiss. For the worshipper of modern rock music—one of Portland's more prominent secular religions—these figures are instantly recognizable. Indeed, catching them out sharing drinks is not unlike a devotee of modern literature ambling past Paris' Les Deux Magots café circa 1948 while Richard Wright, James Baldwin, Jean-Paul Sartre, and Albert Camus are gathered on the patio, smoking cigarettes.

As chief songwriter for the hugely influential band Pavement, Malkmus essentially reoriented the sound of "underground" rock music. Countless garage bands in nameless bedroom communities have imitated the tangential lyricism and distorted, shambolic melodies of their 1992 debut, *Slanted and Enchanted*. Malkmus still records, but has largely passed the gilded microphone to Daniel, whose rock quartet, Spoon, has found dizzying success in recent years playing deceptively simple, not-quite-straightforward indie rock that rewards the repeat listen. And as the drummer for the all-female "queercore" band Sleater-Kinney, Weiss helped put the Northwest on the musical map in the 1990s, in particular as a welcoming place for female and queer-identified musicians.

It is on the strength of such pop music celebrity that this aggressively cloudy city has been basking in a bit of the national spotlight of late. The popular online cultural journal *Slate*, for one, recently named Portland "America's Indie Rock Mecca." As the writer, Taylor Clark, explained at length, Portland's famous rock denizens are far more numerous than Malkmus, Daniel, and Weiss.[1] Indeed, the pint-sized city rolls out the beer-soaked red carpet for several other notables, including James Mercer of The Shins, Colin Meloy and The Decemberists, Isaac Brock of Modest Mouse, Chris Walla of Death Cab for Cutie, and Beth Ditto and Gossip. These artists have achieved national—even international—fame, outgrowing the independent labels that weaned them and embracing much more lucrative deals with major labels based in America's flashiest cities.

What's interesting is that, with the exception of Gossip, none of these rockers' fame was actually incubated in Portland. Malkmus formed Pavement in Stockton, California. Spoon is from Austin, Texas. Sleater-Kinney is from Olympia, Washington. They are all transplants. And in this they are no different from the veritable infantry of rangy young musicians who have migrated to this city in recent years. While it is difficult—if not impossible—to put a number on, anecdotal evidence for this mass migration is formidable. "Everyone is coming here," says Mark Janchar, an Ohio native and co-owner of the art gallery-cum-music venue Worksound.[2] "Every month of the summer I have five friends who move here from Ohio. I can't remember anyone I know who is actually from [Portland]."

Indeed, the city's unique appeal has achieved the status of received wisdom, a laundry list of urban desirables that are easily ticked off. "I don't know what more I can say about this that hasn't been said," Janchar says, slightly exasperated, before reluctantly proceeding. "It's a perfect mix of town and city, it's accessible, it's kind of affordable, it's low key." Add to that walkability, open-mindedness, a historic friendliness to the arts, solid public transportation, intelligent and interesting denizens, and a healthy and sustainable worldview. Add it all up and Portland becomes a place where music cannot only be well made, but also well lived.

BANDS, BOOZE, AND INDIE LABELS

LOCAL BANDS HAVE BEEN GIGGING around Portland bars since the mid-1970s, when the Oregon Liquor Control Commission finally lifted an odd ban that had previously confined them to coffee shops and other sober locales. Since then, the musical nightlife has flourished and proliferated, first taking root downtown, then up and down the vibrant eastside. Today Portland boasts a sprawling, booze-fueled live music economy that offers the music aficionado a menu of entertainment options on any given night of the week. Competition for crowds among venues can be formidable.

At around the same time that those star-crossed lovers, booze and bands, were finally united in Portland, the possibility for local artisan economies in recorded music was also taking shape. In short, the emergence of punk in the 1980s was attended by a democratic re-imaging of the recording industry. Small independent record labels emerged in cities across America, effectively breaking the long-standing monopoly on recorded music that the New York- and Los Angeles-based major labels had enjoyed. Armed with nest eggs worthy of piggy banks and a do-it-yourself ethos, bands began recording and releasing their own records—in lots of hundreds, not thousands—with the help of friends and small-time beneficiaries.

Viewed through an economic prism, early heads of independent labels were clever entrepreneurs. Most punk rock would have difficulty selling in the tens of thousands (that's major-label territory), but niche markets for the music were growing. People stepped in to fill the void. Thirty years and thousands of new indie labels later, however, one thing seems clear: nobody is getting rich. Not exactly moneymakers, these small companies are more usefully understood as vehicles for the proliferation of an aesthetic ethic. Their mission is to put out creative, sometimes risky, always "authentic" music—whatever that might mean. *Haute cuisine*, if you will, that stands in marked contrast to bland, predictable, universally digestible fare cooked up daily in the major-label cafeteria.

"Most bands don't want to be on a major label. The major labels can suck the vitality out of artists in no time at all," says S.P. Clarke, a fifty-eight-year-old music writer and music distribution professional who has been intimately involved in the Portland scene since the 1980s. "Most bands are artists who really want people to hear their music and hear what they have to say." The point is to make music, not money, and to share it with friends and fans—even if you can count them all on two hands.[4]

ROOM FOR ONE MORE

FOR THE PORTLAND NOVITIATE who wants to get acquainted with the local music happenings, a good place to start is the annual PDX Pop Now! Festival. In 2008, Rotture played host to the popular three-day music-a-thon. A hip two-story club in Portland's shambolic eastside industrial area, Rotture announces itself in subtle fashion, its name written backwards in masking tape in a small second story window, almost as an afterthought. The implication: If you don't know where it is, you're probably not cool enough to be there.

Once you find the club, however, the atmosphere at PDX Pop Now! is jovial, even welcoming. How could it not be, with Portland's best local bands playing free, on two stages, for an enthusiastic all-ages crowd? The breadth, depth, and collaborative spirit of Portland music are showcased there. On one night, the breezy alt-country songsters Blind Pilot were followed by precocious high school hip-hoppers Living Proof. On a second stage, up-and-coming Loch Lomond teamed up with local favorites Portland Cello Project, a cohort of classically trained musicians with a taste for popular music (they've covered "Hey Ya!," the catchy Outkast track, among other modern classics).

For Brandon Eggleston, a local jack-of-all-trades who prefers the moniker "music professional," it is this collaborative spirit that really sets Portland apart musically. "Musicians in Portland are really close-knit. People are not so much about bands as about musicians playing with each other. Loose, improvised sound—you don't know what's going to happen because they're not really a band."[3]

This penchant for cooperation seems to reach past the musicians themselves, out to the people working in music's supportive industries. While the traditional economy operates more or less on the Willy Wonka model, constructing large, vertically integrated enterprises that jealously guard the next windfall idea—their personal Everlasting Gobstoppers—these folks tend to have a kindergarten-ish propensity for sharing. Steve Schroeder, owner, CEO, and lone employee of States Rights Records, can easily tick off the names of other local label heads—buddies at Hush Records, Marriage Records, and Audiodrag whom he calls by first name.[5] He turned to many of them for guidance and support when he was getting States Rights off the ground in 2001.

This is not to say that a healthy competitive spirit doesn't simmer under the surface. Speaking of recording professionals, Eggleston notes, "They're a little bit protective of their secrets—you know, everybody wants to think they have a few techniques that nobody else knows about—but everyone's usually open to share ideas and to help everybody else become better and better at what they do." This room-for-one-more spirit stands in sharp relief against an economic landscape that is often sketched as a zero-sum game. It is hardly surprising, then, that Portland is home to more than sixty independent labels, almost all of which have fewer than five employees.

DOING BUSINESS

"SO WHAT EXACTLY IS WORKSOUND?" I ask Mark Janchar, an energetic twenty-six-year-old with close-cropped hair and an easy smile. We are seated side-by-side on the sidewalk at dusk, propped up against a warehouse across the street from the facility in question. "It's a tough question to answer," Mark offers, gazing up at Worksound's humble façade. "Our concept of what it is, is changing all the time." In broad strokes, Worksound is a visual-arts-meets-music concept, a "punk rock art gallery" of sorts for which Mark serves as "music curator." The contours of the project mirror those of the ambling space itself: a central gallery, replete with a stage and a set of turntables, dominates the whitewashed warehouse. To the left and right are two smaller galleries; an office space that houses Worksound's affiliated record label, Hovercraft; a practice space for Hovercraft bands; and a small bar.

These disparate elements come together on the first Friday of each month, when Worksound throws open its doors for a party. With new work from local, national, and international visual artists lining the walls, a bill of bands—selected by Mark—provides the aural entertainment. The bar is open, and the revelers stay late into the night. Though Mark is a guitarist, he reports getting more creative fulfillment from organizing the Worksound events. The Worksound openings are about creating a one-of-a-kind, hand-crafted experience where visual art and music speak to the attendees in novel ways. It is, in a way, an artisan way to *doing business*—an approach not uncommon in the local music economy.

Indeed, Steve Schroeder of States Rights likewise prioritizes personality in his business model. Affable and bearded, the thirty-year-old Minneapolis native exudes an endearing playfulness that permeates the product he puts out. A longtime lover of maps and geography, Schroeder christened his label States Rights with the idea that, rather than number releases chronologically, as is the custom, he would let the artists choose a state that they felt embodied some aspect of themselves and their music. While some insisted on cities or regions outside the United States ("Rules are made to broken," Schroeder says), the result, humorous and predictable, is that he isn't certain of exactly how many records he has put out (His estimate is around forty).

Those forty-or-so records were, however, carefully selected, even if they weren't meticulously logged. "I've generally been almost too much of a stickler about being passionate about the music released," Schroeder laughs. "I take the creation of the entirety of everything I've put out really seriously. I see that as my role as an artist."

Though not a musician himself, Schroeder has always run with an artsy crowd. One day he found himself (somewhat unexpectedly) offering to underwrite the cost of putting out an album for a friend, and a record label was born. He put out a few more records, still holding on to his day job, but soon found that he could not only recoup the overhead, but also actually turn a humble profit—enough to live on. He became a full-time record label head.

Working thirty-five to forty hours a week, flexibly scheduled from an office space in his home, Schroeder stays afloat largely with a DIY ethic. He takes care of marketing and distribution—functions often hired out—while relying on reasonably priced local services for things like manufacturing that he can't do on his own. While he works directly with a few select stores in bigger American cities, Schroeder sells most of his records through mail orders that he personally fills. This makes him happy because it means he will personally touch each CD. "I wouldn't like sending off a couple hundred records and later the money would show up," he says. "It wouldn't really feel like I was dealing with anybody. It builds a bunch of steps that create separation between the music listener and the music makers." Instead, Schroeder focuses on strengthening connection, taking time to include a hand-printed note with each order he sends.

For his part, Eggleston, the music professional, is always juggling aesthetic preferences with the practical need to bring home a living wage. A native of Vancouver, Washington—a city just across the Columbia River from Portland—Eggleston cobbles together a living as a freelance record producer, engineer, and sound technician for touring bands. "At this point I try really really hard to work with people that I believe in musically, that I really like, or that I see are trying really hard and believe in what they are doing. I like to tell myself that I wouldn't take a huge record simply because it paid a lot."

Starting out in music as a young singer, Eggleston eventually picked up drums, bass, guitar, and even a little piano. He also got a bachelor's degree in music that endowed him with technical skills and literacy in the musical idiom and music theory. Eggleston has been quite successful, recording and touring with some famous (for the indie world) artists, such as personal friends The Mountain Goats. Those bigger bands can pay a more generous wage, and Eggleston likes to use the extra money to subsidize the "bro deals" he gives to local bands and friends. "I'm not very financially-minded," Eggleston says. "I just tell bands that if you're successful—and I hope that you are—remember me." This could mean simply passing his name on to other musicians they meet along the way. It's classic social networking, and it's how the local music economy does business.

WORK AND PLAY

THE JULY SUN IS BEATING DOWN hard on Alberta Street, the main thoroughfare in northeast Portland's freshly hip "Alberta Arts" district. It's a Wednesday afternoon and freedom for the nine-to-five set is still a few hours off, but there is no shortage of patrons milling about on the sidewalk patio adjacent coffee spot Random Order. As it turns out, it is a prime location to surreptitiously observe the subtle workings of the local music economy.

One table over, a woman in a torn black T-shirt is giving full attention to her laptop, a smattering of tattoos crawling up both exposed arms. She looks up and spots a friend ambling past. He is tall and languid, with unkempt hair tucked beneath a dirty trucker's cap that is cocked stylishly askew. "Hey, is there a secret show tonight?" he asks, taking a seat. From there, the shop talk jumps tangentially, from the record the young man's band is presently recording to an upcoming show the woman will be playing in Seattle. "You guys wanna come play with us?" she offers, and, just like that, an informal deal is struck.

In any environment where resources are scarce, nepotism will abound. Thus it is not surprising to find that from musicians to recording engineers to label heads to bookers, the currency of the local music economy is social ties. Though Eggleston long ago moved from Seattle to Portland, he still counts on jobs from Seattle bands and their friends for a good chunk of his income. His work with The Mountain Goats, whose star has shined brightest in Australia, has led to jobs with Aussie bands. For Janchar at Worksound, the process of musical discovery "works like a spider web," with bands that he admires introducing him to bands that they admire, and on and on.

While there is certainly a practical aspect to doing business this way, conflating economic life and social life also plays out as a form of idealism. Schroeder at States Rights put this notion at the center of his business model, at least originally. "I had this policy for a while to only work with people that I'm friends with. I mean, why would I want to work with somebody that I'm not friends with?" Schroeder wonders aloud. "But that's been getting a little more difficult because I've burned through all my friends."

One result of this connectedness is that the line between work and play can be difficult to locate. Friends flow easily into business associates and vice versa. Before a big show, Janchar will often spend hours drinking beer and helping the artists get their work ready. "This work is my social life. It's kind of sad, I guess," Janchar laughs. "I'm intimately involved with all these artists, but sometimes I feel like I don't have any friends." Schroeder has had friends on whom he relied to do album art who charged little as they were starting their careers, but who have become too successful for the little amount he can give them. "It's bittersweet," he says.

ECONOMICS OF INDIE MUSIC

THE LOCAL MUSIC WORLD is no doubt "economic." Money changes hands. Schroeder and Eggleston are in this sense very passionate entrepreneurs, having found places to dip their buckets along a crowded and shallow stream of revenue. But the degree to which a thriving local music scene actually generates revenue for a place is more difficult to call. On any given night at one of the dozens of Portland music venues, five bucks buys a cocktail and the bar lines can be long. Certainly the bar owners are cashing in, but who else is?

The music economy is built on the backs of an army of cheap—sometimes free—labor: the hundreds of musicians who enthusiastically perform for the crowds. Most gigs offer a few dollars and a tab at the bar, and the vast majority of musicians don't support themselves playing music. The typical young artist works to live rather than lives to work, and the best jobs for young musicians are those that allow flexible scheduling, ample time for practicing, and the chance to interact with like-minded folks. Some of the most coveted jobs are serving, bartending, and barista gigs, especially for arts-amenable local businesses like Stumptown Coffee.

In addition to the underpaid entertainment, money from the traditional economy can be directly donated to local music. Worksound and its affiliated label, Hovercraft, are yet to generate a profit or even break even, and Janchar is uncertain that they ever will. Janchar and his brother and co-owner Tim, are medical professionals, while their third business partner, Modou Dieng, is an art professor. Each pitches in from their private funds to subsidize the venture. The money they generate on First Fridays helps, but the records that they finance under the Hovercraft label are effectively gifts to the artists, handed over without the expectation of recouping the money. "It's a really expensive hobby," Janchar says.

It's not that economic sustainability for Worksound/Hovercraft is an impossibility, it's just that it's not really on the agenda. For Janchar, sustainability is an attitude and approach that is both ethically and practically unfeasible. Selling records requires a lot of legwork, the e-mailing and press-release writing and package shipping that fills up Schroeder's days. Not only are the Janchar brothers too busy to perform those tasks, they are fundamentally uncomfortable with the notion of making money off artists. While galleries typically ask 50 percent commission on work sold in their spaces, Janchar's comfort zone hovers more closely to 20–30 percent. He dreams of sculpting a career out of curating music, but maintains a sober perspective on the possibilities and limitations of musical economy for himself and other young creatives.

"Looking at this glut of CDs, the CD industry, just these mounds of plastic things. I look at that like, how can you win?" Janchar says. "I could spend my life writing pop songs and trying to make ends meet, touring constantly. And I've known people who have done that and who do that but it's like, you can't win." Like many others, he combats such hopelessness by defining success in music in non-economic terms. "It's like, you have a record, you have three-hundred copies of it, all your friends have it, some people that don't know you get really enthusiastic about it, you play great shows, you know, you might drive to somewhere and play there as well. That's satisfaction to me, that's life, this local economy. It's really, in the end, what everyone is looking for."

SOPHISTICATED AND ACCESSIBLE

THERE IS, OF COURSE, little of the artisan in music-as-physical-product, commonly articulated in the form of the compact disc. Indeed, those "mounds of plastic things," as Janchar calls them, in some ways epitomize the modern economy: cheap, non-durable, uniform, designed for mass consumption. Rather than enhance or personalize a product, a flaw in recorded music negates its functionality, renders it useless.

But while bowing to the socio-technical necessity of uniform recorded music products, artisans do look for opportunities to impart originality into the otherwise blasé. Cover art is often labored over, as it serves as both introduction and visual accompaniment to the musical product inside. Thoughtful label heads like Schroeder personalize otherwise anonymous product delivery with individual attention to orders. Conscious that CDs emanate an aesthetic of the cheap, LP records remain popular among many music aficionados for their larger cover art and less polished sound; Hovercraft, Worksound's affiliated label, recently joined a coterie of other labels that have stopped releasing CDs altogether in favor of the LP.

Ultimately, of course, sound itself is the primary avenue for artisan ingenuity in the independent music economy. While the modern economy shores up the old gulf between fine and popular art—Puccini crones for the old money while The Monkees placate the masses—the best of local independent music is at once sophisticated and accessible to all. The barrier to entry is low for the musician and listener alike. The internet propels this effective democracy, where sites like MySpace allow any musician to upload and share music for free. The music fan, rather than the music executive, is emboldened to decide what counts as good music, as worthy art.

Quite often, what makes music "good" to the ear of indie music aficionado shares few qualities with the finely bred sounds of classical music pedigree. In music-as-high-art, a mastery of theory meets prodigious physical and sensory talent to create a complex and often ornate soundscape. In independent music, bands can be called "genius" for disparate, even oppositional reasons. The Ramones kept it primitive by pumping out a litany of almost indistinguishable three-chord punk anthems, but are remembered for their raw energy and daring; Beat Happening was admired for atonality and the propensity of its members to switch around among instruments despite pedestrian ability in each one.

Many musicians playing independent music—especially rock and roll— were not formally trained. They taught themselves what they decided they needed to know, cobbling together enough skill to express themselves musically in the manner that they preferred. Just as what makes a "good" rock musician is subjective, attempts to objectively determine a "good" band will inevitably bottom out in the murky intangible. It comes down to something like authenticity, a sound, and lyrical content that rings truer, more real, more visceral, more genuine than other sounds.

Chapter 10
Indie Media: Books, Comics, Zines, Radio, and Film

Joshua Roll
Serenity Madrone

Books and publishing

PORTLANDERS ARE BOOK-CRAZED. During any given year, the average Portlander checks out twenty-nine items from the county library. That makes Portland's library number one in annual circulation among similarly sized library systems in the United States.[1] And then there's Powell's City of Books. Nestled between the Brewery Blocks and Portland's downtown, Powell's Books claims to be the largest independent bookstore on the planet. With one million new, used, and rare books on the shelves of its flagship store on Burnside and four million available online, it may be so.[2] But Powell's has not crowded out other independents. In Portland's thriving book culture, as many as sixty independent bookstores serve diverse interests, from mysteries at Murder by the Book to leftist titles at Laughing Horse. These bookstores differ greatly from their big-box counterparts in more than just size. Many place an emphasis on being part of their surrounding communities, and open their doors for social and civic events. In Other Words, a shop that specializes in feminist, queer, and trans literature and non-sexist children's books, hosts weekly courses, exercise classes, and discussions. They also co-sponsor events with Portland State University's Women's Resource Center and support students by carrying textbooks for less than campus bookstore prices. According to Rebecca Luxenburg, one of two paid staff members, they chose their current location to connect to their community. "We wanted to be a part of a neighborhood that felt more like a community and less like a shopping mall."[3] And a part of the community they have become. In addition to providing meeting space and resources for women's groups and others, the store sells buttons, scarves, purses, pillows, baby clothes, and other articles made by local patrons.

Complementing Portland's bookstores are its many independent publishers. Some, like Timber Press, which publishes high quality horticultural titles, have been around since the 1980s and have developed deep portfolios in their particular niche. But most are relatively new—often one- or two-person operations. Getting a count on these is difficult. Dennis Stovall, executive director of Portland State University's Ooligan Press, places the number of publishers in the metro area between three hundred and five hundred, but includes in this number print-on-demand and custom e-book publishers.[4] Cameron Marschall, founder of Ink & Paper Group, believes that there are around fifty local independent presses that are actually sustaining themselves.[5] Quantity seems to beget quality. Between 2003 and 2006, Portland publishers won over half of Literary Arts's Oregon Literary Fellowships for publishers. These included Chiasmus, Hawthorne Books, Poetry Northwest, Burnside Review, The Organ, Stumptown Printers, and Gobshite Quarterly.[6]

Portland's reading culture and literary infrastructure create wonderful synergies with Portland's prolific community of writers, including superstars like Beverly Cleary, Ursula K. Le Guin, and Chuck Palahniuk, as well as Jean Auel, Joanna Rose, and the numerous other local authors who participate in organizations like Willamette Writers and the Oregon Writers Colony and attend Wordstock, Portland's largest annual literary event.

How this productive literary social network functions may best be understood by examining several organizations that bridge these various literary worlds. Chloe Eudaly's Reading Frenzy sits less than a block away from Powell's City of Books. The small store has been cited by some as a literary cornerstone for DIY authors in Portland. Founder and owner Eudaly realized a major goal in 2001 when she opened the zine-focused Independent Publishing Resource Center (IPRC). Four years later another dream was realized when she initiated Show & Tell Press.

Providing an outlet for self-published work from local authors represents one of Reading Frenzy's primary concerns. "The main point of the store is to provide a conduit for small press and self-published work," stresses Eudaly.[7] Stocked with over 95 percent independent or self-published titles, the bookstore offers an enormous selection and a diversity of written work. This proportion of independent and self-published work is mostly due to Reading Frenzy's policy to take any work produced by a local author. "That's part of the hub; people come here to buy their stuff, come here to sell it, come here to see their friends' stuff. It's kind of the wild card of the shop. Our consignment works because we never know what's going to come through, and to a certain degree what we have here is up to the local community," explains Eudaly.

It was that sense of wanting to serve Portland's writing community that led Eudaly to start the IPRC. The center was a hit, and helped produce some surprising early successes. Pete Jordan, who wrote *Dishwasher*, a zine chronicling his experiences as a dishwasher in a variety of locations around the country, was one of the IPRC's early members.[8] In 2007 Jordan published a full-length book of the same name and appeared on the *Late Show with David Letterman* to promote its release. Another early member of the center, Ariel Gore, founded *Hip Mama*, a zine that offers readers engaging political commentary and stories about her experiences raising children. In addition to her thriving print and online zine, she has authored a number of books about parenting, as well as several novels.

The center has worked hard to meet the growing demand for their services. Director Justin Hocking recalls, "When I first started here, we offered two to three workshops per week; now we offer around twelve to thirteen per week." In addition to hardworking board members, Hocking cites the unique nature of Portlanders for the success of the center. "The supportive Portland community has donated money, taught classes, and been overly accepting to what the IPRC is trying to accomplish; the Portland culture spawned IPRC."

The IPRC helps people publish all types of literature, but has found a certain focus in facilitating the production of zines. The range of zine topics published at the center includes politics, poems, transportation, guides to writing and publishing zines, and nearly any other topic, broad or obscure. The gathering of creative people at the center has spawned a community

The Independent Publishing Resource Center's zine library in downtown Portland.
Photo © Whitney Gayer

that allows for people to collaborate and initiate projects of their own. The graphic zine *Daydreams* was created when a volunteer working for the center organized fellow artists and produced a collaborative art and comics anthology. Another zinester leads the bicycle adventure group Urban Adventure League for tours around the city. The IPRC also acts as a space for artists and writers to come together and share information about jobs and living arrangements.

Some of the production capabilities of Portland's literary scene come from Portland State University's own teaching press, Ooligan Press. Started in 2001 by Dennis Stovall, former labor organizer, literary activist, and owner of Blue Heron Press, Ooligan Press is a completely student-run press that uses real book projects to teach and help students familiarize themselves with the publishing process. Stovall identifies the core values that guide Ooligan, "Fundamental to the press is the notion that the students are capable of doing all of the work. Faculty are mentors and advisors, but we don't intervene in the work. Students make the decisions about the direction of the press and decide what books are published. Our job, if anything, is to keep them from going off the edge of the dock." Ooligan focuses on the Northwest region, publishing titles such as *The Portland Red Guide*, a geographic and historical guide to social dissent and radical organizations in Portland, but their catalog also includes some translated versions of German and Croatian titles, one title published in English and Chinese, and alternative history novels.

Ooligan Press is typical of many parts of Portland's literary network, which emphasizes resource sharing and collaboration. Stovall explains, "For instance, in *The Portland Red Guide*, *Fort Clatsop*, and *Deer Drink the Moon*, we have maps. Those maps were done by graduate students in geography. It was a student in the publishing program that went to the geography department and created that relationship." In another work, *Dreams of the West: The History of the Chinese in Oregon, 1850–1950*, co-sponsored by the Chinese Consolidated Benevolent Association of Oregon, students from the history department conducted underlying research that became part of the book. These relationships with other departments and students around campus occurred because of the initiative taken by the students at Ooligan Press. In the genesis of their publishing careers in Portland, these students are putting to use the resources around them in an effort to produce worthy pieces of literary work. This ethos has stuck with many of the alumni who finish their degrees at PSU and go on to start small publishing-related businesses of their own.

One of those alumni, Cameron Marschall, founded Ink & Paper Group in 2007 after he and fellow students from Ooligan decided they would use the lessons learned from PSU's program to create a press with a focus on helping writers find the resources they need to get published. "One of our goals is to become known as a Northwest resource for publishers," Marschall says, explaining his practice of sharing information with other publishers.

Part of this philosophy comes from the reality of being a small business. Ink & Paper does not have a large advertising budget, and word-of-mouth promotion can be effective in spreading a message. "We need to reach out and form more individual relationships with people who might buy our books, who might then go off to the library and say to the librarian, 'Hey, you should carry this publisher's books," continues Marschall. Sharing potential work and offering resources to authors and other publishers lies in stark contrast to a large publishing house's model of business, where the focus is on recognized authors, books with large markets, and the bottom line. But Marschall believes that the collaborative and resource-sharing model of independents can work. "If I go out and help another publisher keep his or her business strong, that's not a sale lost to Ink & Paper—that's somebody who is, ideally, going to pass business on to us."

While a great literary social network is partially responsible for the dynamic nature of the independent publishing scene in Portland, other factors also contribute. Victoria Blake of Underland Press cites Portland's ability to provide the necessities of life at a less than prohibitive cost to aspiring artists as a primary factor. "The thing that I think makes Portland an attractive place for writers is that you can live here pretty easily and have a good quality of life. Writers do a lot of sitting and waiting.... You would like to be sitting and waiting someplace where every minute that you're waiting is not another minute that you're getting yourself deeper into debt."[9]

Marschall agrees that Portland writers and publishers have an edge. "The benefit of being here in Portland would be that you can get paying work easier," says Marschall, explaining the effect of the communal nature of the literary scene. "There is right now, and I don't see this going away, a wonderful community and wonderful sharing of information that other places don't have, either because they don't have the numbers of creative people or they have more of a culture of maintaining proprietary relationships."

COMICS

IN THE SUMMER OF 2008, *Hellboy II: The Golden Army* opened as the number one movie in the United States. The movie is adapted from a comic series published by Portland's Dark Horse Comics. Four other movie adaptations, either in production or due for release, are also taken from series developed for Dark Horse or Portland publishers Oni Press and Top Shelf Productions.[10] Dark Horse is the steed that has pulled Portland into the comics world. With a staff of one hundred, and with sixty film and TV projects completed, it's the big boy on the block. When he established Dark Horse in 1986, founder Mike Richardson changed the comics world by giving artists extensive creative control.[11] *Reading Comics* author Douglas Wolk gives Richardson credit for attracting talent to the area: "Someone at Periscope Studio said that after Mike Richardson stopped collecting comics [he was first a comic store owner], he started collecting cartoonists. And he does seem to be responsible for a lot of them moving here."[12]

To talk with Matt Dryer, digital art technician and former editor for Dark Horse Comics, one would think Portland was the Shangri-La of comics: rich with diverse local talent, an arts culture that takes comics seriously, and some of the largest independent publishers around. Dryer isn't the only one who thinks so. According to Eric Gitter, Los Angeles producing partner for Oni Press, "Portland is the Hollywood of comic books."[13]

Is it the concentration of comics and graphic novel publishers? Is it the city's big-yet-small stature, where people working in the same industry are bound to run into each other? Is it the supportive patron base, or public recognition and support?[14] Most likely it's all of the above; each element of the scene nurturing the others to form a magnet for comics creators and fans alike.

While a job at Dark Horse initially brought Dryer to the Portland area, he soon learned that Portland has a broader base of comics publishers than he expected. The city is home base for Oni Press, Top Shelf Productions, Periscope Studios, and others. He recalls how in recent years the comics creators themselves have started arriving in droves. A thriving comics scene in a town Portland's size generates both benefits and hurdles, Dryer muses.[15] Face-to-face interaction fosters creativity in a way electronic correspondence simply can't. An editor, writer, and artist might end up having beers together and scribbling out a stuck scene on bar napkins—such impromptu meetings are impossible when the individuals in question are on opposite coasts, or continents. Yet Portland's comics scene camaraderie also has its downsides, including the stacks of unsolicited portfolios brought in to Dark Horse's Milwaukie office, leaving Dryer the unpleasant task of turning away unpolished art from die-hard comics fans.

At one of Portland's nine bookstores that sell comics and graphic-novels, you discover that "creators" and "fans" are often one and the same. Andy Johnson, majority owner of Cosmic Monkey Comics, meets many artists when they come in to his store as customers.[16] Johnson has built several strong friendships with comics crafters and other regulars because of their common passion for the art. At times, he gets books directly from artists, instead of through a distributor or book dealer, to get a better rate for his

Graphic artist Sarah Oleksyk hard at work in her northwest Portland studio. Photo © Whitney Gayer

store and to increase profits for the creators. And cooperation often extends to include the "competition." Johnson has worked with other comics stores to go in on ads for large events, or by trading overstocked books.

Johnson is a lifelong resident of the city. Half-jokingly, he equates Portland's comics magnetism to the abundant rain and residents' resulting adoration of all kinds of books. "Bad" weather may foster indoor activities like reading and inking comics, and the city does boast an impressive number of bookstores.

With Portland acting as such a supportive incubator, it's no wonder that annual events like Stumptown Comics Fest have sprung up in recent years to celebrate local artists and publishers and promote Portland to the larger comics community. Cosmic Monkey Comics plays host for several Stumptown events like an afterparty, awards ceremony, and Drawpocalypse. Participants in Drawpocalypse have twenty-four hours to create a twenty-four page comic from start to finish. David Chelsea sat in Cosmic Monkey alongside other professional and amateur artists for 2008's event, amid bloggers and spectators, to create his tenth twenty-four hour comic—two of which have been published by Top Shelf as *24 x 2*.[17]

The connectedness of literary workers in Portland appears to operate on the assumption that an agglomeration of creative types fosters even more creativity. According to graphic artist and cartoonist Sarah Oleksyk, this agglomeration has created a critical mass of like-minded individuals that promotes greater creative thinking. This process happens both formally and informally and through many different groups of people—what Oleksyk calls "tribes of cartoonists" that come together through different venues to collaborate. If it is not an organized event like Stumptown Comics Fest, First Thursday, or a life-drawing session at Dante's punk-rock club, then it's a few hours of drinking and drawing at someone's house, or spending time in a nearby coffee shop putting together a comic. Oleksyk described the importance of writing and drawing with others, "Like writing, drawing comics can be an isolating act, but when you're doing it alongside someone else, it feels like you're there with your community, you can get feedback, you can have company, and that's priceless to me...and now I can go out and meet in a coffee shop and talk to people."[18]

ZINES

DARK HORSE, LIKE OTHER Portland area comics publishers, has attracted top talent in part because of its commitment to artists' creative freedom.[19] Such independence is valued in the zine world as well. The *Zinester's Guide to Portland* has come out with an expanded fourth edition full of hand-drawn maps and illustrations of city sites. Sixteen artists and writers collaborated on the guide, and copyrights for all work are retained by their respective creators. It started as a travel resource, a little photocopied and folded pamphlet handed out to Portland Zine Symposium attendants in 2001, and has grown into a book professionally printed by Microcosm Publishing.[20]

Publishers, bookstores, and other support structures have certainly contributed to the zine scene, but they are not alone in their support. Several branches of the Multnomah County Library now boast zine collections, and a reading series called Zinesters Talking can be found at the North Portland Library. Only six other U.S. cities have zine collections in their libraries.[21] The IPRC also maintains an extensive zine collection,[22] further contributing the city's status as "zine capital of the world."[23]

Events like the annual Portland Zine Symposium create an intense networking and collaborative experience and may attract new fans to their work. Like Stumptown Comics Fest, the Zine Symposium inspires related events in the same artistic vein. Reading Frenzy, ever the supporter of self-published art, has hosted a showcase of women comics artists and their self-portraits in celebration both of the Zine Symposium and the Pearl District's monthly First Thursday Art Walk.[24]

What does all this mean for community building? Personal zinesters' stories can express the art's social glue, and in time of need, the community can respond with both emotional and financial support. For some artists excelling in self-promotion, through blogs and other media, their community may stretch far beyond the city's boundaries.

Take Martha Grover, creator of *Somnambulist Zine*. Martha devoted her recent *Number 10* in the series to her home town of Portland, with a list of favorite bars and two short stories drawn straight from her own experiences in the city. Other contributors to *Somnambulist Number 10* provided a Portland-inspired poem, a third story, and illustrations.[25] On the zine's blog Martha exposes her creative thought-process, Portland tidbits, and the challenges of living with Cushing's Disease.[26] Her brain surgery and its related expense prompted friends and supporters to organize a benefit, held at Portland State University and promoted by Reading Frenzy.[27]

Poets on national reading tours, both sponsored and self-promoted, often make stops in Portland. Local coffee shops and bookstores provide venues and connections for authors to locate cheap or free housing during their visit to the city. Selling self-published zines of their work at readings is an easy way for poets to fund their tours, though it is not uncommon for them to trade wares with other poets and zinesters as well.

People who create zines make a natural reader base for their colleague's work, but does this mean the scene is little more than a tight circle of insiders? Has content changed over time, becoming less political or more self-absorbed? While many zines seem at first glance to be little more than diaries of personal experience, these can often be ways of personalizing larger social issues. In *Somnambulist Number 10*, Grover shares a story of her walk through rapidly gentrifying North Portland. While on the surface it is a parable of late-night entertainment-seeking, it exposes prejudice and social equity in Portland in a way that many avoid discussing.[28]

Another seasoned zinester, Sean Tejaratchi, has edited volumes of ad-art for his zine, *Crap Hound*. Filling pages with political and religious propaganda, Tejaratchi allows the images to speak for themselves.[29] He minces no words in explaining his philosophy on his unauthorized use of copyrighted works. "Over the course of my life, I've been subjected to a stunning amount of advertising, and I can't recall anyone ever asking me for permission," he states boldly, while still adding later that "*Crap Hound* officially urges you to obey all laws, all the time."[30]

Other zines connect people to place by appealing to specific groups, such as scooter riders in Karen Giezyng's *Bumpstart*. Zines may educate or spark critical inquiry by asking unpopular questions. Such diversity in voice is a valuable commodity in a world of increasingly corporate media. Perhaps, in an increasingly computerized world, people are seeking confirmation that they are normal, that others are just like them—therefore seeking out media that speak to them as equals and romanticize the mundane and day-to-day. Perhaps people have grown less trusting of corporate media as their only source of news and are turning to zines and blogs for exposure to less-commercialized perspectives. If so, these trends may not hurt the market for zines, but may actually boost both the sales and creation of small-press works.

Portland has the indie and comics publishers and a deep patron base. It has the IPRC and the zine creators. Portland State University and the city's numerous independent bookstores and comic stores have become "third spaces" for community-building events. With festivals, symposiums, and speaking tours to showcase the diverse local talent, the comics and zine scene could scarcely be richer.

INDEPENDENT RADIO

INDEPENDENT RADIO PROVIDES yet another outlet for the artisan community in Portland. Rather than being driven by advertisers and mainstream music, independent radio depends more upon volunteer power and the engagement of its audience. Portland has a wealth of non-commercial radio stations, many of them affiliated with local schools. Benson High School's KBPS is Portland's only all-classical radio,[31] and Mt. Hood Community College has played host to jazz and blues in the metro area for nearly a quarter-century with the independent KMHD.[32] In 2009, KMHD affiliated with Oregon Public Broadcasting, drawing on its substantial resources to continue its special mission.[33] Both KBPS and KMHD host unique offerings, while at the same time providing opportunity for student involvement and training.

Many universities in the city also run stations, including Portland State University's KPSU[34] and Reed College's KRRC.[35] While these stations have a smaller broadcast range, they also webcast live on the internet. This phenomenon has transformed radio by allowing alumni, as well as the curious, to tap into programming from remote locations across the globe. Because of college radio's history of promoting independent musicians, even jumpstarting careers, the increasing ease of access has particular relevance for the local arts scene.[36]

Portland public radio thrives off-campus as well. Oregon Public Broadcasting hosts quality radio programming to complement its non-commercial television fare.[37] Portland's Indymedia website features both live-stream radio and extensive archives, and is an invaluable outlet for people to create and share web radio.[38]

The iconic community radio station in Portland is KBOO,[39] whose mission is specifically to meet the needs of unserved or underserved populations by airing content not found in other media, and to provide training and air access to the same underserved groups.[40] In existence longer than Oregon Public Broadcasting, KBOO has 6,700 subscribers, an estimated 70,000 listeners, and 450 volunteers who support its nine staff members.[41]

Posted on KBOO's studio walls, the House Rules define a safe space for community building, free from oppression and discrimination. With such diverse groups sharing the station, one might expect to encounter more antagonism or conflict. Not likely. According to the House Rules, "Every volunteer, board member and staff member [is] empowered and encouraged to act immediately to de-escalate volatile situations." There is programming for every taste—shows on bike culture, gardening, labor issues, Islam, and poetry—and the station remains a welcoming space for all.

The station's Youth Collective is one stunning product of an engaged, collaborative community. Two shows each month are produced, recorded, edited, and broadcast by members of the all-under-twenty-one collective: current events and local youth issues on The Underground[42] and tidbits from Portland's youth music scene on Randomonium.[43]

The view from inside KBOO's sound studios. Photo © Rachel Moore

Collective member Annie Soga continues to volunteer at the station during her summer break from college in New York, drawn back to her hometown of Portland.[44] Soga plays several instruments herself and has, for years, been a part of the Rock 'n' Roll Camp for Girls as a camper and later as an intern. Several friends she met at past camps have gone on to start their own bands, and through her work with the KBOO Youth Collective, Soga has been able to support their music by inviting friends to perform live on the air. Now a seasoned collective member, and inspired by the station's House Rules, Soga acts as a mentor for the younger set. With the skills she learned at KBOO, she now does a radio show at her campus station in New York, promoting music from Portland.

KBOO Youth Advocate Erin Yanke helps Soga and other collective members navigate the station's equipment, empowering young Portlanders to do the programming on their own. Yanke moved to Portland from the Bay Area in 1994, attracted by the atmosphere of public collaboration among artists. Although she knew few specifics about the local scene, she was able to tap in immediately. "People have a tendency to get an interest and create a space where they can teach what they know to other people, to bring them all together," she says.[45] When not working with the Youth Collective or on her own programming at the station, Yanke plays in a band—with no desire to score a recording contract, or to ramp up the scale of her art.

Yanke feels instinctive resistance to "selling out," and many at the station where she works share this mistrust. Radio stations have been consolidating, following a trend towards monopolies echoed in the business world. Recent national studies, such as *Community Radio and Public Culture* by Charles Fairchild, have encouraged stations to rely less on volunteer power and to target listeners who are more likely to contribute financially.[46] These strategy shifts have led to cutbacks in local news coverage and ethnically diverse programming. KBOO resists this model in order to preserve its core mission.[47]

KBOO continues to be driven by member support, both financially and philosophically. Chris Merrick, program director for the station, has remarked on how unique it is to have members elect their entire board of directors. Rather than appealing to global corporations for support, what little underwriting there is comes from small, local shops. Listener feedback and participation is constantly encouraged. Because KBOO produces almost all of its own programming, volunteers have the opportunity to learn all aspects of broadcasting, including public policy.[48] Radio in this vein is far more than entertainment.

Community members have greater ease of access to airtime at non-commercial stations, and listeners with tastes outside the pop box can also find their niche. House Rules that focus on "peace, justice, democracy, human rights, multiculturalism, environmentalism, freedom of expression, and social change" might seem out of place at a larger, commercial station, but shared respect for these values is at the very heart of KBOO's community. And while some have interpreted an uncertain economy as necessitating a bit of "selling out," KBOO has stuck to its ideals—increasing listenership, and membership, at the same time.[49]

FILM IN PORTLAND

MUCH LIKE THE COMICS and zine sectors of Portland's artisan economy, the film sector is a mixture of well-funded productions and yet-to-be-discovered passion. In film, perhaps the best-known director associated with Portland is Gus Van Sant, whose mid-career *Good Will Hunting* gave his name Hollywood status. Van Sant was born in Louisville, Kentucky, and though Portland has been only one of his many homes, it nonetheless plays backdrop for many of his feature films, including *Drugstore Cowboy* and *My Own Private Idaho*.

After garnering support from major studios, Van Sant returned to Portland for inspiration, shooting *Paranoid Park* here. The film premiered at Cannes in 2007 and won the 60th Anniversary Prize. International critics have praised Van Sant's work, and it all started with his first feature film, *Mala Noche*, taken from the novella of the same name by Portland writer Walt Curtis and filmed on the city's streets.

Something about the City of Roses became Van Sant's muse. He has often directed films dissecting street culture, finding much in its complex realities to document and discuss with his camera. One crucial strength for any artisan scene is its reinvestment in the local, and Van Sant has been a longtime supporter of Outside In, a Portland agency serving homeless youth and low-income adults.[50]

Van Sant isn't the only filmmaker who has created films drawn from Portland life. A local medical illustrator who crafts custom acrylic eyes for his patients inspired Vance Malone's *Ocularist*. Malone set the film to the chilling music of Auditory Sculpture, while the intro and title designs are the work of digital production studio Videominds, both based in Portland.[51] The eight-minute *Ocularist* was a finalist at Sundance in 2003, yet Vance still considers film "a balance to his day job." When asked about the prospect of moving to Los Angeles, Vance responds, "I feel lucky every day I get to live in Portland making films."[52]

Animated movies are also bringing considerable attention to Portland. Dark Horse Comics has had one huge hit, adapting its action hero Hellboy to the big screen. Laika Entertainment House (formerly Will Vinton Studios) is becoming a presence in the industry with the success of its innovative 3D animation film, *Coraline*.[53] Yet small-time artists are the heart of the animation movement in the city. Portland's first Platform International Animation Festival[54] attracted over one thousand animators from around the world in 2007.

Portland has routinely ranked highly in *MovieMaker* magazine's annual survey of independent film hotspots. Several rising stars help build this reputation: Todd Haynes (*I'm Not There*), Miranda July (*Me and You and Everyone We Know*), and Irene Taylor Brodsky (*Hear and Now*). Film festivals, like the Portland Queer Documentary Film Festival, Portland Underground Film Festival, Longbaugh Film Festival, Portland Documentary and eXperimental Film Fest, and Portland International Film Festival, now in its thirty-third year, give the independents energy and cohesion.

The depth of the independent film sector was highlighted by Shawn Levy, the *Oregonian*'s film critic. In his presentation for the City Club of Portland, Levy observed that, within a ten-minute drive of city hall, there are twenty-seven screens dedicated to independent, alternative, or specialty cinema, as compared with only twenty-six screens carrying mainstream Hollywood fare. He noted that in his experience only Paris, France, can make a similar claim of featuring more independent than mainstream films. He also noted that his discussions with indie film distributors confirmed his sense that Portland screens indie films longer than nearly any other major city, including New York.[55]

Underserved groups of emerging directors—youth, women, and minorities—can find support in several Portland nonprofits that serve the local film industry. Film Action Oregon (FAO) was created by governor's decree in 1992 and assists independent filmmakers with everything from fundraising to editing and screening. FAO restored and now resides in the stunning Hollywood Theatre, from which it operates the Women's Film Initiative and the Project Youth Doc program for teens.[56] Each year Docupalooza screens at the Hollywood Theatre to showcase the most recent teens' work, with all proceeds going toward the following year's program. The Northwest Film Center also has the Young People's Film & Video Festival and funds the Oregon Latino Youth Video Project, among numerous other endeavors.[57]

Several of the city's classic theaters also feed residents' hunger for independent and obscure films. The volunteer-fueled Clinton Street Theater— one of the oldest operating movie houses in the nation—hosts both the Portland Underground Film Festival and a weekly screening of the cult hit *Rocky Horror Picture Show*.[58] And the PDX AV Club meets in the theater once a month or so to have a short film festival, sipping beverages from the attached Clinton Street Brewery.[59]

CONCLUSION

FORMAL STRUCTURES SUCH AS publishing houses and major comics distributors have helped make Portland a draw for creative types. But without an artistic philosophy supportive of independent work, the city would look nothing like it does today. Small bookstores and eclectic symposiums are equally important here, though not necessarily in "competition" with their big-name counterparts. There is potential for a writer or illustrator to link up with Dark Horse or with zinesters, depending on their own personal motivations. Independent radio, media, and film add depth and richness to the mix. It is the diversity and complexity of the scene—not one strict focus within it—that has, over time, nurtured Portland's artisan economy. Such multiplicity makes change over time inevitable; the wealth of talent and a supportive consumer base ensure that the local art scene will continue to grow and evolve.

CHAPTER 11
PORTLAND CRAFTERS: MOBILIZING A COMMUNITY ONE STITCH AT A TIME

Renée Bogin

INSIDE THE BARELY LIT, moody basement of the Doug Fir, a retro-fitted hotel turned swanky lounge, Portland's hippest crafters display their latest creations of ironic, sophisticated, and even utilitarian wares at Crafty Wonderland. We see business-savvy moms, single women, and even a few potential superstars. Collectively, this scene conveys communitarian values and organization at their most grassroots and effective. These ladies are serious about crafts, but "this ain't your grandma's sewing circle."[1]

The setting is off the beaten path, frequented only by those in the know. More than a shopping event, it's a culture and scene rampant with visual spontaneity and DIY ethic. Cara Buchalter's "ladies,"—pop art illustrations of independent women—adorn handmade cards and journals. Elsewhere, cleverly designed animals on patches with frayed ends, are sewn on hand-knit caps with visible uneven stitches—like everything on display, unabashedly made by hand. Unlike mass-produced items, the process of making these goods becomes a part of the design; the rough edges and irregular recycled material are celebrated as a statement of uniqueness, authenticity, or sustainability. An evident ethic infuses the process, product, producer, and consumer at Crafty Wonderland.

Across the river, Art in the Pearl is going strong with crafts of a more traditional style on display. This event showcases the region's finest artisans and artists who attract Portland's artsy clientele—locals and tourists alike. Well-designed booths adorned with market-oriented displays and stocked with fine crafted goods are spread over several park blocks in the upscale Pearl District. At the booths, vendors describe to potential customers the exquisite details of their works, calling attention to refined edges and complementary color schemes. The patrons are older and dressed more conventionally than those at Crafty Wonderland; fewer frayed-edged skirts and mismatched knit caps are visible. Instead, neat and stylish clothing matches superbly fabricated pottery bowls, glass ornaments, metal statues, and fine leather handbags. Master skill and aesthetic appreciation are clearly prioritized at this venue. Also more evident is the producer/consumer division; the patrons are shoppers. Initially drawn to the area's chic boutiques and elegant chain shops, they may have stumbled upon the outdoor artisan market on a pleasant summer day.

This introduction to Portland's rich and varied craft scene reveals the rough geography of two strong yet distinguishable communities—DIY/indie and traditional/fine craft. Distinctions between DIY and traditional crafts are not decidedly clear. DIY artisans acknowledge the refinement of older crafts like pottery and glassware but see DIY's potential for refinement. Others highlight DIY's simplicity and affordability. Sometimes aesthetic and function set DIY apart. While indie crafts are often more functional than fine decorative crafts, they don't always attain the high functionality of other durable crafts, like leather jackets or ceramic serving ware. Thus, while DIY crafters might embed functionality into their products, it's the deliberate aesthetic which brands them as indie, despite much crossover with traditional crafts.

PORTLAND: MECCA OF INDIE CRAFTS?

WHY IS THERE such a concentration of crafters and craft events in Portland? Crafters consistently identified community support as the reason, including favorable public policies, cooperative use of public and commercial space, strong neighborhood culture, and artisan networks.

Support from the city is essential. Year-round arts and crafts events in public spaces would not happen without the city's permission. Artist markets fill public parks with booths and patrons, pedestrians meander down sidewalks during art-walks, and streets shut down in neighborhoods all across the city for summer street fairs. Ultimately, this is all possible because city policies encourage the transformation of public space into art markets, art walks, and street fairs.

Events like neighborhood street fairs and art walks contribute to the reclamation of public space when public authorities and businesses relinquish some control over sidewalks and street space. While First Thursday, frequented by Portland's more elite patrons, features fine art and craft, Last Thursday is Alberta Street's free-spirited response—a wild, anything-goes street party filled with street vendors, music, fire dancers, jugglers, and other experimental arts and crafts displays. At both events, vendors, entertainers, and visitors experience unusual freedom of movement as the requirement for vending licenses is loosely enforced. This leniency sustains those who operate within an informal economy and circumvents commercial or state control over street and sidewalk space. While some street and sidewalk spaces are reserved at most artisan events, free space prevails on the fringes. Meanwhile, commercial spaces support or adapt to the culture with flourishing cafes and bohemian boutiques to serve the local community.

The character of Portland's neighborhoods also contributes to the rise of crafter communities and markets. On the east side, neo-bohemian neighborhoods with shops and cafés pop up at regular intervals from the north to the south. Each of these artsy enclaves houses a few crafters, craft shops, or other DIY hot spots. Private residential space is altered as indie crafter households operate as flexible workspaces, transforming the household from a unit of consumption to a unit of production. On the west side, the more traditional crafts typically thrive in downtown galleries or in the northwest Pearl District. Big arts and crafts events happen along the west side Park Blocks, either in the Pearl, or at the south end of downtown.

In addition to advocacy from the city and the character of Portland neighborhoods, support for the craft sector comes from key individuals and support networks. DIY leader Diane Gilleland loves the work, community, and opportunities she found in Portland. She was christened Sister Diane when she founded Portland's Church of Craft, an organization so successful she could no longer manage it. Now she focuses exclusively on her podcast and blog that feature local crafters. After watching talented artisans struggle, Jen Neitzel founded DIY Lounge to offer space for artists to share skills in DIY workspaces. DIY Lounge now hosts thirty different teachers and numerous classes including design, recycled crafts, and business management topics for mostly female students, aged seven to seventy.

A cluster of nonprofit and educational organizations strongly support Portland crafts. In addition to several smaller educational institutions, Portland has two colleges, Oregon College of Art and Craft and the Pacific Northwest College of Art, that offer undergraduate programs and a Master of Fine Arts in applied craft and design. The Museum of Contemporary Craft, a nonprofit organization, offers public educational opportunities in addition to its contemporary displays of fine craftsmanship. Trillium Artisans, a community development program, promotes local artisans. Portland Saturday Market began as an independent nonprofit organization in 1974 and has grown into the largest craft market in the country.[2] Portland also has a number of traditional guilds and studios for workshops.

Apart from formal institutions, informal DIY networks provide vital community support. National women-oriented and crafter magazines regularly feature Portland indie crafters. Meanwhile, the internet serves to connect

Artists showcase their wares at Crafty Wonderland, at the Oregon Convention Center in northeast Portland. Photo © Rachel Moore

Portland crafters to their local, national, and global community through online markets, magazines, zines, blogs, and podcasts. Sites include resources for crafters to get organized and develop business skills, how-to pages, and directories that profile artisans and their wares. Etsy, a virtual, global marketplace for crafters, has a very active Portland presence. The Black Apple and Ashley G, both of Portland, are the site's top two sellers of art prints.[3]

Connection to other artisan communities provides an expanded network of mutually supportive and non-competitive sectors. For example, Buchalter explains how local indie artisans support each other through work, social links, and a larger community of crafters, writers, cafés, and the music scene. "The gals are in the DIY scene, and the guys are musicians."[4] She designs concert posters for local bands and then attends their performances. Through mutual patronage across indie artisan scenes, Portland's DIY craft sector flourishes.

"Portland is the mecca" for indie crafts, claims Sister Diane, because it's "very tribal…fiercely indie…with a creative community [that] supports local artisans." Moreover, she suggests the city's attractiveness, sustainability, and affordability make it a "great bubble." Neitzel also acknowledges support for local economies, while Buchalter believes affordable home prices sustain independent living. Portland's thriving independent culture, community support, and formal and informal networks are crucial to craft's boom. While these supports help weave a tightly knit community, does this community constitute a movement?

MOVEMENT OR MARKET?

A MORE IN-DEPTH EXAMINATION of DIY craft necessitates an introduction to earlier DIY culture. Historically, the nineteenth century Arts and Crafts Movement "arose in England and the United States [to elevate] well-designed and finely crafted handmade work above common mass-produced goods."[5] Over the last few decades, resistance has shifted from traditional forms into new stylistic, political statements. Seventies punk launched a DIY ethic into the community through stylistic statements meant to show resistance to mainstream culture: deliberately ripped clothes; self-created, anti-aesthetic designs; and radical accessories like jewelry made of safety pins.[6] Nineties DIY fashion softened punk's resistance-based aesthetic but pushed new styles that suggested neo-tribal affinity and a continued predilection for spectacle.[7] While current styles are generally less provocative, elements of resistance pepper the movement, and an ethic of sustainability is revealed through material and market choices. This includes an enthusiasm for "found" art—recycled or reclaimed products. Recycled craft eliminates a component of the classic capitalist model by circumventing the extraction and conversion of raw materials into a new product. Moreover, labor exploitation is avoided because material extraction has already occurred, and the crafter is usually the sole laborer as designer, producer, and seller. The downscale digs of DIY events also hint at a mode of resistance. No investors reap huge benefits from the sale of crafts.

Resistance through markets also occurs as Portland DIY connects to the virtual, transnational DIY community through a shared intention to create alternatives to mass production. Goods are cheaper when mass produced, yet DIY consumers and producers share an ethic that supports product integrity. This may not rise to the level of what Tim Costello refers to as "globalization from below" or the activities of "peoples' transnational coalitions"—social

Vendors at Last Thursday on Alberta Street often find new and adventurous ways to display their art. Photo © Rachel Moore

Artist Cara Buchalter stands by her work in her north Portland home. Photo © Whitney Gayer

movements mutually supporting workers in different parts of the world.[8] However, the DIY community does create global and local linkages through information technology networks, where it freely shares information, promotes accessibility, attempts to revalue labor, favors community over competition, and generally generates a "series of connections, contacts, coalitions, and networks of cooperation."[9]

A look at today's craft circles, especially DIY, suggests that wealth accumulation is far from the primary goal of Portland's prominent artisans. Economic inter-competition is rare; rather community alliances, ethics, and craftsmanship drive participation and production. In reference to DIY crafters, PDX Super Crafty's Rachel O'Rourke suggests, "The core energy [isn't about] competitiveness or hierarchy… That comes from being a collective."[10]

In summary, acts of resistance in the current crafter market are less "counter" cultural than their DIY predecessors and generally promote sustainability, local community, and ethical exchange, rather than revolution. Portland's indie crafters don't directly challenge globalizing forces, but provide alternative models through local and transnational networks. Without promoting economy of scale advantages or exploiting cheaper, foreign labor, they expand into international markets and participate in a network that is accessible across borders through the internet. Consumers who choose DIY over mass-produced goods potentially remove support for globalization. Thus, local production is global action. Essentially, DIY culture is primarily an alternative, not a counter-movement, and is characterized by an integrity that drives the local community and provides a substitute for globalization models of production.

ETHICS AND MARKETS

WHAT ARE THE TRADE-OFFS between the need of crafters to sustain themselves and their desire to express themselves creatively, work independently and maintain their values? And how have DIY crafters responded to the 2009 recession?

Crafters are confronting the economic downturn with resilience and adaptability. Neitzel encourages others to become recession-proof by considering usability and asking practical questions like, "Can I wear it?" Likewise, Sister Diane warns that when funds are tighter, "nonessential" indie crafts move off the radar screen. She suggests that artisans should enhance functionality and self-promote beyond Portland through online markets. She is concerned that the indie craft community is "starting to hit a point of saturation" as Portland is mainly a "town of producers, lacking [enough] consumers." To survive, Klepp modifies products based on consumer demand. Her higher-end, labor-and-design-intensive items—mosaic glass lawn ornaments—are pricey, so she created smaller, simpler suncatchers to sell quickly.

Potentially, market tensions could force other crafters to similarly adapt, become more competitive, or take advantage of corporate opportunities in design, production, and marketing. Artist and illustrator Amy Ruppel, a local superstar, was thrilled to work with Target to create a design for a product line they were developing. She has also developed a relationship with a small museum company. While this arrangement produces steady revenues, it also diminishes her control of the production process. Emily Martin, another Portland superstar and owner of Black Apple,[11] welcomed the opportunity to promote her work on the Martha Stewart Show despite some local criticism.[12] Are Ruppel and Martin achieving

Bonnie Organ, Richard Fox, and Jen Neitzel at DIY Lounge. Photo © Rachel Moore.

deserved recognition for their products or selling out? Would most indie crafters resist the flattering, marketable prospect of widely distributing their designs through corporate accounts in order to preserve the purity of their craft? Indie crafters are facing such dilemmas as changes in markets push diversification.

Pursuit of wholesale accounts raises the possibility of increased production, and potentially an expanded workforce, to meet demands for economies of scale. If work stays local and small and maintains integrity of process and product, there's no ethical contention. Less clear is whether working with large wholesalers ultimately diminishes DIY credibility and compromises resistance to commodification. Moreover, does it become a type subculture exploitation in which styles are mainstreamed and production processes morph into mass production?[13] Indie crafters face other challenges from large-scale companies and corporations who capitalize on DIY's popularity through imitation, exploitation, and co-optation. Some items sold at big-box stores are imitations of impromptu styles seen at DIY events and sites like Etsy. Sister Diane recounts a recent predatory practice: companies promote contests geared toward indie crafters and then retain copyright, not just of the winning entry, but of all entries. They tempt with rewards, including new cars, cash, or product distribution of winning designs. Artisans achieve wide distribution of their designs, but they sign off their rights by entering the contest. The companies eliminate design fees and obtain creative products at minimal cost.

If artisans don't critically analyze the impact of co-optation within a global framework, they may inevitably become engulfed by the globalization forces they initially resisted. But if survival or opportunity demand it, is there a way to enter mainstream markets? Buchalter's experience may serve as a model of how some compromise may be both sustaining and ethical. Most of her work is done by hand, by her own design, in an atmosphere of integrity. However, she also contracts with one small company that commissions designs and manages production. While she sustains herself through both hand work and contracted work, she feels that she operates predominantly within the DIY ethic.

CONCLUSION

AT THE HEART of Portland's thriving craft sector is community support and commitment to ethical production, despite vulnerability to market forces. This support strengthens a rich, evolving sector and a community accentuated by ethical guidelines of integrity toward production. While unable to entirely circumvent globalized models of capital and production exchange, Portland's crafters clearly make serious efforts. In this capacity, Portland's craft sector is not just a market niche, or local culture, but exhibits elements of a social movement, particularly in the DIY community.

Essentially, Portland's craft communities rely on both formal and informal networks and support structures to thrive. Formal institutions like Museum of Contemporary Craft and Portland Saturday Market continue to support traditional crafts, while informal networks, enhanced by events, online forums, websites, blogs, and podcasts, give DIY circles organization, recognition, and cohesion. These latter community networks are built not only on a desire to create, teach, or introduce crafts, but also on a shared set of ethics that drive production and markets. Despite a new aesthetic, the DIY community conveys an ethic reminiscent of the original Arts and Craft and DIY movements. Portland, a longtime champion of craft, is now the center of the DIY craft movement.

If the movement survives, some compromises of ethics may be necessary. It's not a perfect model, but then Portland's craft sector, even the DIY community, is not an anti-globalization social movement out to actively push a new, post-capitalist model. Moreover, market forces exist to compete with and potentially co-opt crafter products. Yet, if some artisans, like those profiled here, create products with a mark of integrity, they contribute to their local community of producers, consumers, and artisans, as well as to the global DIY/crafter community, through commitment to their ethic and participation in an economy which supports globalization from below.

CHAPTER 12
IN THE CHURCH OF COMMUNITY REUSE AND TRANSFORMATION

Alison Briggs

IN THE CHURCH of Community Reuse and Transformation, followers worship the holy trinity of Free Geek, the Rebuilding Center, and City Repair. These three nonprofit organizations have attained iconic status in Portland for their ability to articulate a vision of community and to attract a cluster of devoted supporters and volunteers. However, the products of their work—a nine-year-old laptop, a bucket of tiles leftover from a bathroom remodel, and a giant sunflower painted on a city street—are not what first comes to mind when thinking of an artisan economy. The physical products of these organizations are not artisanal in the sense of, say, locally distilled vodka. Rather, the tangible creations are a byproduct of their missions, and these missions are consistent with an artisan world view of improvisational learning, collaborative organizational structures, respect for materials, reconnecting with place, and building social wealth. Free Geek exists "to recycle technology and provide access to computers, the internet, education, and job skills in exchange for community service."[1] The Rebuilding Center "is a vibrant resource working to strengthen the environmental, economic, and social fabric of local communities."[2] The City Repair Project "educates and inspires communities and individuals to creatively transform the places where they live."[3] Portland looks to these organizations for new solutions to urban issues such as the digital divide, overflowing landfills, and urban isolation.

FREE GEEK: HELPING THE NEEDY GET NERDY

"THE DATABASE IS DOWN—I can't process this donation! Where's James? Someone find James!" It's 11:01 AM on a Saturday morning in the lobby of Free Geek, a nonprofit community technology center in southeast Portland, and it has just opened its doors for the day. At first glance the scene appears as pure chaos. A line of forty volunteers stretches out the door as they wait to check in for their shifts, a child stands mesmerized by a rotating hard-drive disk nailed to the wall, and two staff members are frantically checking in volunteers ("Where's James?"). There is method to this madness and, like the famous "sidewalk ballet" observed by urbanist Jane Jacobs, this is the vibrant daily routine for Free Geek. By 11:10 AM all the volunteers have started their shifts, the child has snapped out of her hypnosis, and James, our thirteen-year-old hero, has fixed the database.

Free Geek was founded in 2000 to recycle computer technology and provide low- and no-cost computing to individuals, nonprofits, and social change organizations in the community. What does this mean? Anyone can show up at Free Geek's doorstep and donate their old Commodore, sign up to volunteer time in exchange for a free Linux computer, or peruse the Free Geek Thrift Store for that special SCSI cable they so desperately need. While there are roughly twenty paid staff members, the majority of this operation is run by Free Geek's seven hundred active volunteers.

Free Geek accepts donations of computers and other gizmos from the public and refurbishes them to redistribute back into the community in a variety of ways. Volunteers can either contribute twenty-four hours of time to earn a free computer or, if they have more time to spare, they can learn how to build computers and eventually take one home that they built for themselves. Alternately, folks who are both strapped for cash and lack twenty-four hours to spare can get outfitted in the thrift store with a fully functional set-up—including the main computer and its peripherals such as monitor, keyboard, mouse, speakers, and printer—all for under one hundred dollars. The set-up is so affordable in part because Free Geek installs free and open source software (FOSS) on all its computers (the operative word here being *free*). Using FOSS on older hardware breathes new life into these machines, and even the oldest computers that Free Geek refurbishes are entirely effective for basic uses like checking email, listening to music, or typing a resume.[4]

The choice to use FOSS is not just grounded in financial reasons, but also philosophical ones, and this philosophy resonates throughout all of Free Geek, including their particular choice of operating system. Free Geek installs the user-friendly *Ubuntu* operating system on its computers. The word Ubuntu is African, meaning, "I am what I am because of who we all are."[5] FOSS embodies this spirit of collaboration, and the belief that working cooperatively on a project makes the product even more worthwhile. The Volunteer Build Program at Free Geek is a peer-to-peer learning experience, and it exemplifies the Ubuntu spirit. Although an instructor is always present, volunteers are encouraged to ask questions of whomever is standing nearby. If the volunteer on the left doesn't know why the hard drive won't show up in BIOS, perhaps the volunteer on the right does. Or maybe a group of volunteers temporarily assembles to solve this minor crisis. These interactions contribute to an ever-growing collective knowledge base. Volunteers sustain this cumulative wisdom by taking on the role of instructor; in fact, the majority of the instructors who teach computer assembly and troubleshooting are volunteers themselves.[6]

Hundreds of pounds of computer parts await processing by Free Geek's volunteer staff. Photo © Rachel Moore.

Proponents of FOSS believe in access and use; there is a keen emphasis on making one's computer into the tool one wants it to be. If you want to create a bookkeeping system for your nascent small business, you not only want a computer that has the appropriate software, but you also want to be able to manipulate that software to your personalized needs. There is a distinct attitude of "do not touch, experts only" with closed-source software, as if the experts "know best" and present the perfect final product to the homogeneous consumer. But in order for the average computer user to become fully comfortable actually *using* his or her computer, one must break through this "experts only" mentality. Free Geek computers (which bear the amusing moniker "Freekbox") are designed to be used and are made comprehensible for volunteers as a means to empower them to use the computers for their own specific needs.

Volunteers are truly the lifeblood of Free Geek. Free Geek's goal is to help bridge the digital divide and get working technology into the hands of people who need it, but Richard Seymour, a staff member at Free Geek whose actual job title is "That Man Behind the Curtain," adds that the mission is also "to educate them about it and to demystify that technology…to change their relationship with how they use computers."[7] This new relationship is fostered from the moment an individual starts volunteering. Seymour explains that all the education at Free Geek is hands-on and the volunteers "learn by actually doing what we need done in order to produce the computers." Volunteers are inextricably integrated into the overall functioning and production of Free Geek; they dismantle printers and computers, test keyboards and mice, and help sort through the massive piles of incoming gizmos. As the volunteers engage in each of these tasks, the technology becomes less intimidating. After all, by taking apart a computer, one realizes that it's mostly filled with air.

Free Geek volunteers receive an introductory class on how to use and personalize their computers, a year of free tech support, special deals on internet access through a local internet service provider, and the opportunity to take about a dozen specialized classes for free. Classes include education on such topics as how to edit digital pictures, how to master the Open Office spreadsheet program, and how to get an email address and surf the web. For these computers to be an authentic product, Seymour maintains that this education is absolutely necessary:

> If we can continue to educate people about how to use the com-
> puters and how to repair or maintain them, then I think [the com-
> puters] can remain authentic. Lacking that, they become just one
> more commodity. You see an ad about a computer, and it will tell
> you it can do anything, but if you don't know how to actually
> make it work it's not that authentic.... Free Geek is better than that.

When regular Joe buys a sexy new laptop from a big-box store, he
may plug it in at home and be so completely baffled by all its cutting-edge
software that he never turns it on again. Seymour relates this to the artistic
process in that "you have to have some kind of inspiration, but you also
have to have your technique down. And if you don't have your technique
down, that inspiration really doesn't do you any good.... The more you
know about the computer as a tool, the more you're going to be able to
express yourself through it."

The educational framework of Free Geek is not the only connection to
FOSS philosophy. Free Geek has no bosses; the staff is non-hierarchical and
is run by a collective of fourteen dedicated members. All collective members

Volunteer Daniel White, hard at work on one of Free Geek's rebuilt laptops. Photo ©
Rachel Moore

are paid the same and receive the same benefits (including full health benefits, paid vacation time, and an employer-matching retirement account). Free Geek uses consensus decision-making in all its committees, including the board of directors. While the staff is collectively responsible for the day-to-day operations, the big-picture visioning is guided by the community council, a group comprised of board and staff members as well as volunteers. Seymour, who has been involved since day one, notes that "it's a very central thing for us to be democratically managed, and that means that everybody who is affected by decisions has a say in those decisions." As emphasized in Chapter 2, the actors in an artisan economy organize their work not by "command and control" but rather by "an organization of coordination, cooperation, and assemblage." Free Geek is heavily dependent on the support of its seven hundred active volunteers, including FOSS supporters, computer hobbyists, DIY activists, environmentalists, and community members who enjoy the welcoming social aspect of the Free Geek community. Free Geek is truly a community organization, and has relationships with such diverse groups as the city government and the Red and Black Café, a worker-owned vegan coffeehouse. Indeed, even from the beginning, Free Geek has relied on a widespread network of skills and moral support, and was founded by folks involved with the City Repair Project.

Employees don't make much money, but they have comprehensive control over their work environment. Seymour describes the type of person who is attracted to this kind of environment as one who appreciates not being micromanaged all the time by some arbitrary hierarchy and who relishes being actively involved in the formation of decisions that affect how they work. Like true artisans who live for their craft, most Free Geek staff struggle with having Free Geek bleed into every aspect of their personal life, and many must remind themselves that "Free Geek is not my boyfriend." While each collective member has some expertise in a specific area, they have their hands in a myriad of projects. These projects are constantly in flux as new opportunities or challenges arise.

However, FOSS philosophy is not the only way Free Geek embodies the substance of the artisan economy. Like the example of the artisan baker described in Chapter 2, who builds a narrative of her product and shares this with her patrons, so too do Free Geek staff and volunteers attempt to create narrative linkages between those who work on a computer and those who eventually own it. All Free Geek computers bear a large sticker with handwritten notes about that particular machine's components: how many RAM slots and which kind of RAM? Does the motherboard have an AGP slot? Which keystroke allows you to enter BIOS? If an artisan is one who applies skills, judgment, improvisation, and passion to their work, then Free Geek is certainly cultivating its volunteers to be artisans. Free Geek works with donated computers of all different brands, shapes, and architecture. For this reason, every computer that is rebuilt must be an act of improvisation. Maybe the USB port on the front doesn't work on one computer, or the sound is a little tinny on a particular laptop; this forces the builder to make a judgment call—how reusable is this machine? Is there a creative solution to this problem?

Seymour makes a telling point when he explains the contrast between the original manufacturing process and the refurbishment that Free Geek does. Computers are largely made by robots in an industrial factory, but when Free Geek gets them, "we take them all apart by hand and cobble them together in lot of different ways…in a Frankenstein process, pieced together in a hands-on way." Luckily, computers are more easily revived than an assemblage of cadavers. Seymour believes that "a lot of times people are very focused on the end goal…but if you can somehow step back from that and just enjoy the work you're doing, you'll be a happier person." To Seymour, this is evident at Free Geek by the fact that so many volunteers who are drawn to Free Geek to earn a free computer or learn a new skill keep coming back because of the community. "Being in the moment really makes that happen," He believes people think of Free Geek as a virtual community because the organization deals with technology, but "we're really very based in a local, physical space, and I think that's key to the organization because people can see each other face to face in the context of something that's otherwise considered very abstract."

Free Geek is also an excellent resource for the community in that it serves as an incubator for local businesses and nonprofit organizations. The thrift store offers a diverse range of inexpensively priced computers, gizmos, and accessories. It is not uncommon for budding entrepreneurs trying to set up a small business to get their computers inexpensively through Free Geek. Additionally, through Free Geek's Community Grants program, local nonprofit organizations receive free computers and other related hardware, saving them hundreds, or even thousands, of dollars on new hardware and closed-source software. Seymour succinctly phrases this as "[w]e take stuff that nobody wants, and we make cheap or free things out of it." What was formerly junk becomes highly desirable. Through a partnership with the City of Portland, Free Geek refurbishes all the outgoing computers from the city and redistributes them to Portland Public Schools.

Except for the final processing of electronics bound for recycling, everything is done at Free Geek. Free Geek is financially self-sufficient; it supports itself through cash donations and thrift-store and recycling income. Foundation grants are only solicited to seed new projects, such as the purchase of a box truck for performing pickups for local businesses upgrading their computers. According to Seymour, this reflects the character of Oregon:

> Oregon is an obvious western state where there's a "go at it on your own" kind of attitude and a lot of permissiveness when it comes to expressing yourself. Oregon has that contrariness that you find in the West and that independent rugged individualistic spirit, but Portland specifically has attracted a lot of very bright young people from all over the country…interlopers into that Western individualistic mentality that come in with all these alternate ideas and make a very vibrant culture.

Free Geek has certainly benefited from its Portland location. The environmental scene has always been strong here, and since Free Geek has diverted approximately 2,500 tons of e-waste from the landfill since its inception, it can definitely be described as environmentalist. Free Geek has benefited from the support of other environmentalists, as well as a selection of ethical recycling vendors. Such vendors don't simply ship off boatloads of toxic e-waste to countries with lax environmental regulation, but rather are fully accountable by demonstrating a transparent process.

Seymour sees the future of Free Geek in terms of replication rather than expansion. Because all documentation necessary to copy the Free Geek model is publicly available, there are already about a dozen other similar organizations popping up across North America. Replication of the Free Geek model by other dedicated individuals makes sense because in each different region there exists a distinctive flavor of community. One can't replicate the community that Free Geek in Portland has cultivated over the last nine years in Kansas City or Mexico City. It is precisely this unique community that defines Free Geek. Seymour eloquently summarizes how Free Geek fits into Portland's artisan economy in this sense:

> It's hard to scale up a craft. I go all the way back to the dawn of the industrial economy when, prior to that, you had artisans making everything by hand and then you introduced factories. We're at the end of the industrial economy (sort of, or we're into something that comes after). What Free Geek is doing is taking the tailings coming out of that Industrial Era, and we're applying the old craftsman skills to it.

REBUILDING CENTER: FROM TRASH TO TREASURE

IN A POOR NEIGHBORHOOD in North Portland in the 1990s, a group of neighbors congregated on the sidewalk one day to discuss the most recent drive-by shooting. They asked themselves, how did we get to this unhealthy place as a society despite all our resources? The conversation proved so stimulating that the group continued their discussion around kitchen tables for weeks afterwards. One day someone mentioned David, a young teen in the neighborhood. Everyone knew of him, as David was quite the problem, but no one knew much about him. So a member of the group decided to get to know him a little better, and the next time she saw him, she asked, "What's important to you? If you could have anything in the world, what would you want?" David replied that he wanted a million dollars, a motorcycle, and braces for his malformed teeth.

When the neighbors met again they discussed David's comments and eventually decided that they would endeavor to get braces for David. The group found an orthodontist who was willing to offer reduced fees, and the neighborhood rallied to raise the remaining funds. Soon after David received his braces, the woman who initially approached David was cleaning out her garage when David walked by and said, "If I didn't know you, I'd take these bikes lying out here." The group realized that they had not changed

David, but they *had* changed their relationship with him. It was a "eureka" moment for them—there should be an organization that promotes this sort of transformation. The Rebuilding Center was born out of this realization that the power to improve one's community lay in changing the interpersonal relationships amongst the community members.

The Rebuilding Center's website describes the organization as a project of Our United Villages, which is a "vibrant resource working to strengthen the environmental, economic, and social fabric of local communities."[8] It does this primarily by accepting used (but still usable) building and construction materials from the public and, in turn, selling these at 50–90 percent market value in their thrift store. The Rebuilding Center recovers nearly six million pounds of building materials each year and is the largest nonprofit reuse center for salvaged building materials in North America. The Rebuilding Center's mission is guided by a faith in reuse as an integral factor in environmental sustainability. This faith resonates throughout the spectrum of their programs and services. The building itself is a "showcase of reuse," in the words of Executive Director and Founder Shane Endicott.[9] Everything down to making a sign—from reused materials, of course—reflects the mission.

Through their Deconstruction Services program, the Rebuilding Center sends a licensed and bonded crew out to a deconstruction site to salvage reusable materials. Deconstruction is a slow process that involves a great deal of improvisation as each part of the building is removed by hand. The Rebuilding Center claims that they are able to recover up to 85 percent of reusable building material this way and, in doing so, are able to decrease building removal costs, reduce the environmental impact of conventional construction practices, conserve landfill space, and create living-wage jobs. Deconstruction Services is attractive to businesses and homeowners because all salvaged materials can be claimed as tax-deductible donations.

The cleverly titled ReFind Furniture is the creative outlet of the Rebuilding Center and is a shining example of how the organization fits into Portland's artisan economy. Artist/builders at the Rebuilding Center utilize salvaged materials to create entirely handmade, functional works of art such as tables, benches, or picture frames. These exquisite pieces of unique furniture are designed to be durable, to be celebrated and enjoyed for the long haul. The reclaimed materials reflect periods of regional architectural history, and, when possible, these stories accompany the finished piece via an attached tag. These historical details enhance the value of the pieces in the artist-builders eyes, and therefore, sharing these narratives with the customer is a meaningful link, even a bond, between them. The artist-builders celebrate the history and individual character of the salvaged materials by spotlighting specific features or irregularities of the items. For example, a knot in a salvaged piece of wood might become the focal point of the new piece of art rather than have its presence diminished by being painted over. Endicott revels in the idea that "every single item has a history, has a story, had a life before." The glass used in Refind construction is cut from old windows, windows which may be one hundred years old, and Endicott creates his own story for this: "Somebody for years looked out those windows... Some kid saw their first snow through that window... somebody made those windows.... I love the fact that it keeps living on."

The Rebuilding Center also cultivates functional reuse by providing affordable educational opportunities to community members eager to flex their creative muscles. Classes span such topics as "Found Object Printmaking," "Jewelry Making with Recycled Materials," and "Introduction to Traditional Joinery." These classes seek to inspire community members to reconceptualize used materials and transform them into works of art. The hope is that these individuals will feel empowered by this new perspective and continue to critically examine old materials in other aspects of their lives.

The Rebuilding Center is a resource for the community in many other ways, as well. Through its gamut of services, the Rebuilding Center has direct financial benefit for the community. Endicott summarizes this contribution adeptly:

> Basically we're taking what society has said for a long time is a liability, is waste, and was paying to throw away or have crunched up and thrown into the ground in a landfill. And by reusing it, we're turning that waste into an asset for the community. We're able to create locally sustained jobs, we're able to provide a local, affordable resource to the community, and it benefits the environment—everything that's getting reused here is something you don't have to buy new, which preserves natural resources and prevents manufacturing of things that cause pollution.

Every fifteen minutes, something is coming or going out of the Rebuilding Center. All of these materials are from the local region, and these assets remain in the region. The Rebuilding Center refuses to ship out any items or sell them on the internet, and the thrift store's bargain prices provide affordable access to materials for Portland residents. Additionally, Deconstruction Services employs six people for every one person used for standard demolition. Preston Browning, former program manager for Mercy Corps' reclamation work in New Orleans, states that deconstruction jobs are essentially a job-skills training program, and that in less than a year a worker is ready for entry-level work in the building trade.[10] If Browning is correct, then the Rebuilding Center can also add job-skills training to its repertoire of community services. And since 83 percent of staff live in the surrounding zip codes, the Rebuilding Center is directly improving the local work force.

In the same vein as Free Geek, the Rebuilding Center is committed to openly sharing its business model. Endicott describes this as an obligation as a nonprofit "to give away whatever we create here...[and] the more we give the more successful we'll be." People interested in starting their own local deconstruction companies are encouraged to visit the Rebuilding Center and shadow staff, gather documentation, and inherit the wisdom of the Rebuilding Center's trial-and-error development. If society is one day subject to a great awakening—if we cease throwing things away and start working together—the Rebuilding Center would no longer need to exist in its current form. Far from fearing this, the Rebuilding Center would welcome this societal shift and consider it a great success. At this idyllic point in the future, the Rebuilding Center and Our United Villages would then adapt the organization into a new community resource. To a certain extent, the particular items the Rebuilding Center deals in don't even matter; they're simply a means to an end. That end is fostering interpersonal relationships that enhance the social fabric of the community.

For this reason the Rebuilding Center refuses to expand. Location is pivotal to its success and its value as a resource. Indeed, the organization grew out of a desire to cultivate the relationships in its own north Portland community. Endicott argues that "[t]he Rebuilding Center and Our United Villages [have] become part of the social fabric of our community. You can't replicate that; it has a relationship." This relationship exists in myriad ways, many elaborated earlier, and can manifest from even a seemingly minor instance—a local resident dropping off the original cabinets from her newly remodeled kitchen, and the feeling of this donation being genuinely appreciated by the Rebuilding Center. To open up a branch location, even within the greater Portland metropolitan area, would run counter to this type of localized relationship-building. This is not to say that the Rebuilding Center is done growing its services. Endicott wagers that the Rebuilding Center is at about 60 percent of its full capacity.

CITY REPAIR: MENDING THE URBAN FABRIC

WHILE PASSING THROUGH the peaceful, residential Sellwood neighborhood of Portland, one cannot help but marvel in the vibrant and quirky beauty of Southeast Sherett and 9th Avenue. An enormous mural occupies the intersection—actually, a more accurate description would be that the mural *is* the intersection. A beautifully designed whirlpool invokes the four elements: a brilliant red burst of flame, a calming deep ocean blue, an earthy emerald green, and a whimsical swirl of sky blue. Some capricious silver stars seem to make the mural sparkle. The corners of the intersection feature a community bulletin board and chalkboard, a twenty-four-hour free tea station, a kids' playhouse, and a food-sharing station where neighbors can come trade their surplus beets for another's overabundance of kale.

This mirthful display, known as Share-It Square, is no accident; a determined group of neighbors came together in 1996 because they wanted more of a community focus in the place where they lived. The City Repair Project was born out of this grassroots, neighborhood-initiated project with the belief that localizing culture, economy, and decision-making is fundamental to sustainability. City Repair's website maintains that "[b]y reclaiming urban spaces to create community-oriented places, we plant the seeds for greater neighborhood communication, empower our communities and nurture our local culture."[11]

Share-It Square was the first of City Repair Project's Intersection Repairs, initiatives which seek to reclaim a space dominated by single purpose auto-oriented functionality and recontextualize it as a place where the individuals in that neighborhood can interact as human beings. Mark Lakeman, one of the visionary founders of City Repair, explains this concept:

This was the primary thing, more than anything. I understood that in the [Roman] Grid the intersection is made to be no place, and I knew that in the Village the intersection was the greatest place. So the catalytic stroke that would change the world was to say, let's take the Village heart and put it back to the place where it's so terribly missing. That point will become the possibility of change.[12]

City Repair does not invade neighborhoods and impose their doctrine on those who live there. Rather, they function as a cultural democracy, responding to invitations from local groups asking for help facilitating a community-building project. Lakeman's description of the "timeless core principle" of building community through participation echoes the tenets of the Open Source Movement. Ultimately, this is the essence of City Repair's mission, "to inspire people to both understand themselves as part of a larger community and fulfill their own creative potential, and activate people to be part of the communities around them, as well as part of the decision-making that shapes the future of their communities."[13]

South Tabor Commons, one of City Repair's many community spaces, comes equipped with a handmade pizza kiln for neighborhood meals. Photo © Whitney Gayer

In addition to the Intersection Repair, City Repair invokes the rejuvenation of the "village heart" via a diversity of projects including the Village Building Convergence (VBC), the Depave Project, a widely-attended annual Earth Day celebration, and City Riparian: the Village Planting Convergence. VBC, started in 2000, is a "ten-day event held each spring, where a convergence of citizens, natural builders, and activists come together to help neighborhoods design and build their own community amenities."[14] The Depave Project, as its name suggests, mobilizes individuals to remove impervious asphalt and concrete pavements from urban areas to minimize stormwater pollution and connect city folks to the natural world. City Riparian "engages neighbors in a collective process to design and install forest gardens and other permaculturally informed landscapes in the commons."[15]

Given City Repair's focus on civic engagement, Lakemen is surprisingly uncomfortable with the concept of citizenship; he prefers to think of himself as a villager. He argues that "a sustainable culture is not going to be made up of citizens. Civic or civil infrastructure is the beginning of unsustainable culture." This infrastructure is "designed to concentrate power, stratify people, [and it is] a system for organizing the landscape, the living ecology." In the city, people can become consumed by greed because they are starving from lack of ongoing, meaningful human interactions. Alternatively, these interpersonal relationships thrive naturally in the village. By supporting neighborhoods to spearhead their own community building efforts and cultivate these relationships, City Repair is thus building social capital. According to Lakeman, these projects help "people to feel more connected to each other [and foster] the possibility that they can be friends with the people they've been interacting with." His argument is that the primary way to "build a deeper association with place…is for people to really care about each other in that place." By building something that is permanent, individuals develop a deeper connection and become more committed to living in that place. This is unique to Portland, Lakeman believes, and because of it, he feels that residents are less likely to leave. Indeed, to him city-dwellers are "desperate" for this sense of place and belonging, "to have something in common with other people and to feel so connected to them that they are creating together." Mike O'Brien of the Portland Office of Sustainable Development recognizes City Repair as playing an integral role in the realm of sustainability via this process:

They're doing what I would call social building. It's social, so people in the neighborhoods design the projects, and the volunteers are building them. They're creating the social bonds that are so important to having a sustainable community. Really, that's the foundation of everything. Having trust in the ability of your neighbors is what sustainability's all about.[16]

The Village Building Convergence (VBC) is a composite of citizen/villager-initiated projects that foster human interaction amongst local residents. Each year numerous proposals are submitted. The City Repair Project relies nearly exclusively on its dedicated and passionate volunteers to realize these projects, as there are only two part-time, paid staff members. The ubiquitous cob (a mix of sand, clay, and straw) structures around Portland, such as benches and other gathering places, were largely born out of VBC. These structures are built by the neighbors with some generous help from a slew of City Repair volunteers. Every structure erected by City Repair is entirely handmade and unique, and expresses the creative aesthetic and improvisation of all who help construct it. Community building by participation is a core value of City Repair, and Lakeman emphasizes that it is important to "leave room for other people to be creative…for the sake of community building" and to conceive of the whole process as a conversation open to improvisation and suggestions.

The cob structures are rarely linear, and never homogeneous. In the words of *Portland Tribune* journalist Jennifer Anderson, " if Walmart represents all things corporate and non-local to many, the cob bench symbolizes all things grass-roots, organic and creative."[17] A key facet of these cob structures is their unification of aesthetic beauty with their function of fostering human interaction. Their elaborate, sweeping curves are like arms welcoming neighbors to sit and chat. Random nooks are visible here and there, sheltering candles or little treasures, and one frequently finds a bulletin board where neighbors share news, poems, or ideas. Tree imagery symbolizes the branches of social networks and the roots one puts down in those networks. In fact, all of the cob structures integrate natural materials such as driftwood or fallen branches.

None of the founders of City Repair were formally trained in the use of natural building materials. Rather, the use of cob and other sustainable and recycled materials was part of an ethic they developed collectively. City Repair receives many design awards, sometimes to the bafflement and irritation of local design firms. City Repair designs represent an alternative to the big-concept, high-fee approach of traditional architects. City Repair projects are human-scale, low-cost, use locally sourced products (often free) and rely on heavy participation by volunteers. Volunteers flock to participate in these projects because City Repair teams "sit down with communities and let the thing emerge from them." To Lakeman, the design community misunderstands sustainable design because they are too "ego-logical" and focused on the appearances of things. In contrast, City Repair is "process-oriented—things are simply emerging in a way that's more integrated from the start." City Repair begins all of its projects thinking of this, which Lakeman describes as "human social culture is an ecological function." Elitist architects don't listen to other people, but in City Repair projects—especially VBC ones—the entire community approaches design with their eyes, ears, and hearts open to others in the group.

Lakeman believes that the greatest power to enact social change resides in the creative function of artists. The way he describes it, artists hold the fate of the world in their hands:

> Look at the city. We've separated economics and ecology and politics and all these other departments of the city. Who [else] in this society is supposed to be integrating all of this stuff into a story or a form that enables us to understand how it all fits together?

Lakeman explains that City Repair's "main strategy for outreach is to do stuff that is provocative enough for people to want to carry those stories with them."

BUILDING SOCIAL WEALTH

THESE THREE ORGANIZATIONS exemplify the artisan moral economy in their devotion to reuse, sustainability, and building a local community. Portland is transforming its economy by fostering such organizations, and transformation ties all three nonprofits together. Free Geek reinvigorates older computers and transforms them into functional machines. The Rebuilding Center offers one man's garbage to another who will transform it into treasure. The City Repair Project seeks to "educate and inspire communities and individuals to creatively transform the places where they live."[18] These organizations are invested in transparency and collaboration rather than proprietary trade. Each organization readily shares their business model; in fact, each organization *wants* to see others like it across the country. Additionally, they design their products to be used, celebrated, and understood; not one of these organizations portrays itself as a group of omniscient experts, nor presents its products as museum pieces of high art.

Wealth is generated in an artisan economy differently than a traditional economy. Free Geek, the Rebuilding Center, and the City Repair Project enrich the community in a wide spectrum of ways. Free Geek gave away 1,200 computers in 2008 to individuals and nonprofit organizations, the Rebuilding Center diverted nearly 6 million tons of alleged waste from the landfills, and the City Repair Project continues to enliven neighborhoods throughout Portland by giving neighbors a reason to work together. These three groups have all collaborated with one another at some time in the past, and would consider one another valuable resources for the community.

These organizations are decidedly "Portland" in their character, and part of their success is the support from the folks who live here. Where else is there not only a thriving market for reused building materials, but also a distinct pride in the aesthetic of reuse? In what other city would the local government partner with a wacky nonprofit to redistribute computers into schools? How many cities could muster up enough passionate and dedicated volunteers to keep something like the Village Building Convergence going for nine years?

CHAPTER 13
LEATHER

Melissa Cannon

THE NONDESCRIPT STUCCO BUILDING with its brown and beige sign doesn't seem hip enough to be the place where Bruce Springsteen, Marlon Brando, Bob Dylan, and Neil Young buy their leather jackets.[1] But this is it; this is Langlitz Leathers, perhaps the most internationally recognized artisan business in Portland. Langlitz Leathers is a family-owned enterprise that offers high-end leather outfits favored by motorcyclists. Bikers purchase about 90 percent of the company's products, paying about $1000 for either a pair of pants or a jacket. A reputation for high quality has made Langlitz and Portland famous in the global biker community, especially in Japan, where about half of all Langlitz products are sold.[2] Articles about Langlitz Leathers have appeared in popular media such as *Esquire*, *People*, and the *Wall Street Journal*, as well as trade and international publications.[3]

ALL IN THE FAMILY

FOUNDER ROSS LANGLITZ grew up in McMinnville, Oregon, where he lost his right leg in a motorcycle accident at the age of seventeen. Despite being told by doctors that he could no longer ride, Ross defiantly returned to biking upon his release from the hospital. He moved to Portland, and in 1947 founded Langlitz Leathers after making several jackets for friends and relatives. In the mid 1980s, Ross handed the business operation over to daughter Jackie and son-in-law Dave Hansen, who became general manager.

Production at Langlitz has changed little since Ross first opened for business. All garments are made on four cutting tables and eight sewing machines. One cutter and one seamstress are assigned to each garment. Workers typically build six garments a day, but a custom set of leathers may take a few weeks to several months, depending on backlog.[4] Custom-made jackets may be ordered, cut, and sewn in the same room while the customer watches and interacts with workers who willingly discuss the intricacies of their work.

Philosophy

DAVE HANSEN ANSWERS QUESTIONS freely and honestly as he guides me around the shop. According to Dave, at Langlitz they "don't do things like a normal company would," and his own philosophy is "180 degrees out of whack from the normal world."[5] While other businesses find ways to cut corners and save money, Dave emphasizes quality and customer satisfaction, claiming he would rather sell one expensive, high-quality jacket to a happy customer than several cheap jackets that need constant repair or replacement. He believes that most chain stores are "here today and gone next week," and that, although they claim to put customers first, they simply do not give the same quality of customer service as Langlitz.

Customer happiness is at the peak of what Dave refers to as his "priority pyramid." While it is important to strike a balance between fashion and functionality, fashion is usually at the bottom of the priority pyramid. Traditionally, every aspect of a Langlitz garment is designed for a specific reason pertinent to a motorcycle, and Dave is not afraid to tell the customer if his or her aesthetic preference is compromising function.

Operation

LANGLITZ HAS NO ADVERTISING BUDGET and will not consider moving its operations, increasing production, or contracting out. It has stayed small-scale and has remained resilient even during drastic fluctuations in the economy. Dave claims that craft-based businesses are more resilient because they avoid being drawn into boom-and-bust cycles. Langlitz lets backlogs increase during periods of strong demand so that, when the economy weakens, they still retain one- or two-week backlogs.

Dave Hansen, current owner and manager of Langlitz Leathers, takes a moment to relax in the shop. Photo © Whitney Gayer

Dave has observed the problems of competitors who expand production and outsource their manufacturing to foreign companies. Sometimes they've expanded just as the market contracted, or exchange rates changed, forcing them to close production facilities. Another problem is quality control. Langlitz offers a complete satisfaction guarantee. With a small local operation, if a Langlitz garment faces a problem during production, the problem gets solved immediately. Everything happens in real time and within the building, a luxury lost if the production is far removed.

Dave's commitment to keeping the business close to the customers is strong. He wants customers to feel they can talk directly to him about a problem, even refusing to allow the business to use an automated message system. As the business grew its Japanese customer base, Dave feared that they would not experience the same level of connection as local patrons who can visit the business to personally check the progress of their orders. The solution was Club Langlitz, a unique webpage for each customer that displays pictures of the entire process of making their garment, allowing viewers to see everything from filling out the initial paperwork to loading the finished product into a truck and driving away. It is clearly a success for both the business and the customers, who often add pictures of themselves wearing their new leathers.

TALITHA LEATHER

NATE BAGLEY, OWNER of Talitha Leather, makes a variety of affordable and high-end courier bags, purses, journals, and wallets.[6] Like many artisans he discovered his medium and his love of craft by making gifts for friends and family. Now Nate sells his work at Portland Saturday Market, First Thursday in the Pearl District, Last Thursday in the Alberta neighborhood, and through his website. He estimates that abut half of his business is local, and half comes to him through word of mouth. A good share of his non-local sales come from his network of friends in Southern California.

Nate splits his time between three vocations: working as a counselor for a mental health agency, managing his own private counseling practice, and doing leather work. Ultimately, he would like his leather crafting to provide a quarter to half of his income. With a new family, he expects that the need and convenience of working at home will cause him to focus more on his leather work and less on counseling.

Currently, he makes about one purse, three wallets, and half a bag per week, so he thinks twice that amount would be ideal. About 30 to 40 percent of his products are made-to-order, and the backlog of orders tends to vary from time to time. To increase his sales, he recognizes the need to develop a more streamlined process to ensure a steadier flow of orders. He has considered partnering with a major outlet or manufacturer but decided against this because he believes his product would change, quality would be compromised, and that such a partnership could create a moral conflict if it involved paying employees less than he thought they deserved.

Nate considers himself both an entrepreneur and an artisan, saying he has good business sense as well as artistic skill with leather. But his top priority is to ensure that "each product is designed and constructed with the goals of simplicity, quality, functionality, and style in mind."[7] He identifies with all definitions of an artisan: someone who works with the hands, head, and heart; desires to do a job well and for its own sake; and applies skill, judgment, improvisation, and passion to his work.

Nate believes that his leather products are better designed and more durable than mass-produced items. For example, he uses only real leather instead of cardboard inside thin leather casing as leather goods manufacturers do. Surprisingly, he has noticed that the prices of handmade goods are fairly competitive with those in the mass market, so artisans are increasingly having an easier time selling their work.

Nate also operates with a moral base for his craft and business. He won't use leather from an animal killed primarily for its hide, and is also very conscious of reducing leather waste by skilled layout and cutting. He has, on occasion, talked someone out of buying something or lowered the price, if he thought that person could not afford it. He tries to give his customers space and to avoid pressuring them to buy anything. He believes staying local has economic and environmental benefits, since it cuts down on the use of fossil fuels and keeps the money circulating locally.

Nate doesn't see himself as competing with other leather crafters in Portland because his products are unique enough to have their own market. For example, many of his courier bags fall into a unique niche with hard-to-find, retro-looking styles. He engages in collaboration with other artists, which often helps him get references or custom orders. He feels like part of a community within craft fairs and the Saturday Market and enjoys hanging out with others in Portland's art community.

A resident of Portland for five years, Nate senses that living here has made him more conscious of the environment, sustainable practices, and staying local. He believes that Portland is definitely ahead of the rest of the country in supporting these values and local artisans, but that people nationwide are becoming more likely to purchase products that are consistent with their values.

TWILIGHT AND FILIGREE

ELIZABETH ROBINSON, OWNER of Twilight and Filigree, uses her creative spirit to infuse unique and beautiful qualities into her leather products.[8] She entered the world of leather through bookbinding and making hats and costume pieces for festivals. Her current line includes purses, shoulder bags, wallets, hats, and hand-bound journals, as well an assortment of special order items. She sells her work through Etsy, at the Last and First Thursdays, at the Frock Boutique on Alberta Street, and at the Faerie Worlds Festival in Eugene. She works from home at least five hours a day, five days a week, but keeps a fairly flexible schedule depending on her other life engagements and level of energy. The personal, social, and occupational parts of life typically blend together, as she does much of her business with friends.

Elizabeth started this work to fulfill her creative spirit and to feel in charge of her life. She draws inspiration from the natural world, art nouveau, Asian art, fairy tales, and what she refers to as the "magic" of leather. She loves working with leather, she says, for its feel, look, and strength. She believes it is completely unlike any other material with its natural variations of texture, thickness, and dye absorption, and she also has a deep respect for its source and feels this in all aspects of her craft, from choosing the hide to cutting and stitching. Because of this, she tries to keep waste to a minimum and sometimes leaves in marks and scars because she so highly values the beauty and origin of leather. As a former vegetarian, Elizabeth sometimes struggles with the idea of using animal products; however, she believes that she is honoring the life of the animal that was killed for its meat, because using the hide byproduct means that it is not wasted. Using vinyl does not appeal to her because it is less durable and is made from non-renewable petroleum.

216

Since moving to Portland in 2002, Elizabeth has enjoyed the city's varied creative scene and its focus on reused and recycled materials and vintage and handmade looks. She believes there are lots of interesting, courageous artists with great ideas in Portland, and the scene is an inspiring reminder to follow her heart and pursue her ideas. She feels that she is part of Portland's community of artists, and takes advantage of the wealth of available venues where she can sell her work. While she is concerned that the Portland market may be getting saturated, she sees little direct competition in her niche, since few other makers of bags use heavyweight leather, rich colors, and detailed appliqués in a shoulder-bag style. Elizabeth notes that Portland and the Northwest are already known for having independent styles and up-and-coming trends in music, fashion, and crafts, so this may add to the intrigue of artisans producing in the area.

As to the future, she would like to use more recycled leather, maybe offering wool as a leather alternative. She wants to donate a percentage of future sales to nonprofit organizations and buy materials and supplies that are produced locally. At this point she does everything—design,

Langlitz Leathers on Division Street in southeast Portland. Photo © Whitney Gayer

construction, marketing—but would consider hiring others, saying she would enjoy the extra help and advice. Her optimum business size would include two other workers: a bookkeeper and a seamstress/cutter; however, she doesn't intend to sell to the mass market, because her products would lose their handmade feel.

ARTISANS ALL

BROADLY SPEAKING, THE THREE LEATHER CRAFTERS represent somewhat different value orientations to their work while still remaining within the frame of artisan production. Langlitz Leathers is, in many ways, a typical small business, but its decisions about product quality and limited production reflect artisan ideals. Despite competitive pressures, Langlitz maintains its tradition of handmade leathers and personalized experiences. The unity of design and production allow patrons to oversee all aspects of construction. Langlitz jackets and pants are intended to be used and appreciated over long periods of time.

Dave Hansen is determined to maintain small-scale production so as not to compromise the quality of the products. He feels obligated to keep Langlitz local because the roots of the business are firmly planted in the city. While he is not always happy with Portland's attitude toward small business, he enjoys living in the city and appreciates its cachet. He proudly displays the name Portland on many Langlitz products, including the various accessories that have become popular in Japan. He is determined to remain self-reliant so that external forces will not affect the business too greatly, and he remains loyal to those with whom he has done business so long as they maintain the same high standards of quality.

Some of Dave's perspectives reveal an interesting contrast between Langlitz and other artisans. Dave is not particularly responsive to the term "artisan," openly admitting that he does not view his business as an outlet for creativity or artistic expression. Nor does he relate to Portland's artisan community, since he sees most of their activity as a hobby rather than a business. Because Dave is around leather and the motorcycle culture all day at work, he wants to be far from it outside the shop, a desire that seems especially reasonable since he must take medication to mitigate his allergy to leather.

As important as it is for Langlitz to remain in Portland, Dave does not see his business as dependent on a local market. Customers do not typically patronize Langlitz simply because it is in the neighborhood. Rather, he believes that Langlitz serves the larger community of bikers, in particular those who buy top-quality bikes and expect to pay high prices for functional leathers.

While many of today's artisans consider the ethical aspects of production such as equity, environment, human rights, and animal rights, Dave maintains that the quality of his products and satisfied customers remain his only guiding principles. He does not claim to be overly empathetic with workplace concerns, and expects his employees to work hard and maintain high quality standards. He has never been asked about the ethical practices of tanneries from which he buys his leather and prefers to assume that they are operating in a legitimate manner.

Talitha Leather bears little resemblance to Langlitz. It is a one-person, home-based, art-inspired endeavor that provides supplemental income. The views and practices of Nate Bagley are consistent with an artisan worldview, including a loosely structured work life, a collaborative approach to business, and an artistic, creative outlook for his work.

Another quality that seems part of the emerging artisan economy is a mode of production that is inspired by an ethic of humanitarian ideals and environmental consciousness. Twilight and Filigree follows a path very similar to Talitha Leather, and like Nate, Elizabeth Robinson strives to use sustainable practices and places great emphasis on locality. As leather artisans, both expressed a deep respect for the source of the leather and a desire to produce goods that are unique and very high quality. Unlike Langlitz, both feel that their personal, social, and work lives blend together, that they greatly benefit from others in the artistic community in Portland.

Despite the differences, these artisans share a common thread; they seem to be part of a broader phenomenon of changes in the characteristics of production that has taken off nationwide. By reaching a reliable customer base and offering high-quality, handmade products, the participants all indicated they are less affected by changes in the economy and the presence of large firms that may act as competitors. Dave Hansen notes that the success of craft-based firms hinges on their low output and small size, because they can easily fix the problems in their production and remain self-reliant so that they don't get tangled in the economy or financial problems of other firms. He maintains that by keeping prices high, production low, and by staying level, a smaller company can survive while large firms that move their manufacturing overseas are struggling.

Although he doesn't attribute his success to living in Portland specifically, Nate Bagley points out that Portland is unique in that people here tend to consider the social implications of the purchases. He sees this happening nationwide, however, and has also found that problems with the national economy and the weakened dollar have allowed prices of handmade goods to become fairly competitive with those produced in the mass market. Elizabeth Robinson also identifies a unique environment in Portland that allows the existence of many outlets from which to sell handmade work, and believes that the trendy, independent reputation of the region has helped artisans sell their wares.

The market for authentic handcrafted products is increasing, and people are yearning for meaningful labor through which they can truly express their creativity and humanity. While handcrafted products seem to be more expensive and therefore exclusive, there is a sense that other factors of mainstream economies—such as costly advertising, distribution, and retailing, not to mention poor-quality products—are making quality handmade items economically competitive. There is also some indication that minimally leveraged, small-scale operations that maintain a reliable customer base are able to ride out the unpredictable swings in the global marketplace.

Chapter 14
The Rhythm of Portland's Instrument-Making Community

Alison Briggs

Portland resonates with makers of fine instruments. Although guitars are by far the most prevalent instrument made, there exist craftspeople who make a myriad of instruments including flutes, trumpets, electric kalimbas, ukuleles, marimbas, violins, didgeridoos, mandolins, and bass guitars. No statistics exist to confirm that Portland is home to more instrument makers than anywhere else in the United States, but among those interviewed there is consensus that Portland is indeed a mecca for instrument makers. Just as the fecund Willamette Valley provides the ideal environment for abundant agriculture, the city of Portland fosters a fertile culture of cross-pollinating artisans. The artisan instrument makers' scene is but one facet of this vibrant Portland community, and it is distinguished by the openness and cooperation that reverberate throughout, nurturing the evolution of the craft.

This cooperative spirit manifests in a variety of ways: local luthiers (those who make and repair stringed instruments) casually meet up for lunch to share their current projects, while events such as the annual Northwest Handmade Instrument Show and organizations such as the Guild of American Luthiers keep the instrument-makers' community humming along. Portland's thriving music scene feeds into the cycle, as well. While most local musicians cannot afford artisan instruments, the supportive music environment in Portland is nevertheless intertwined with the evolution of the instrument-makers' scene. Jeffrey Elliott, a successful Portland guitar maker with a fifteen-year backlog of special orders, says that:

> We kind of all feed off of each other. We find out what [the musicians] want, how they want it, how it will evolve because of their needs, and we do that and we feed them and it evolves some more. And the people who come and support the musicians are part of it too; it's just a great big link in the chain.[1]

Portland's dynamic music scene is described vividly in Chapter 9, but an introduction to some of the noteworthy craftspeople who comprise the artisan instrument-making scene is necessary to understand just how unique and alive Portland really is.

DAVID KING: KING BASSES

DAVID KING WANTS YOU to "get closer to your music."[2] One step into the basement of his north Portland workshop is enough to convince any bass player that her ideal instrument could be easily born here. When an individual seeks out King to purchase one of his unique, entirely handmade electric bass guitars, there is no middleman—only King on the other end of the line. And while a potential customer can select exactly what she wants from an elaborate web-form on his website, he also encourages the customer to call or email him directly. For anyone who has ever entered a typical music shop and needed only to choose the color of a Fender bass, this level of customization can be mind-blowing. King's basses express a stunning aesthetic sensibility, particularly his peculiar-looking signature instrument, the headless King bass.

King began his musical career as a violinist, but eventually traded in a lightweight, high-pitch instrument for something on the opposite end of the spectrum, the electric bass guitar. His first electric bass was an incredibly heavy and clumsy instrument that "screamed out to be redesigned." Despite his lack of experience, King resolved to create a lightweight, well-balanced electric bass. He maintains: "I had a very clear idea of what I wanted to do and I knew that no one else was gonna do it for me, so I had to get there

David King works on one of his custom headless electric basses in his home workshop.
Photo © Whitney Gayer

myself."[3] The result is the King bass, a headless bass that King believes is more ergonomic and easier to play than a traditional bass guitar. In designing this instrument, King discovered an alternate way to position and design the electronics on the bass. Part of King's ingenuity, and what separates his basses from other artisan basses, is the fact that King creates his own hardware to accompany his unconventionally shaped instruments.

Now with more than twenty years of bass-building under his belt, King has earned a solid international reputation. Despite this, however, a career in handcrafted bass guitars is unfortunately not accompanied by a high income. King has been living at or below the poverty line since he began his career, and he estimates that, after factoring in all his costs, he earns about five dollars an hour.[4] Yet impoverished is the last word he would use to describe his life:

> I lead a very rich life compared to lots of people. I know this is because I've been isolated from the economic forces that drive so many. I come from a very bourgeois background, if I may use that term. I inherited a simple lifestyle with a lot of "nice" things, like traveling, painting, reading, and playing classical violin. Once you get used to the idea of paring down the toys in your life, you can find time to really enjoy the good things like food and music, which hardly cost anything.[5]

King is committed to a lifestyle that affords him more than just a pursuit of material goods. Building basses is more than a career for King, it's a vocation: "It's like being a monk—you commit to it and you don't have any way out once you're in." Like any vocation, King contends that it's precisely this mentality that inherently drives all artisans: "you do it not because you want to so much as you feel you have to, there's something that drives you from inside, and there's no explaining it.... You do it because you can't stop doing it."[6] King's testimony to the artisan spirit resounds clearly, as he is connected to the Portland scene in many ways; he is a member of the Guild of American Luthiers, as well as an exhibitor at the Northwest Handmade Instrument Show, and he lives in the heart of the Mississippi neighborhood, a quirky community dotted with all sorts of artisan shops and innovators.

DAVID BELLINGER: ELECTRIC KALIMBAS

DAVID BELLINGER FELL IN LOVE with African music upon hearing the rhythms of a marimba band. He set about creating kalimbas shortly thereafter in his southeast Portland home. Kalimbas, also known as African thumb pianos, are handheld members of the percussion family. In the small realm of artisan kalimbas, Bellinger's electric kalimbas are unusual because they can be plugged into an amplifier. Through his creativity, craftsmanship, and engineering, Bellinger has transformed the beautiful simplicity of a thumb piano into a modern, electronic masterpiece.[7] This innovation has attracted the popular indie-rock band Modest Mouse as a client, which is noteworthy because a kalimba is hardly an instrument one would associate with the indie-rock genre.

Bellinger modestly describes his craftsmanship as a "finite engineering project" and claims that "it's nowhere near as hard as making a guitar," but he clearly applies the same level of precision and passion. Each of his entirely handmade kalimbas are distinct, and each instrument bears a unique serial

Master builder David King takes a break from work to play one of his hand-built instruments. Photo © Whitney Gayer

number stamped in its aluminum bridge.[8] Bellinger attests that he is always trying to learn "what sounds good" and thus, each new kalimba is the result of creative problem solving and improvisation. It would certainly be difficult to replicate any of these instruments, as he collects the bulk of his materials secondhand at the "Bins," a Goodwill outlet store. In his words, "Usually I make [the kalimbas] as found objects"[9] He designs the electric kalimbas in a variety of keys, including a dramatically powerful bass and a rich pentatonic. He is immensely proud of his craftsmanship. As he says on his website: "there is no factory, no sales force, just one dedicated artist-inventor making sawdust and magic."

Although Bellinger has been making kalimbas for over twenty years, it wasn't until his first website in 2000 that he began selling them, primarily to professional percussionists from around the world. Indeed, the internet has played a major role in the expanding the audience for his kalimbas. Starting in 2008, Bellinger took on an assistant who helps make the kalimbas more accessible by handling eBay sales and posting sound samples of individual kalimbas on Bellinger's website.[10] A frequent exhibitor at the Northwest Handmade Instrument Show, Bellinger's kalimbas are accompanied by a handwritten sign: "Please play and touch the kalimbas."

David Monette: trumpets and mouthpieces

As a trumpet player, David Monette was utterly disappointed by the intonation and inconsistent playing qualities of conventional trumpets he encountered, so he decided to fashion a superior one himself. Monette knew little about making horns when he started; he'd never even taken a high school shop class.[11] But with determination and practice, and a little training at an instrument repair shop, Monette taught himself. He began building horns in 1983, but realized quickly that "the only way to fully realize his new and revolutionary trumpet designs was to redesign the trumpet mouthpiece." Two years later, Monette's first mouthpieces were discovered by such high-profile clients as Wynton Marsalis, the acclaimed jazz trumpeter, and Charles Schlueter, former principal trumpeter for the Boston Symphony Orchestra. Indeed, Monette's unparalleled mouthpieces are the core element of his instruments. Monette will not sell a horn without one of his mouthpieces unless the customer already has one.[12]

The caliber of Monette's horns has led to solid growth for the Monette Corporation; Monette currently employs ten others at his large northeast Portland workshop. That most of these people are former customers is a rather strong statement in itself and perhaps is part of the reason why every trumpet remains special. Each trumpet Monette creates is individually tailored to the player; no instruments are standard models made in advance. His most elaborate horn, the Elysian Trumpet, was commissioned by the New Orleans Jazz Orchestra for Irvin Mayfield, the official cultural ambassador to New Orleans. With hand-sawn details, this exquisite and intricately adorned trumpet took over two thousand hours to build. Monette finds these trumpets the most rewarding to make, as the instrument eventually tells both a visual and an acoustic story.[13]

Getting in tune with each other

Cyndy Burton is well known in the handmade instrument scene as a hub of information among artisan instrument makers; she keeps her finger on the pulse of the community. Burton and her partner, Jeffrey Elliott, both make classical guitars, but Elliott is primarily the builder. Burton's craft comes into play after the guitar has been assembled, for her art lies in a rare style of finishing known as French polish. French polish is applied by hand and, as Burton says, "it's sort of an ancient art, and I've made it kind of a specialty."[14] Burton and Elliott contend that historically, the luthier community tended to be quite protective of their trade. This secrecy is the root note of competition, an attitude that simply does not resonate with the contemporary Portland scene. This wasn't always the case, though. Lacking any mechanism to unite their craft, in the '50s and '60s the Portland luthier community was a collection of individual artists rather than a supportive community. Burton and Elliott believe that two local resources have played a pivotal role in harmonizing this community: the Guild of American Luthiers and the Northwest Handmade Instrument Show.

Headquartered in nearby Tacoma, Washington, the Guild is "a nonprofit educational membership organization whose purpose is to facilitate learning about the art, craft, and science of lutherie."[15] It was formed in 1972 by a small group of luthiers and has matured into an organization of 3,600 members from forty different countries. The Guild has published eight books, compiled from over one hundred articles previously published in their journal. Elliott notes that it "started out as information-sharing group…[because we] all pool our information, the collective level rises for everybody, and everybody gets something out of it."[16] Burton elaborates on this philosophy:

> The Europeans have the old guild tradition…. [The Guild of American Luthiers] is not a guild in that sense at all; it's completely the opposite. The attitude is "a rising tide floats all boats." [The Guild] provided a mechanism through the magazine…and through conventions every two or three years where people give lectures and presentations.[17]

The hub of this knowledge network is the Guild's quarterly journal, *American Lutherie* and its interactive website and blog. The Guild firmly believes that the contributors to both are motivated by a desire to share their knowledge, successes, and failures with a worldwide audience that will use this information to advance the field of lutherie. It believes that "this broad base, and wide outlook, and open attitude is basic to the success of the Guild."[18]

The Northwest Handmade Instrument Show, held annually in the Portland area, heralds the diverse community of instrument makers in the Pacific Northwest. Burton and Elliott have been involved for more than fifteen years, and they believe that the show, organized by a volunteer group, functions as a celebration of the resonant artisan scene. It invites the general public to participate by charging a very modest admission fee: three dollars per adult with children free. In recent years many luthiers have taken to arriving a bit early to participate in a swap meet of sorts, whereby they trade or sell tools and materials to other luthiers. In addition to the instrument makers' exhibits, the show features woodworking demonstrations and performances on the handcrafted instruments. These twenty-minute musical performances continue back-to-back all weekend, part of what Burton refers to as a "three-ring circus."

The 2009 show featured over seventy exhibitors. The show is often unable to accommodate all the people who want to exhibit, because it only costs fifty dollars for the weekend (and this includes breakfast). The show is not organized as a fundraiser, and Burton contends that "one of the philosophies underlying the show is to keep it affordable for people who are just doing it, maybe making one or two instruments a year, and it gives them a chance to be around other people who are making instruments, too."

Many of the visitors are fledgling instrument makers coming to get a feel for the scene and connect with those already entrenched in it. Establishing these connections can be an excellent way to get started with the benefit of tapping into the collective wisdom, of lessons already learned. Indeed, it was the Northwest Handmade Instrument Show that served as the linchpin for budding instrument-maker and new kid on the block Kurt Ungerer.

Jeffrey Elliott adds one more guitar to his fifteen-year backlog. Photo © Rachel Moore

NEW KID ON THE BLOCK

AS A CHEF, Kurt Ungerer developed a taste for high-quality ingredients, slow food, and attention to aesthetic presentation. This taste for quality spilled over into other aspects of Ungerer's life. As a musician, Ungerer desired a higher-quality electric bass guitar but his modest income prevented him from buying a high-priced factory made instrument. So, despite a lack of knowledge about electronics or woodworking, Ungerer resolved to build his own bass. He states, "basically, I was interested in it originally because it was an economically viable option to get what I wanted...to get all the bells and whistles without having to pay upwards of a thousand dollars."[19]

Without the resources readily available in Portland, Ungerer's plan to build his own electric bass could have fizzled quickly, but he soon discovered just how extensive the network of easy-access information was in Portland. Through Portland Community College, Ungerer enrolled in an electric instrument-building workshop, which focused on designing and assembling guitars. The class ended before Ungerer had finished his bass guitar, and since he no longer had access to woodworking equipment, he sought the advice of friends who encouraged him to attend the upcoming Northwest Handmade Instrument Show.

At the show, Ungerer met David King, the well-known electric bass builder profiled earlier. King was incredibly friendly and invited Ungerer to visit King's shop, an offer that proved pivotal for Ungerer's budding hobby. Indeed, Ungerer maintains that if it were not for King's welcoming attitude, he never would have finished his first handmade bass. The show itself was a major confidence booster, and many friendly luthiers encouraged Ungerer to check out their instrument demos that day. Ungerer realized that even experienced luthiers were still honing their craft:

> They weren't building the same thing over and over, so they constantly had to revise their way of working because people want different things...and I realized that part of the beauty of the handmade instrument is that people pointed out mistakes they'd made, people pointed out flaws in the wood that they used that added additional beauty.[20]

Portland's friendly and open culture is what initially attracted Ungerer to Portland and that mentality reverberated throughout the Northwest Handmade Instrument Show. Indeed, according to Ungerer, everyone he approached commented that Portland was the place to be for building guitars. Building one's own guitar not only saves you money, but "it's much more beautiful and much more connected to you."

CONCLUSION

"PORTLAND IS A MECCA for instrument makers…and the attitude of sharing is right up near the top." Cyndy Burton's statement is clearly valid, but why Portland? Burton suggests that a confluence of climate, critical mass, attitude, openness, access to materials, and proximity to the Guild of American Luthiers all contribute. Many of the artisan instrument makers in Portland find support and knowledge in each other, whether by plugging in to the Northwest Handmade Instrument Show or the Guild of American Luthiers, proximity to an artisan neighborhood, or informal meet-ups with fellow craftspeople. The rich diversity of instrument makers has lessened competition and nurtured cooperation. Considering the smorgasbord of artisans in Portland, perhaps it is the Portland way of life that plays a key role in nurturing an environment of cooperation and thus a healthy artisan community.

The characteristic artisan trait clearly echoes in each instrument maker: each craftsperson creates instruments because, as they say, they can't not do it. Most got started, despite a lack of experience, with little more than the motivation to produce a superior instrument that was simply unavailable anywhere else, as well as the willingness to experiment to get it right. While some have successfully expanded their businesses, others have kept their craft small but find fulfillment in the freedom their lifestyle affords them. Today, nearly all of the instrument makers have their own little niche, whether by their own design or by chance of their instrument being unique. The future looks quite bright for the symbiotic community of Portland instrument makers, from Jeffrey Elliott with his fifteen-year backlog, to Kurt Ungerer just starting out.

CHAPTER 15
DOWN THE RABBIT HOLE:
PORTLAND'S LEGION OF TECH START-UPS

Amanda Hess

IT'S A BEAUTIFUL SPRING EVENING, and I walk quickly within the shadows and fading light of downtown Portland, looking for the offices of Oracle, the IT company where Web Innovators is hosting one of the five tech events happening this evening. Web Innovators hosts quality speakers from some of the best tech start-ups in Oregon, and this could be an excellent introduction to the Portland tech scene.

When I find the Oracle offices, I am directed to the event space. At the door, I'm offered a local microbrew, and I take this as a welcome sign that this may not be your typical tech talk. Everyone in the room is unapologetically "plugged in." In the dimmed light, the warm glow of smart phones and laptops complements the images projected at the front of the room. As the speaker moves through her presentation, she is accompanied by a silent dialogue as participants check related links online or add their tweets to a running commentary about the presentation. The scene is intriguing, puzzling, and for the uninitiated, somewhat disconcerting. It's as if I have fallen down the rabbit hole into the land of Portland's Legion of Tech—a generation of geeks fiercely devoted to their craft and to their on- and off-line community.

I adopt the phrase "Legion of Tech" (or Legion) to describe this new generation and community of Portland IT because it comes straight from one of Portland's first, and still arguably most influential, tech community organizations of the same name (legionoftech.org). The Legion grew out of the founders' long term relationships, which were created in planning two signature events of Portland's geek culture: the ad hoc BarCampPortland, where participants actually set the agenda of the conference when they arrive; and Ignite Portland, a conference begun in 2003 where participants get five minutes to present a "burning" new idea.

Like the founding members, the individuals who make up the Legion are not your traditional four-eyed geeks. They do not wear pocket protectors, hide behind cubicles, or develop computer code in order to turn a major profit or become the next Bill Gates. The Legion is hyper-connected and highly versatile. They are self-proclaimed entrepreneurs, web designers, coders, marketers, artists, proud geeks, and non-geeks, sometimes all wrapped into one.

As I learned through in-depth conversations with some of Portland's geek elite (leaders like Rick Turoczy, Scott Kveton, and Adam DuVander, as well as up-and-coming stars like Michael Richardson and Adam Lowry), what they share in common is that they are passionate about technology and devoted to crafting new ways to use technology to solve basic problems, satiate their intellectual curiosity, and engage the user. Likewise, they share a sense that their pursuit is not about reaching a higher status—it is, in itself, a craft that should be appreciated for the process and for the community that it creates. And if it ends up paying the bills, all the better.

As Rick Turoczy, creator of the Silcon Forest blog and self-proclaimed head cheerleader of the Portland tech scene, explains, "The tech scene here in Portland is really pure in that way. For these people, technology is a tool to solve problems and grapple with issues that they are passionate about... They enjoy the pursuit of figuring out the problem or solving the puzzle and, much like any art, (they) enjoy eliciting a reaction from others."[1]

The problems and puzzles that the Legion grapples with are diverse. Some examples include figuring out how an individual can have one username and password across the entire web (OpenID.net); how to find the location of your friends at any given moment (Shizzow.com); how to listen to DJ sets as if they were albums (Mugasha.com); or even how to get the best bacon in the world over the internet (Bacn.com). The underlying assumption, however, is that a well-crafted code, application, or website can solve the problem—or at least get you a lot closer to your goal.

WEB 2.0 AND OPEN SOURCE CITIZENRY

THE PORTLAND LEGION OF TECH is part of a broader, more globalized generation of Web 2.0 developers who focus on creating collaborative and interactive web services. As defined in Wikipedia, "Web 2.0 facilitates communication, secure information sharing, interoperability, and collaboration on the World Wide Web…. [It] has led to the development and evolution of web-based communities, hosted services, and applications, such as social-networking sites, video-sharing sites, wikis, blogs."[2] Some of the best known Web 2.0 services are Facebook, YouTube, Twitter, political blogs like the Daily Kos and, of course, Wikipedia, the free content, openly edited online encyclopedia.

A wiki is one of the first examples of a Web 2.0 innovation. It is a collection of web pages that allows anyone to contribute to and edit the content. Wikis can be used to create resource sites like Wikipedia, but they can also be used for any collective composition project, including writing a book.[3]

Many Web 2.0 generation technologies are built from open source development, which epitomizes the open community and collaborative ethos. Open source development, unlike proprietary software development, lets anyone view and alter code (not just content like wikis or blogs), thereby allowing peers to learn from each other while concurrently building new approaches from someone's original source code. One of the most successful open source software products, the GNU/Linux operating system, is based on Linux source code, which was created and named after a current Portland resident and major player in the tech scene: Linus Torvalds.

In Portland, open source has evolved from a development tool to something more like a moral code or even a social movement. In 2009, Portland welcomed the open source community to its first-ever Open Source Bridge conference "for developers working with open source technologies and for people interested in learning the open source way." Several aspects of the conference, such as its collaborative, improvisational, and civic focus, made it a quintessential Portland event. The conference was organized and run completely by volunteers. During the last day of the event, designated the "unconference day," individuals who wanted to lead a session briefly explained their idea from the conference podium and then posted their session on the board. During the day, attendees filled these impromptu sessions.

The local distinctiveness of the conference was reflected in the event's civic theme: "What does it mean to be an Open Source Citizen?"[4] Audrey Eschright, one of the co-founders of the conference, explained in her blog: "We're exploring what open source means to us, what it offers, where we struggle, and why we do this day in and day out, even when we're not paid for it…We are, like citizens of a country, engaged in the practice of an interlocking set of rights and responsibilities."[5] She hinted at what exactly these rights and responsibilities are: the intellectual property rights inherent in developing code, and the responsibilities of all open-sourcers to build a respectful community that fosters creative development. Even so, Eschright left the question open for the conference participants to answer together. This, of course, is the open source way.

This open, collaborative, non-proprietary ethic is an artisan-like aspect of open source development and Web 2.0 innovation, as is the desire to collectively discover an optimal solution using improvisational problem solving. Like artisans in other fields, Web 2.0 and open source developers are truly devoted to the beauty of the craft and not the monetary rewards. They are dedicated to finding unique and artful solutions to complex design problems. While the touch they leave on their product is not exactly visible like a potter's thumbprint, when an application really works—does just what it was designed to do, and in a particularly elegant way—that becomes a signature of sorts.

THE SILICON VALLEY VS. THE SILICON FOREST

WHY HAS WEB 2.0, as exemplified by the Legion of Tech and the open source ethic evident in the Open Source Bridge conference, become so deeply rooted in Portland's tech sector? Some attribute this to the open and cooperative culture of the Silicon Forest, as Portland is playfully nicknamed. Unlike its namesake, the IT mecca of Silicon Valley, the Silicon

Forest easily facilitates a feeling of community. "In the Bay Area and Silicon Valley, you get an idea, you get a couple million in venture capital—or tens of millions in venture capital—and you run that idea to the ground.... It's extremely competitive—you are at the office from 6 AM to 7 PM or later, and you burn out quickly," explains Michael Richardson, an up-and-coming developer who chose to stay in Portland rather than relocating to the Bay Area for a better-paying job.[6] Adam Lowry, of the startup Urban Airship, a developer of mobile device applications, agrees that the focus here is different. "In Portland, people take their time and you get a lot more cooperation between people who might be competitors."[7] Unlike in much of Silicon Valley, venture capitalists do not run the game, and there is little underlying incentive among the Legion to make it big quickly and reap a fortune through the next Amazon.com. Portland developers have an approach, common to artisans, that is more focused on doing good work; they're willing to sacrifice immediate rewards to maintain personal autonomy and exert control over their craft, and participate in a community of others who share their worldview.

The importance of the Legion's sense of community is illustrated in yet another example of the collaborative approach of the tech scene: the tag cloud. A tag cloud, or "weighted list in visual design," allows you to physically map the weight of user-generated tags to describe an overall concept. To demonstrate, Rick Turoczy created a tag cloud that would encapsulate the Portland tech scene. Rick asked geeks, via his Silicon Florist blog, to describe the Portland tech scene in their own words. Their collective responses are displayed as the tag cloud in Figure 1. From the visual representation, several things become evident. First the descriptor "community" is the largest in the cloud, indicating that Legion of Tech responders used that word most frequently in describing the Portland tech scene. Several other prominent descriptors, such as "folks" and "open" and "collaborative," all suggest a collegial, even familial orientation. Overall, the viewer is struck by the overwhelming number of positive words. Perhaps as telling are the words that do not appear, such as "competitive," "money-driven," or "intense."

The Legion community has not always been around, however. In fact, according to Turoczy, who came to town in the early '90s, Portland rode the dot-com boom just like San Francisco and Seattle—"everyone thought that they were going to get rich fast and buy a boat on the coast." But after the bust, Portland geeks were left with little money, few venture capitalists, and an underlying feeling that their skills could be used to build something that held deeper value.

Into this vacuum stepped visionary "community organizers" for the Portland tech scene. These include Legion of Tech founders Todd Kenefsky and Dawn Foster; Silicon Florist blogger Rick Turoczy; Igal Koshevoy creator of Calagator, an all volunteer effort to provide a unified calendar of technology happenings in Portland; Adam DuVander, the force behind Web Innovators, a once-a-month get-together that focuses less on the technology technique and more on considering the purpose and function of technology; and Beer and Blog's Justin Kistner, among many others. While each organizer focuses his or her craft on a unique service to the tech community, all are devoted to completely volunteer-run, nonprofit causes that provide free events and support to anyone who is interested in getting involved.

As the cost of tech development gets less expensive (all you really need is a laptop and internet access), more people are attracted to the Legion. Having an open and organized community with events gives newcomers a chance to jump in and learn from veterans of the trade. A prime example of this is Justin Kistner's Beer and Blog. Kistner started Beer and Blog at a

Figure 1. Portland Tech Scene tag cloud.

local brewpub in 2008 as a means to help out his friends, who were having trouble setting up and managing their blogs. Now over sixty people, from developers to marketers, come every Friday to network and troubleshoot. The event has been so successful that they have moved to a bigger micro-brewery, can claim credit for facilitating several successful start-ups, and have spurred the creation of ten similar chapters across the United States. Kistner only sees this as the beginning. "This is just the first step in a much bigger, long-term plan to reach our potential," he says. "We are building the power and getting to the point where we can impact and better integrate into other industries in Portland and around the world."[8]

The efforts of Kistner and other tech "community organizers" to make technology more accessible, understandable, and useful are similar to the vision of Free Geek described in Chapter 12. This vision is about recon-ceptualizing technology as a tool that fits the hand of the user, one that can be controlled and directed to solve a problem, one that liberates rather than intimidates. This is the core principle of Web 2.0 and the open source movement, and it is embedded in the vision and operation of the Legion of Tech, Free Geek, and the many other volunteer efforts to build a com-munity of tech artisans. Implied in this effort, and sometimes explicitly engaged, is a conversation about the relationship of tools to society. To those who know the history of the turn of the century Arts and Crafts Movement, these themes have a familiar ring. During the last great technol-ogy revolution, when industrialization was creating a new set of relation-ships between tools and users, the Arts and Crafts Movement developed a philosophy of using tools for liberation and creativity, putting humans, rather than machines, in control, and reclaiming the quality and elegance of craft production.

SIDE PROJECT OR START-UP

WHEN IT COMES TO MAKING A LIVING from their craft, the Portland tech sector faces some special problems. Because they are willing to contribute to projects developed through open source or for the public domain, their work is free to the user. Since most events and community-organizing sites are entirely not-for-profit, this also limits the ability of contributors to get paid for doing the work they are passionate about. Given this reality, most developers are either forced to resign their passion to a side project or take a leap of faith to secure capital to fund their start-ups.

In the "side project" category, this means that individuals must supplement their craft with a full-time job in consulting or coding firms, if possible, and in service industry jobs if needed. For those who take the leap to tech start-up, the road is even more difficult. If they find a venture capitalist in Portland (not an easy task), they must have a persuasive argument as to why the project deserves funding. And the risk for developers and funders is high. Technology changes so quickly that a promising application may not get to market or to scale before it is made obsolete by a rival application of a new game-changing development like Google or the Smart Phone.

Furthermore, many of the Legion are reluctant to work with venture capitalists because they fear their vision will be undermined by a competitive and profit-driven ethos. These geeks prefer the artisan approach, even if that requires them to supplement their work through less-desirable paying jobs. As Rick Turoczy argues, they should not be pushed to "mature" before they are ready. "Pushing these people to be business people is wrong; it's like pushing an artist to be an owner of a gallery—it doesn't mesh."

But other geeks in the Legion are more entrepreneurial, at least in the sense of their willingness to create small-scale start-ups that do not require huge infusion of venture capital. Several weeks after the Oracle event, a group of developers and coders, including up-and-coming Legion members Michael Richardson and Adam Lowry, were laid off from their internet security company due to declining revenues. When I met with them at a local geek hangout shortly thereafter, they explained that they were actually elated at this development. They had, over a couple of microbrews, come up with yet another great way to solve a problem through IT, and with their newfound unemployment, they now had the freedom and time to pursue it. "I can finally fully devote myself to building something I am passionate about," said Richardson. "Yeah, I'm excited!"

Falling down the rabbit hole of Portland's technology community can be a strange and beautiful trip, and the excitement is contagious. Portland's Legion is earnest and passionate about their craft. They are less driven by the extrinsic rewards of a lucrative job or big money start-up; rather, they're motivated by the intrinsic satisfaction of contributing to a well-crafted application and building a technological world that is more open, accessible, and creative.

CHAPTER 16
ARTISAN SAMPLER

Alison Briggs

THIS CHAPTER IS OUR ADMISSION that the artisan economy is broader than even we imagined. So here we celebrate a few of the artisan endeavors that we were unable to cover in more depth. Some of these crafts may not typically spring to your mind, but all embody the artisan spirit that radiates from within the Rose City. So think of this chapter as a series of dessert samples—just a little taste to pique your interest. And what better way to introduce the menu than with some delectable chocolate?

CHOCOLATE

PORTLAND IS ONLY A MID-SIZED CITY, yet it surprisingly boasts a diversity of artisan chocolatiers that rivals much larger cities. Many of these chocolatiers began selling their decadent confections at local farmers' markets before finding a more permanent storefront in which they could expand their operation. In a vibrantly decorated and extremely quaint shop nestled on hip Northeast 28th Avenue, Alma Chocolate creates exquisitely fabulous chocolates. Owner Sarah Hart started out experimenting with chocolate molds in her kitchen and selling at the farmers' market before moving into this shop in 2006.[1] Using fresh, fair-traded, and organic ingredients, the mouth-watering chocolate treats are entirely handcrafted. Their trademark creation is a solid, single-origin dark chocolate fashioned into intricate icons from their custom-designed original molds that are then hand gilded with twenty-three karat edible gold leaf. No two batches of Alma chocolates are exactly alike, and "they are as individual and unique as the people who enjoy them."[2] The exquisite French-style bonbons come in a variety of delectable flavors, such as smoked paprika, cardamom with burnt sugar sesame, tequila and pomegranate with candied orange peel, and habanero caramel.

Sahagún is a cozy little northwest Portland shop that showcases the region's bounty. Locally sourced lavender, marionberries, cherries, filberts, and herbs compliment the high-caliber chocolate Elizabeth Montes creates. She relies on real spices, seasonal herbs, and fresh fruit flavors (not flavorings) to create pure tastes, and limits ingredients to preserve the balance of complimentary flavors with chocolate's intrinsic flavor.[3] Like Alma Chocolate, Sahagún also got its start at the farmers' market. Such success rooted in the farmers' market bodes well for fledgling Missionary Chocolates, whose entirely vegan morsels are sinfully succulent. Lest anyone think that the

Sarah Hart and her gold leaf-encrusted chocolate icons. Photo © Whitney Gayer

abundance of chocolatiers in Portland breeds competition, consider how on a recent visit to Alma Chocolate I was provided with a list of half a dozen other chocolate shops in town, encouraged to visit them all, and informed about the specialty of each one!

GLASS

THE GLASS ART SOCIETY is a nonprofit organization promoting and supporting the worldwide community of glass arts.[4] Executive Director Pamela Koss describes Portland: "The Northwest has a high concentration of glass-working people, and Portland is a jewel in the crown.... It's become kind of a center for kiln-formed glass that really doesn't exist in a lot of other places."[5] Kiln-forming refers to a process by which glass is pieced together and fired in a kiln. Offering more than a thousand different glass products, Bullseye Glass is the epicenter of Portland's glass industry.

Bullseye Glass is hardly a simple glass manipulation shop. Tucked between the railroad tracks and a local park, Bullseye has created the Research and Education Studio adjacent to their southeast Portland factory to foster craftsmanship and innovation in glass art. Seven artist/technicians teach glass kiln-forming and torch-working, test glass products, and provide technical support to customers and visiting artists from around the world. Bullseye is devoted to advancing the craft of glass art, and in addition to their educational publications, they openly share all technical advances they make via free lectures and on their website.[6] Bullseye organizes a biennial international conference geared towards professionals, BECon, to advance the art of kiln glass via comprehensive workshops targeting the artistic, technical, and business direction. BECon 2009 featured twenty-eight presenters, nine of whom call Portland home.[7]

Bullseye Glass is but one of many players in Portland's glass industry. Elements Glass, Uroboros, and Glass Alchemy also play an integral role in fostering the dynamic artisan glass industry in Portland. The thriving local glass industry is, in part, fueled by the abundance of customers. Portland's ultra-trendy Pearl District features a wide range of local glass products in its contemporary architecture, including the Casey, a luxury condominium whose developers specifically sought out Bullseye's talent.[8]

HOUSE, WALL, AND GARDEN

THE ARTS AND CRAFTS IDEAL is evident in neighborhoods throughout Portland, where much of the housing stock was built at a time when craftsman style was influential. This ideal is seen in the Tudors, foursquares, craftsmans, and modest bungalows that have been preserved and renovated. It is also apparent in the artisan businesses that have grown to meet the demand for period fixtures and furnishings. Rejuvenation Hardware, begun in the 1970s to recycle deconstructed house parts, now employs over 260 workers who make and market reproduction period lighting fixtures, hardware, and house parts for its mail-order and retail business.

YOLO Colorhouse, an environmentally responsible business developed by formally trained Portlanders Virginia Young and Janie Lowe, features paint with a natural palette.[9] Their experiments with old recipes using milk and clay ingredients led to the creation of their line of zero-VOC paints, which have been featured in over sixty articles in dwelling magazines from *Metropolitan Home* to *This Old House*.[10]

One of the pleasures of living in an older Portland neighborhood is the chance to see the diversity of styles evident in that ubiquitous landscape feature, the retaining wall. One of Portland's more popular artisan builders is The Wall. The Wall recycles broken concrete from municipal sidewalks and turns it into beautiful structures that have the look of natural stone. In this way, they reuse about 600 tons of discarded concrete each year.[11]

Gardening, one of the most popular outdoor activities in the United States, goes beyond passion in Portland. The same climate and topography that make the Willamette Valley a premier U.S. location for production of nursery stock and grass seed also make for ideal year-round gardening. In central city neighborhoods, the neatly mowed and primly landscaped front yard is becoming more rare, having given way to an abundance of decorative and edible flora. Seeding this resurgence is the venerable Portland Nursery. More than a place to buy plants, it is now a community educational institution and a gathering place for a variety of festivals and music.[12]

Tile

THREE ARTISAN TILE MANUFACTURERS have their roots in Portland: Pratt and Larson Ceramics, Ann Sacks Tile and Stone, and Design and Direct Source. Portland artists Michael Pratt and Reta Larson began collaborating in the production of art tile in 1980. Since then their company has become a national leader in tile design and has grown to a staff of more than one hundred individuals engaged in all phases of design and production. They proudly claim that each "handcrafted product reflects the art, interest, [and] spirit of all those involved in its production."[13] All production transpires in their shop, which is tucked away in close-in, industrial southeast Portland. Pratt and Larson's beautiful tiles are currently distributed throughout North America. Representative of the eco-friendly city it calls home, Pratt and Larson launched a new line of tile using a reclaimed byproduct from their signature metallic glazes.[14]

Both Design and Direct Source and Ann Sacks Tile and Stone are the creations of Ann Sacks. Sacks made a name for herself developing custom color tile for homes. Such customization enabled the customer to precisely match tile hues to the furnishings already present. This is an integral part of interior design; "tile brings a space to life because it is a personal expression of those who live there."[15] Though she later sold the company, her product line still bears her name.[16] The Ann Sacks Collection of artisan tiles continues to be produced entirely in Portland by skilled designers.

After a brief retirement, Sacks jumped back into the tile industry with Design and Direct Source, a company geared towards providing tile and stone for commercial projects.[17] Design and Direct Source's tiles can be seen on hotels, condominiums, public and commercial buildings across the country.[18] In true Portland fashion, each product listed on their website includes a line describing the sustainable practices used in the creation of that particular product. Sustainable products are gauged based on five criteria: recycled content, natural or renewable material, resource-efficient manufacturing, ecological responsibility, and efficient sourcing and transportation of materials.[19]

LEATHERMAN KNIVES

LEATHERMAN KNIVES ARE UBIQUITOUS, even in Hollywood: MacGyver sported one, as did Keanu Reeves in the blockbuster film *Speed*, and Gillian Anderson on the popular TV show *The X-Files*. The company's story is the ultimate American dream. An engineer-turned-inventor, founder Tim Leatherman started making his multi-use knives in his basement in the late 1970s. Leatherman Tool Group incorporated in 1983 and, within the next year, sold nearly thirty thousand knives. More than a quarter century later, Leatherman has grown to a team of more than 550 employees that focuses on high-quality artisan production backed by a twenty-five-year guarantee. Leatherman knives have remained quite popular, and the company has sold millions of knives despite relatively few changes to the original design. Rather than mass-produce a single product, Leatherman has diversified their product line to create tools for specific purposes, including gardening pruners and bicycle tools.[20]

Leatherman is proud of his company's Portland roots and argues that "being from Portland, Oregon, means a lot of things, but ordinary definitely isn't one of them."[21] The company has remained in Portland since day one, and Leatherman believes that this is part of what makes them such a special company. Indeed, their local customer base is related to proximity to the activities of the Columbia River Gorge outdoors scene, such as fishing, camping, and boating. Portland's heritage as a frontier town inspires the company, and Leatherman tools embody "the rugged individualism of those intrepid souls who first pushed our nation west."[22] Nearly 80 percent of manufacturing is done in Oregon. What better way to honor the pluck and courage of pioneers than by keeping the manufacturing close to home?

PUPPETRY

AN ANCIENT FORM OF THEATRE, puppetry continues to be celebrated today in Portland. A host of puppet companies and independent puppeteers flourishes in Portland, delicately fabricating miniature costumes, sets, and figures. Founder of the Olde World Puppet Theatre in 1976, Steve Overton believes that Portlanders "support this not as a folk art, but as an art."[23]

Tears of Joy Theatre, a highly regarded touring puppet company, has been entertaining adults and children for more than thirty-five years. Serving as an incubator for puppetry in the city, co-founder Janet Bradley claims that the theatre has hired 150 puppeteers since 1973, recruiting these innovative artisans from all over the country and luring them to Portland where they eventually settled down. Many of these folks have since started their own puppetry side projects.[24] Outside of their extensive touring schedule, Tears of Joy is a resident company at the Portland Center for the Performing Arts, where they present six productions each year. Three of their productions have been awarded American puppetry's highest honor, the Citation of Excellence in the Art of Puppetry.[25]

Michael Curry, one of the most sought-after puppet designers in the world (he designed the puppets for the Broadway musical *The Lion King*) has his own company right outside Portland and also employs a cadre of budding artisans. The diversity of puppetry is astounding. Consider the Dim Sum Puppet Opera Company, which creates entirely handmade Taiwanese puppets. Or the Mudeye Puppet Company, an educational puppetry arts organization dedicated to reducing waste and encouraging creativity through the reuse of old materials.[26] Portland is so full of sustainably minded folks that it can even boast green puppeteers!

Hats

At least a dozen hatmakers call Portland home. Felted, knit, fleece, velvet, or straw, there is a hat for everyone, and many of these hats can be found on display at the Portland Saturday Market. True to Portland's DIY and eco-friendly cultures, you can find multiple hatmakers who focus on revamping something old into something fashionably new. For example, Nicole Flood of Flood Clothing assembles hats from 100 percent recycled materials. Her funky, flirty hats are less an accessory and more the center-piece of an outfit. Sweater Heads' hats, although made in Astoria, are well received at the Portland Saturday Market. These hats are made entirely from reclaimed sweaters and other found fabrics.[27]

In the realm of high-fashion hatmaking, or millinery, is Dayna Pinkham. The artisan behind Pinkham Millinery, Pinkham is renowned as one of the West Coast's top milliners. Her handcrafted hats have made appearances at

Great Britain's exclusive horse racing event, the Royal Ascot, and have also adorned rock stars, tennis legends, and fashionably minded Portlanders. Every single one of Pinkham's unique hats are designed and created in her downtown Portland shop. Pinkham fabricates all different styles of hats for both men and women, ranging from "the sleek and sexy to the fantastic and absurd."[28] Though some hats are available off the rack, at any given time there are twenty-five to thirty hats on special order with a wait time of two to three months. Pinkham creates roughly three hundred hats a year with the help of seven part-time interns.[29]

ARTIST PAINT

IT'S HIP TO BE GREEN in Portland—there's absolutely no doubt about that. The city is replete with all sorts of artisans incorporating sustainable practices into their work. Gamblin Artists Colors is yet another excellent example of this eco-friendly spirit. Founded by Robert Gamblin, a painter who wanted to make a living doing something closely related to his passion for painting, Gamblin Artists Colors "handcrafts luscious oil colors and contemporary mediums true to the working properties of traditional materials."[30] In the factory in southeast Portland, Gamblin discovered a way to avoid polluting water and landfills with the factory's waste paint. By mixing waste paint with pigment powder trapped by the air filter and adding an oil base, Gamblin created Torrit Grey. By installing the air filter, Gamblin prevented workers from being exposed to pigment dust; by reusing the waste pigment, he kept potentially hazardous material out of the waste stream.

Named after the Donaldson Torrit air filter, this cleverly reused paint product is given away at Earth Day events to artists, students, and teachers. In 2008, more than eleven thousand tubes were distributed.[31] Every batch is always grey and always free. Indeed, Gamblin prominently announces on each tube of paint that it is "always complimentary, not for sale."[32] Gamblin Artists Colors hosts the Gamblin Torrit Grey competition each year. Artists from all over the world submit paintings using only black, white, and Torrit Grey. The winners are judged by Gamblin and serve as an example of how artists need not leave their mark on the environment, but rather on canvas.[33]

Founded in 1980, Gamblin Artists Colors is currently the largest producer of artists' oil paints in the country and employs twenty people who, on a busy day, produce about five thousand tubes of paint.[34] Now that the company has grown, Gamblin has been able to ease off the business side and is able to speak to many artists and groups one-on-one. Chris Saper, winner of the 2008 Torrit Grey Competition, accurately sums this up: "Of course the personal contact and advice is unique—who would think you could actually call a company, talk to a live human being, and get amazing help?"[35]

Eyeglasses

While many artisan creations are consumed, hung on the wall, or even used on a regular basis, few become a daily expression of oneself. Eyeglasses serve a practical purpose, yet they also represent an individual's personality. Unlike a bicycle, which may be used every day to get around town, or even a piece of clothing, which can serve as an expression of self on the occasions it is worn, eyeglasses are perched in the most conspicuous place on the body and present an image of the wearer. So why should wearers of eyeglasses be forced to frame themselves in mass-produced objects? Even eyeglasses bearing a prominent designer label, like Dolce & Gabbana, are produced by large corporations to appeal to a large demographic.

Though eyeglasses are hardly the first things that come to mind when thinking of artisan craftsmanship, Portland has two eyeglass manufacturers: Amy Sacks and Reynolds Optical Co. This is no surprise, as Portland is a hotbed of artisan fashion designers. Distinguished tile designer Ann Sacks is the mastermind behind Amy Sacks eyewear. Sacks named the business after her daughter, Amy, and profits from the eyewear company help fund her daughter's nonprofit animal rescue organization. Eyeglasses are expertly crafted yet reasonably priced, and each pair comes with a comprehensive warranty and exchange/return program.[36] In Portland, the city that SustainLane has dubbed the "role model for the nation" in terms of sustainability,[37] it's no surprise that Sacks would incorporate green components into her eyewear. The Masa collection features eyeglasses made of bamboo, a sustainable material.[38]

Reynolds Optical Co.'s INhouse brand was created by current owner, Gary Piehl, and began as a single pair of customized frames for a longtime customer. Today INhouse eyeglasses are sold nationwide. Despite being the alleged competition, Piehl will occasionally consult with Sacks regarding eyeglass designs. In discussing localism, Piehl contends: "I live my life that way. I go to the farmers markets. I shop locally. Why not glasses?"[39]

POTTERY

PORTLAND FOSTERS THE ARTISAN SPIRIT through many support mechanisms. Classes, showcases, formal and informal associations, and social networks all nurture the creativity of Portland's inhabitants. The pottery scene in this city is no different. The Oregon Potters Association (OPA), a professional liaison between the public, galleries, businesses, publications, and arts agencies, organizes cooperative purchases to obtain pottery supplies at discount rates. Additionally, OPA helps and enables members to publicize, exhibit, and sell their work at the annual OPA Ceramic Showcase and in conjunction with other guilds, fairs, and craft organizations.[40] The Members Links page on the Oregon Potters Association website links to dozens of potters, many of whom reside in the Portland area. The 2009 Ceramic Showcase, held in Portland, attracted more than 150 exhibitors.[41]

Larry Nelson signed up for Beginning Ceramics at Portland Community College and began to discover his talents with the help of experienced potter and OPA member Richie Bellinger.[42] Nelson, now a professional potter and an OPA member himself, was honored by the OPA as Member of the Month in March 2008. His interest in pottery was sparked by a vase made by his wife, Debra. The handmade vase contained marks made by her fingers and the unevenness of a hand-applied glaze, and Nelson realized its perfection in these imperfections: "It contained her spirit and it spoke to me."[43]

Portland potter Careen Stoll echoes this revelation of visible evidence of handcrafted pottery; all her pottery intentionally incorporates little imperfections. Stoll maintains that our contemporary culture needs craftspeople. "Right now we're not making dishes to hold food. We're doing that, but we're also making metaphors for how to see people as individuals and not just numbers. I share a sweet cup of tea with you, served in a handmade mug. There's a story to that mug."[44] Artisans strive to cultivate these connections between craftsperson, consumer, and the story that unites them. For Stoll, this is precisely the goal, as the pleasure and nourishment that comes from sharing food in these dishes goes far beyond the simple act of eating.

CHECK, PLEASE!

IT'S NEARLY IMPOSSIBLE to overemphasize the sheer abundance and diversity of artisan activity in Portland. These short portraits help round out the sense of what comprises this culture of high-quality, handcrafted artisan products. You can see the strong overlap of sustainability and the artisan economy, both philosophically and in practice. The incorporation of eco-friendly materials and techniques reflects the larger-scale support of sustainable practices in Portland. Whether it be Mudeye Puppet Company promoting waste reduction and fostering creativity through reuse of old materials, or Gamblin Artists Colors' ingenious transformation of pigment powder waste into Torrit Grey paint, Portland is a city that doesn't just talk the green talk; it integrates sustainability into all aspects of life and culture.

CHAPTER 17
BEYOND BOHEMIAN ENCLAVES:
SPACES FOR ARTISANS TO WORK AND LIVE

Bridger Wineman
Charles Heying

THE STORY OF THE DEVELOPMENT of an arts enclave is a familiar one. Urban pioneers, such as artists, musicians, and other bohemian types, congregate in a forgotten industrial district with abundant space and cheap rent. Over time, a vibrant street life emerges; the neighborhood becomes known for its authentic cultural products and edgy lifestyle. At first the locale is frequented by knowledgeable locals, but later tourists come to consume the scene and sample the cultural offerings. Sensing opportunity, entrepreneurial developers convert the industrial spaces into residential lofts and urban professionals renovate nearby houses. The success of these early renovations draws public investment and new development to the area. Rents go from affordable to exclusive; local artisan businesses are replaced by upscale corporate retail; edgy artist studios give way to expensive private galleries.[1] In the process, the artisans themselves become "victims of the gentrification process they helped initiate."[2]

This model of gentrification and displacement has played itself out in Portland, most notably in the Pearl District, but in this chapter we show that this process is neither universal nor inevitable. We describe how Portland developers and artisans have attempted to find workable alternatives that preserve spaces for artisans while also allowing them to benefit from the cultural ambience and community aspects of a vibrant arts scene. There is growing awareness among artists, developers and political leaders that solutions must be found to mitigate the usual process of development and displacement. Affordability and access to spaces to live and work are crucial to retaining the creative talent so important to the future of the city. Speaking of the value of affordable live/work space, Portland Mayor Sam Adams states, "I want Portland to be this vibrant city where weird, quirky, wonderful ideas are sparked. That can only happen if you have artists, culturalists, and innovators in your midst." It's a holistic vision shared by project developer Ted Gilbert: "It's the creative talent that's going to bring us, Portland, into the future."[3]

THE CITY AS ARTISAN SPACE: SHORT-CIRCUITING GENTRIFICATION

THE ULTIMATE SPACE for artisans in Portland is the city itself. This Portland space encompasses the lifestyle, spatial and interpersonal connections, and inspiration provided by the myriad interactions that make it a city comfortable for artisans in every sector. At the street level, artisan food producers meet their customers every week at farmers' markets throughout Portland. Crafters head to Crafty Wonderland or the venerable Portland Saturday Market. Organized art walks occur in neighborhoods throughout the city, such as the Thursday and Friday walks in DIY and gallery districts. On First Thursdays, upscale Pearl District galleries open their doors and artist studios. On First Fridays, the grittier Inner Eastside shows off the contemporary art scene that is taking off there. But Last Thursday on Alberta Street in north Portland, where sidewalk space belongs to whoever gets there first, is perhaps the ultimate show of street-level creativity. Food vendors, musicians, artists, and gawkers fill the streets in a brilliant and ridiculous seventeen-block-long circus that shuts down traffic and blends fine arts with absurdity and fun.

Stumptown Coffee Roasters serves as the model for dozens of smaller roasters, cafés, and shops that connect artisan culture to everyday routines. The culture encouraged there is one of collaboration. The works of local artists are displayed on the walls, and baristas are given time off to tour with their indie bands. These artisan coffee roasters, cafés, and their patrons are passionate about the subtlety and diversity of both flavor and ideas. Neighborhood cafés, like the Red and Black, an all-vegan workers' collective in Inner Southeast, and Red Bike in north Portland host art exhibitions, lectures, meetings, and knitting clubs, while serving small-batch coffee and food from artisan farmers and bakers. These spaces and their inhabitants are characteristic of what Portland has become in relation to other large American cities: casual, engaged, experimental, activist, creative, collaborative, and quaint. This active street life, ubiquitous throughout the city, can short-circuit the typical pattern of gentrification and displacement that occur when cultural activities become concentrated in particular bohemian districts.

DISJECTA: ANCHORING INSTITUTIONS AND NEIGHBORHOOD CHANGE

DISJECTA IS A PORTLAND NONPROFIT that focuses on contemporary performance and visual art. It is currently located in the Kenton neighborhood of north Portland in a building that was once a bowling alley but now houses 3,500 square feet of exhibition space. Through fundraising and various grants, Disjecta is set to add offices, as well as artist studios and a café.[4]

Disjecta offers one model for how a community of artists might preserve creative space in a neighborhood. In an interview with local radio station KPSU, Bryan Suereth, Disjecta's director, explained that development pressures that would ordinarily force artists out of an area can be overcome by an anchoring institution that mobilizes the collective energy of individual artists. This is Disjecta's strategy.[5]

Suereth understands the problem of displacement caused by neighborhood change. Disjecta is now in its third home since its original incarnation in an old Masonic lodge on Northeast Russell Street. Before moving to its current Kenton location, it was in the Templeton Building on the east approach to the Burnside Bridge, an area primed for public investment and heavily promoted by the Portland Development Commission. Disjecta had planned to be part of a high-profile artist incubation site at the Burnside Bridgehead until the widely publicized breakdown of the planned redevelopment of the area.

But Suereth accepts the twists and turns of building anchoring institutions for the avant-garde. He is working to create a home for Disjecta into the new scene he sees developing in Kenton and north Portland. Buoyed by increased accessibility from light rail service, he sees the presence of new galleries, like Rocksbox Fine Art on North Interstate Avenue, as evidence of the next big thing, where credibility and creativity again converge. "In some ways arts folks, cultural institutions really should be pioneering the next fertile ground for creativity, and north Portland was just perfect for what we were trying to do."[6]

THE FALCON ART COMMUNITY: RE-CONCEIVING VALUE AND A "MODEST CHANGE" ON NORTH MISSISSIPPI

WE MET BRIAN WANNAMAKER to get his take on Portland's artisan economy and the role developers like him have been playing in creating affordable living spaces for artists. We stopped at Coffeehouse-Five on Albina Street, just across from the Falcon Apartments, a building he owns and manages. "This is one of your guys," Wannamaker commented, as he chatted with the barista about the coffee-roasting venture the barista hoped to start.[7] Across the street at the Falcon, Wannamaker is building a collection of art, but he's really a collector of artists. The basement of the Falcon houses studios for painters, writers, and musicians. Wannamaker seems to rejoice at being at the center of it all.

In redeveloping the Falcon Apartments, Wannamaker learned that creating a building that works for artists requires more than just offering workspaces and affordable rent. It's really about creating community. It involves uniting disparate groups—the art community and the neighborhood community, older traditional tenants and a new creative class, starving artists and young urban professionals—all brought together by the place they share.

Falcon Apartments was built in 1909. It's a medium-sized complex with a basement, three floors, and forty-seven apartments. Located near Killingsworth Street and Mississippi Avenue in north Portland, a traditionally African-American neighborhood, it borders the rapidly transforming Mississippi Avenue business district. "I bought it around '97," Wannamaker explains, "and this was a very difficult neighborhood at the time, very low income and had been left out of the rest of the prosperity that was going on in the city." He began by confronting drug and crime issues in the building and the surrounding neighborhood. Wannamaker explains that he first got the idea of bartering housing when he hired a live-in security guard to help keep track of the building and the surrounding area. "I got into this concept of trading housing for [security].... I started wondering what else I could add to the building and the neighborhood in order to start solidifying the community around this other model that had more to do with prosperity." Wannamaker came to the realization that creating a community of artists was one path toward transforming the Falcon Apartments and the surrounding area into a more prosperous place.

Wannamaker's vision, embodied in the Falcon Art Community, challenges the scenario of displacement that typically plays out as reinvestment comes to a struggling neighborhood. This is accomplished by preserving and encouraging forms of value and vitality that are often neglected in real estate

Owner Brian Wannamaker focuses on community and diversity at the Falcon apartments.
Photo © Whitney Gayer

development. Part of this effort involves retaining residents who have lived at the Falcon for decades. "Community and diversity are two components that I think add a lot of intrinsic value.... I tried to come up with strategies where I could recognize their value, not necessarily from a monetary standpoint so much as from a community standpoint." Toward this end, Wannamaker kept the rent of these long-term tenants much lower than that of those new to the building, creating what he calls a "modest transition" as new tenants supplement rather than displace their older neighbors.

By trading art for affordable rent, artists and their work contribute to Wannamaker's long-term vision for the building. "Part of that vision is to collect...some of their work so that it stays with the building.... There's a lot of wall space for paintings, photography, etc. It would be nice, over the period of the next thirty, forty years, to be able to start filling up all of those spaces with artwork from people who have lived here." Wannamaker found a unique way to use those spaces to honor long-term residents. Fourteen oil portraits by Alexander Rokoff depicting members of the older generation of Falcon residents are the foundation of his art collection.

Wannamaker recognizes the value of art and culture, as well as of maintaining economic and generational diversity for the district as a whole. It's an approach that ties the fate of the Falcon Apartments, and the success of the artists' community based there, to the prosperity of the entire neighborhood. "I think the Falcon is still quite young—and it's almost a hundred-year-old building—in terms of the art-community model and component. There's still a lot of wall space."

LIVE/WORK SPACES

THE CITY OF PORTLAND, beginning with former Mayor Vera Katz, has taken seriously the idea of providing live/work spaces for artists to stimulate the arts and encourage redevelopment in rundown neighborhoods. As chief of staff for Mayor Katz, Sam Adams was involved with the initial development of a policy encouraging live/work developments. Elected Mayor in 2008, Adams continued the City's strong support of initiatives to grow the arts community in Portland.[8] Portland's Pearl District, now chic and urbane, has been the site of much of the city's investment in arts development. One of the first initiatives was Everett Station Lofts. In 1989, developer Martin Soloway secured $2.5 million in public funds to convert a three-building complex into forty-seven live/work units. Drawing on lessons from other cities, Soloway concluded that encouraging a lively art scene would be a good antidote for a neighborhood perceived as dangerous and blighted. The lowest rents were charged for the sixteen storefront units. In exchange, artists agreed to open their studios to the public during regular business hours and during nine First Thursday gallery tours each year. Everett Station was one of the pioneers that sparked the full-tilt redevelopment of the Portland's upscale Pearl District during the next decade.[9]

In 1998, when the tax abatements requiring affordable rents were about to expire, Soloway proposed a sale to existing tenants. The offer to own was not a priority for tenants, but the impending conversion to market-rate units impelled them to seek an alternative that would work for Soloway. Forgoing a higher return, Soloway agreed to sell the building at its appraised value to Artspace, a national nonprofit that develops spaces for artists.[10] Under the management of Artspace, Everett Station Lofts continues to be a relatively affordable live/work space and an important contributor to the now flourishing arts scene in the Pearl District.[11] The success of the Pearl District was a mixed blessing. More established artists stayed on, but new entrants sought other quarters. These needs were partially met by Ken Unkeles' Portland Art Studios. For twenty-five years, Unkeles has defied economic logic by leasing very affordable art spaces in historic buildings in downtown Portland.[12]

Milepost 5 is a contemporary example of an intentional live/work development. The project is located on Northeast 82nd Avenue, a busy traffic corridor populated by used car lots and big-box retailers. Lacking pedestrian ambience and far from the artistic energy of the central city, it's an unlikely and risky location. Milepost 5 consists of two main buildings on the campus of a former Baptist nursing home. It is the brainchild of Ted Gilbert, a Portland commercial real estate developer who is also a board member of two local housing nonprofits. Gilbert brought the idea to Brad Malsin of Beam Development, which recently redeveloped several high-profile buildings in Portland's Central Eastside. Glibert and Malsin partnered to create ArtPlace Development, the company that is developing Milepost 5.[13]

The developers of Milepost 5 are doing all they can to make this intentional creative community a success. When complete, the project will include loft-style live/work condos as well as rental apartments and artist studios. There are also galleries, a restaurant, a performance space, and music studios in the works. Former leader of the Portland Art Center, Gavin Shettler, was hired as the creative director and is organizing exhibitions of residents' work on site.[14]

Like many new developments, Milepost 5 is working hard to find residents and fulfill its ambitious goals to serve as a creative community, provide affordable housing and ownership opportunities, and play a part in revitalizing the Montavilla neighborhood. Some of the units for sale have special rules, following a community housing model, that limit the appreciation of units to cost of living in order to retain affordability into the future. The development originally offered $2,500 grants to condo buyers who met certain conditions. In the current down market, the developers have increased the grants to $8,000.[15]

There is a lot of hopefulness about the prospect of success at Milepost 5, but the jury is still out. Bryan Suereth of Disjecta notes that Milepost 5 came from the development side rather than the arts side, and wonders whether the intrinsic independence of creative lifestyles may not naturally fit the grand schemes of developers. "The bottom line," says Surereth "is how does it serve the arts community? I think that's what they're struggling with right now."[16]

CREATIVE SERVICES CENTER: WHAT MONEY CAN'T BUY

IN SOME CITIES, new ideas are stifled by entrenched interests and public inertia, but in Portland the situation is reversed. Citizen groups, agency entrepreneurs, and vision-driven politicians compete to promote whatever is the next big thing. It's a blessing and a curse. It gave Portlanders a transportation system that is the envy of the country, but it also gave the city the Creative Services Center, a $10 million boondoggle that was intended to be Portland's incubator for the creative services industry.

As with all such projects, it began with the best intentions. A study funded by the Portland Development Commission (PDC) identified a cluster of creative services in advertising, film and video, graphic arts, and design that were demonstrating remarkable growth—11 percent over a six-year period between 1992 and 1998. The study identified over eight hundred firms, 15,500 workers, and roughly two thousand freelance businesses in the creative services that were potential tenants for this new hub of innovation and collaboration.[17] The development plan called for "state-of-the-art loft space for creative services companies and key industry associations," including the newly formed Oregon Creative Services Alliance. The Kalberer building was quickly selected for the signature renovation that would create seventy thousand square feet of new space in the heart of Old Town.[18] With more than the usual fanfare, it opened its doors in fall 2001. Initially, the project attracted some anchor tenants, like the Regional Arts and Culture Council, but after two years, the building remained 80 percent vacant.[19] The costly renovation had forced the PDC to market its space at twenty-three dollars per square foot at a time when similar spaces in the area were renting for half that.[20]

While some of the blame was placed on the 2001 economic downturn, other factors, like significant cost overruns and failure to understand their target market, were at least as important. The PDC appeared to have missed something fundamental about the new economy. Emerging artisan businesses are not usually flush with cash or seeking nicely appointed spaces.[21] Successful projects seem to start incrementally, with basic renovations of old buildings in low-rent areas. But all was not lost for the PDC. In a remarkable confluence of events, the PDC's building lease was up for renewal just as the Creative Services Center was going under. Given the large investment they had made in the building and with no other viable alternatives, the PDC took over the building and moved to all its staff and operations there in late 2004.[22]

SHOP PEOPLE: ARTISANS TAKE THE LEAD

CRAFT AND FINE ART are melded at Shop People, a community workshop in Portland's Central Eastside, which was started three years ago by Richard Ellison and Rebekah Dreske. When Ellison, who builds small boats, and Dreske, who makes custom jewelry, needed more room to work, they leased and began renovating a junk-filled space on Grand Avenue. But at eight thousand square feet it was too large for them, so they invited other artisans to share space and tools and help pay the rent. "Within four months the shop was paying for itself," says Ellison.[23] Since opening in October of 2005, Shop People has expanded four times and now includes seventy members and twenty-five thousand square feet of workspace, remaining financially sustainable throughout this rapid expansion. The shop now includes a jewelry-making room, a woodshop, a metal shop, a pottery and glass studio, and space for unusual projects like building freak bikes or welding large metal sculptures.

Shop People attracts members from diverse backgrounds. Some are hobbyists. Some have left jobs or been laid off and are falling back on other skills. Others avoided traditional jobs altogether, opting instead to work with their hands to earn a living. Like other community spaces for artisans, Shop People provides space, tools, and support services. Members get access to communal workspaces and tools for a base monthly rate of $150 and can rent additional private space for one dollar per square foot. Members can also sell their work in the café/gallery at the front of the shop and participate in the Central Eastside Arts District First Friday gallery walk.

The open workspace and community vibe encourage collaboration. "A lot of projects involve several people in the shop working together," says Ellison. Members benefit from working in a community of craftspeople where advice is available and willingly offered. One example is Lindsay Jo Holmes, a young entrepreneur who launched a successful business beginning with just an idea and support from the community at Shop People. Holmes creates earrings and bracelets from junked-out skateboard decks that she obtains from local skate shops in exchange for home-baked cookies. Ellison and others at Shop People showed her how to use a drill press and other tools to realize her idea. Now Holmes sells her unique jewelry in over twenty stores around the United States, internationally, and on her website, MapleXO.com.

Shop People has become both a community center and an incubator for small businesses. Ellison explains that about a third of Shop People members use the space for personal projects and hobbies, and another third supplement their income by selling wares made at the shop. For the remaining third, work produced at Shop People is their primary source of income. In the short time it's been in operation, Ellison notes that six members have grown enough to move out and lease their own dedicated spaces around town, while other members have moved closer for easy access to Shop People.

Ellison's vision for the future is to make the handcrafted, authentic products created at Shop People more accessible to Portlanders. His plans include developing a website where customers, who might have gone to a big-box retailer like Target, will instead buy directly from local artisans at Shop People.

Portland's support of unique local products and a culture that encourages creativity have been particularly conducive to an enterprise like Shop People. This support has stimulated the creation of similar enterprises like Tool Shed PDX, a nonprofit organization that offers a slightly different model of a community workspace.[24]

The future of artisan spaces in Portland

Some describe Portland as an affordable alternative to Seattle or San Francisco, but the creative output of Portland's artists and artisans suggests a city with its own identity. The visionaries constructing innovative new ways for artisans to live and work are focusing on the development

Lindsay Jo Holmes creating her signature handmade jewelery from used skateboard decks. Photo © Rachel Moore

of physical and social infrastructures simultaneously. Moreover, none of these efforts can be separated from the larger civic environment in which they're embedded. The future of Portland's creative spaces will continue as a balance between the artisan's need for affordable space and development pressures in the neighborhoods they help define.

It's not clear how different models of artisan space—formal and informal, publicly or privately developed, live/work or neighborhood institution—will fare in the future. But it does seem likely that a combination of these initiatives will serve the broader Portland community in the continual cycles of rebirth that characterize the cultural and physical evolution of place. The creative initiative of those behind these spaces reflects the innovative spirit of the artists and artisans themselves. In any case, the need for artisan spaces, and the creativity of its people, is recognized as intrinsic to Portland's success in coming decades. The view from here looks bright. "Culturally, Portland is a large, young, enthusiastic, creative community," says Wannamaker. "It feels like this is Portland's moment in time. In ten years, who knows where it's going to be, but right now it's here, and that part feels good."

BACK TO THE FUTURE

CHAPTER 18
PORTLAND'S ARTISAN ECONOMY: LESSONS FROM THE FIELD

Charles Heying

YOU CAN FIND IT on the web. Search for "200 artisan skills to make a Victorian town functional." As I surveyed the list of skills, I was surprised to find how many were being practiced by Portland artisans; by my count, 112 of the 200. I couldn't remember any Portland bodgers (we have our wood turners but none that go into the field, cut the wood, and turn the chair legs right there), and mud brick makers had me stumped until I thought of the cob builders at City Repair; but we do have our chair makers, leather workers, milliners, bookbinders, knife makers, dry stone wallers, beekeepers, brewers, knitters, and instrument makers. And Portland artisans are not just hobbyists. As we discovered from the interviews conducted for this book, many artisans earn part or all of their income from their craft, and a number of them have enterprises with national reputations and national reach.

So what does this mean? Is it really back to the future? Did we find support for the claim we made in our introduction that "the transformation from an industrial to a post-industrial economy is being articulated in the trend-setting edges of Portland's artisan production"? I would say yes, with reservations. The problem with being immersed in a project like this is that the part of the world you observe soon consumes your vision. You begin to mistake the part for the whole, or more likely, believe that the part will soon become the whole. So, let me be clear, the industrial economy is still here. Most of our economic life has a nine-to-five, not an artisan, vibe.

But something is happening here. The evidence from the chapters cannot be ignored. It is significant. It does suggest that what is emerging after the industrial economy is going to look more like an artisan economy than not. But again, caution is in order. We observed one city at one point in time, so projecting our findings forward and outward is risky. As Indie Music chapter author Laura Cesafsky puts it, "The present is the visible moment in a long story that unravels in unpredictable directions." So, while I sense that what we observed in Portland is part of a larger trend rather than an anomaly, I will leave it to the reader to make that intuitive leap, or to future research to establish.

With that as background, let's turn to the task at hand and address the question, what did we learn from our research? Table 2 provides an accessible summary of the important lessons we collectively gleaned from our fieldwork and interviews.

TABLE 2: LESSONS FROM THE FIELD

An Abundance of Making and Doing

- There is an artisan economy in Portland.
- Portland's abundance of artisan enterprises suggests a return to an economy based on making things.

Product Qualities and Work Life

- Integrating the design and building process, striving for quality and authenticity, and engaging the materiality of the product are integral to artisan work.
- Some established artisan businesses are doing well, but most artisans continue to work because they "can't stop doing it."
- Artisans often learn their craft by doing rather than through formal education.
- Portland has a culture of knowledgeable patrons who expect and appreciate artisan quality products.
- Artisans tend to blur the lines between social and work life.

Artisan Clusters, Soft Infrastructure, and Learning Communities

- Seminal institutions pave the way for new entrants by providing a place to learn basic skills, practice their craft, and sell their creations.
- Festivals, conferences, blogs, guilds, and other types of collaborative events and organizations were universally identified by artisans as important means to create community, network, and share resources.
- Artisan clusters facilitate resource sharing and cooperation but also engage in healthy competition that spurs innovation.
- Portland's wealth of public places, such as farmers' markets, the Saturday Market, and Last Thursday on Alberta Street are important venues for artisans to get their wares before the public.
- Actions by the public sector are important because they can remove barriers to innovation, create structures of support and legitimation, and open markets for artisan products.

Social Wealth and the Moral Economy

- Artisans are attracted to Portland because it provides an affordable, people-centered place to live and work.
- Artisan enterprises engage workers in a way that is more humane, flexible, and supportive.
- Portland artisans demonstrate complex systems thinking about work, waste, and use. Acting ethically and including the best sustainable practices are common themes for artisans.

Paradox of Place

- Some artisan products have a special quality derived from the climate, geography, or unique production practices of the locality. Purist artisans believe this connection should be maintained by producing primarily for a local market. Other artisans believe that unique local products are the very ones that should be sold to distant markets.
- For some, Portland's reputation as a place of artisanal production provides marketing leverage for artisanal producers in all sectors. Others fear overselling will diminish Portland's "coolness" factor.
- The global/local paradox is evident in markets for artisan products that are more dependent on sales outside the locality than expected. This paradox is especially present in the substantial use of web-based marketing.

Scale and Authenticity

- Purist artisans remain small because this allows them to maintain autonomy and keep creative control.
- Locality artisans are willing to expand within a given location but feel that other places should develop their own artisan enterprises.
- Custom-stock artisans produce some handmade items in volume as well as one-of-kind specialty orders. They will grow sufficiently to meet demand but will not get so large as to lose touch with their artisan roots.
- Scale-to-market artisans are willing to scale up and distribute their product as widely as possible as long as they can continue to create a craft-based, quality product.

While many of the lessons are similar to the expectations laid out in Table 1 of Chapter 2, there are some additional insights that were not evident at the outset of our research.

AN ABUNDANCE OF MAKING AND DOING

There is an artisan economy in Portland. The chapters in this book provide ample evidence of the breadth and depth of Portland's artisan economy. Yet the more artisan sectors we discovered, the more we realized how much we missed. Our chapter "Artisan Samplers" was the final throwing up of our collective hands. Even with this, we left some glaring exceptions, including most of the theatre scene, published authors, fine artists, musicians other than indie rock, design-build firms that do one-house-at-time construction or restoration, and small specialty trade workers such as those who do fine tile or masonry. There was no mention of boat builders, blacksmiths, wood-carvers, or toy makers, all of whom have a presence in Portland. Nor did we include body artists or tattoo artisans even though the latter were recognized with their own show at the Portland Art Museum.

I am certain there were many more, but this book is not a glass half empty. It is a book about a city overflowing with artisan talent. In several instances—food, coffee, brew, bikes, distilling, comics—we have evidence of their significant financial importance. And for what it's worth, Portland receives its share of accolades that suggest the prominence of its artisan enterprises: "Bike City USA," "Beertopia," "Zine capital of the world," the "epicenter of independent specialty coffee," the "Hollywood of comic books," and the "mecca" of indie rock, indie crafts, and instrument makers.

If there were a Fortune 500 of artisan enterprises, Portland would seem to have more than its share. Here are a few businesses that I believe could rank in the top tier of their artisan sector: McMenamins Pubs and Lodges, Clear Creek Distillery, Widmer Brothers Brewing, Pinkham Millinery, and Stumptown Coffee Roasters; Rejuvenation House Parts, Pratt and Larson Ceramics, and City Repair; Leatherman, Gamblin Artists Colors, Monette Trumpets, Tears of Joy Puppetry, and Bullseye Glass; the Portland Saturday Market; Powell's City of Books, Dark Horse Comics, and Laika Entertainment; Langlitz Leathers and fashions by Adam Arnold, Seaplane, and Anna Cohen; bikes from Strawberry Cyclesport, Sweetpea, and Vanilla Bicycles; the bands Pink Martini and The Decemberists; and art prints by Black Apple and Ashley G.

Portland's abundance of artisan enterprises suggests a return to an economy based on making things. In the aftermath of the collapse of the financial sector in 2009, there has been some serious national handwringing that we no longer have an economy where people make things. If Portland's artisan economy is a harbinger of a changing approach to economic life, there is something to celebrate. As the chapters in this book illustrate, Portland artisans are very much engaged in making and doing.

PRODUCT QUALITIES AND WORK LIFE

Integrating design and build, striving for quality and authenticity, and engaging the materiality of the product are integral to artisan work. This was a message we heard repeatedly from artisans. Fashion designer Adam Arnold expressed it this way in Chapter 5: "How can you design something you don't know how to make?" In Chapter 13, leather crafter Elizabeth Robinson expressed her deep appreciation for the material's "natural variations of texture, thickness, and dye absorption." She noted her desire to make these variations a part of her work even to the extent of showing flaws that might typically be disguised.

Some established artisan businesses are doing well, but most artisans continue to work because they "can't stop doing it." In the more established areas of the artisan economy, where we find businesses such as Widmer Brothers Brewing and New Seasons Markets that have scaled up without abandoning their artisan roots, they are doing well. However, most artisans we spoke with are just getting by rather than getting rich. For some, who are just starting out or work part time, this is expected. But many artisans are working full time and have established reputations. For them it is truly a labor of love. Instrument maker David King made this case in Chapter 14, as he described his level of commitment to his craft as "like being a monk," saying it's something that "drives you from inside."

Artisans often learn their craft by doing rather than through formal education. We found this to be a common, almost universal theme, whether it was fashion designers, bike builders, indie rockers, or instrument makers. These artisans had an itch and they didn't need formal training to scratch it. This says something about the truly democratic aspects of the artisan economy. It also suggests a distinct contemporary period for craftsmanship where resources and knowledge are sufficiently ubiquitous and the ethic of skill sharing is sufficiently widespread that long periods of apprenticeship are no longer the norm.

Portland has a culture of knowledgeable patrons who expect and appreciate artisan-quality products. Portlanders are rethinking what it means to be a consumer. The operative concept is not more, but better. Those who buy artisan products are looking for relationships, accountability, connection to locality, and the quality and character of the product. Many of those involved in the artisan economy remarked that this expectation has become a cultural norm for Portlanders. In Chapter 4, Brian Rohter, founder of New Seasons Market, noted that that Portlanders expected to know where their food comes from and the practices that were used to produce it. In Chapter 7, Julie Beals, editor of *Fresh Cup* magazine, recognized that this desire for quality and distinction sometimes requires a trade-off that Portlanders seemed willing to make: "People here, more than in a lot of other cities, are willing to drive a fifteen-year-old car but drink really good wine and coffee, eat good cheese, and treat themselves to nice meals out."

Artisans tend to blur the lines between social and work life. For indie music producer Mark Janchar, the blurring between social and work life is a bittersweet reality. He enjoys working closely with the artists on his label, but sees the sad irony that he really has no social life outside of work. Richard Seymour of Free Geek employs humor to deal with the same dilemma, exhorting his staff to not let work take over their life like a romantic relationship.

ARTISAN CLUSTERS, SOFT INFRASTRUCTURE, AND LEARNING COMMUNITIES

Seminal institutions pave the way for new entrants by providing a place to learn basic skills, practice their craft, and sell their creations. Artisans were quick to identify seminal institutions in their sector. McMenamins was the place where many of the second generation brewers and distillers learned their craft. In bicycle frame making, Andy Newlands mentored others like Tony Pereira and Natalie Ramsland who both went on to start their own lines. In comics it was Dark Horse that attracted artists to the area and provided a place to sell their works. Seaplane, one of the first Portland boutiques to offer locally made indie fashions from a variety of designers, was a springboard for later stars like Adam Arnold and Anna Cohen.

Festivals, conferences, blogs, guilds, and other types of collaborative events and organizations were universally identified by artisans as important means to create community, network, and share resources. This partial list, gleamed from the chapters, reveals the richness of support available to artisans: Oregon Brewers Guild, Food Alliance, Chefs Collaborative, Portland Fashion Week, Bikeportland.org, Oregon Bicycle Constructors Association, Pedalpalooza, Oregon Craft Distillers Guild, Burning Still.org, Worksound, PDX Pop Now! Festival, Independent Publishing Resource Center, Portland Zine Symposium, Platform International Animation Festival, Stumptown Comic Fest, KBOO Community Radio, Independent Media Center, Northwest Film Center, Portland International Film Festival, Crafty Pod, Portland Church of Craft, DIY Lounge, Free Geek, Village Building Convergence, Portland Office of Sustainable Development, New Legion of Tech, Open Source Bridge Conference, Northwest Handmade Instrument Show, Guild of American Luthiers, Guild of Oregon Woodworkers, Bullseye Glass and its BECon conference, and the Oregon Potters Association Ceramic Showcase.

Artisan clusters facilitate resource sharing and cooperation but also engage in healthy competition that spurs innovation. At New Deal Distillery they call it "coopertition," a blended moniker that describes how artisans embrace healthy competition that challenges them to improve their skills while sharing information that helps everyone move forward. Generally there is a sense that the work of each artisan is sufficiently unique that they are not in direct competition, so there is always room for one more. Sharing extends to an appreciation of artisan work across sectors and a willingness to buy or trade services. Shane Endicott of Free Geek embraces an even more generous perspective. In Chapter 12, Endicott speaks of an obligation "to give away whatever we create here...[and] the more we give the more successful we'll be."

Portland's wealth of public places, such as farmers' markets, the Saturday Market, and Last Thursday on Alberta Street are important venues for artisans get their wares before the public. As they say in marketing, its "location, location, location." But for the struggling artisan who lacks the means to rent even a small storefront, public spaces like craft or farmers markets are cost effective places for artisans to get a foot in the door, test the waters, and ease the transition from hobbyist to artisan producer.

Actions by the public sector are important because they can remove barriers to innovation; create structures of support and legitimation, and open markets for artisan products. In terms of the public sector removing barriers to emergent artisan industries, the most compelling examples have been in the beer, wine and spirits sectors. Oregon legislation lowered the cost of distilling permits, allowed makers of brew and spirits to sell their products on their premises, and allowed businesses to simultaneously own a brewery and distillery. Oregon has also passed legislation that acted as a stimulus for artisan industry. For example, Oregon's Bicycle Bill, passed in 1971, mandated that 1 percent of local transportation funds be set aside for construction of bike and pedestrian pathways. Ultimately this helped seed Portland's wide-ranging bike culture and its nascent bike frame and parts makers. Local government has also shown that it can be supportive. The Portland Development Commission helped bike and distilled spirits artisans form trade organizations that enabled them to work more cooperatively. Portland city officials have been lenient in allowing public spaces to be used by artisans, and they have enacted workable codes leading to a proliferation of food carts in business districts throughout the city.

SOCIAL WEALTH AND THE MORAL ECONOMY

IN OUR DESCRIPTION of the moral economy in Chapter 2, we attempted to compare traditional conceptions of wealth to a more grounded and communal sense of wealth we expected to find in the artisan economy. The narratives recounted in this book have increased our understanding and appreciation for what we are now calling social wealth. In many different ways, artisans expressed their sense that social wealth makes it possible for them to experience a high quality of life because they rely less on individual consumption and personal accumulation and more on participating in shared benefits of a lively community.

Artisans are attracted to Portland because it provides an affordable, people-centered place to live and work. Portland's reputation as a quality place to live, with a progressive political culture and a critical mass of supportive artisan enterprises, attracts like-minded creative people to the community. Artisans take advantage of the social wealth of invigorated neighborhoods and small business districts across the city that maintain the integrity of current building stock and enhance the supply of low-cost retail space. They use the quality public services that prevail throughout the city; the improved bike, pedestrian and mass transit options that reduce pollution, enhance healthy activity, and increase intergenerational access throughout the city.

Artisan enterprises engage workers in a way that is more humane, flexible, and supportive. Finding employment that pays enough, that is flexible and receptive to artisan lifestyles, and that encourages autonomy and creativity is an important attribute in an artisan-friendly city. This can be difficult where so many artisan enterprises are one-person shops. However, Portland is fortunate to have a diverse artisan sector with a sufficient number of successful enterprises that provide employment. Some, such as Vanilla Bicycles, Monette Trumpets, and Langlitz Leathers, employ fewer than twenty people. Others, like New Seasons Market, Stumptown Coffee Roasters, Powell's Books, Grand Central Bakery, Rejuvenation House Parts, Pratt and Larson Ceramics, and Bullseye Glass, employ hundreds. Many of these enterprises pay well, provide benefits, and take a much broader, flexible, even familial view of employees who they expect to share a passion for their work.

Portland artisans demonstrate complex systems thinking about work, waste, and use. Acting ethically and including the best sustainable practices are common themes for artisans. Numerous expressions of a new moral outlook were provided by artisans across sectors. It is exemplified by enterprises like Hopworks Brewery and Anna Cohen's designs where sustainable practices are embedded in every aspect of production. It is made real in efforts like those of

Stumptown Coffee Roasters that started Bikes to Rwanda, now an independent nonprofit organization that provides cargo bicycles and a bike workshop and maintenance program to cooperative coffee farmers in Rwanda. But it is also found in creative efforts like those of Gamblin Artists Colors that created a new paint, Torrit Grey, from waste pigment powders trapped by its air filter.

PARADOX OF PLACE

ONE OF THE UNEXPECTED FINDINGS of our research was that artisans hold complex and often contradictory views of how they connect to and benefit from Portland as a place. In the lessons that follow, we explore this paradox of place.

Some artisan products have a special quality derived from the climate, geography, or unique production practices of the locality. Purist artisans believe this connection should be maintained by producing primarily for a local market. Other artisans believe that unique local products are the very ones that should be sold to distant markets. The quality and character of Oregon and the Pacific Northwest are an essential part of what makes some artisan products unique. This sensibility was expressed by in Chapter 3 by Portland beer historian Bill Schneller, who noted that local waters are perfect for brewing and that the prevalence of hops growers in the Pacific Northwest has produced a distinctive regional terroir of more bitter and hoppy beers. Purist artisans believe that regional terroir is a reason to limit the range of where they sell their products and that other localities should develop their own, place-based, artisan enterprises. In Chapter 4, Ben Davis, of Grand Central Bakery expressed his intention "to stay where we are" and remain "tight and small." He felt that each city needs its own local bakery like Grand Central, large enough to be effective but small enough to maintain quality and distinctiveness. For other artisans, the reverse is true. They think that high-quality locally distinct products are exactly what should be sold outside the region. These are the very products that will not be devalued by copies or reproductions. Clear Creek Distillery's pear-in-a-bottle brandy is an example of an artisan product that is sold internationally without losing its quality or cache.

For some, Portland's reputation as a place of artisanal production provides marketing leverage for artisanal producers in all sectors. Others fear overselling will diminish Portland's "coolness" factor. The paradox of place also relates to the realization that it would be difficult for artisans to advance their craft and sell their wares without the critical mass of other artisans in Portland, as well as the educated local population that provides a receptive base of supporters. These artisans believe that Portland's reputation is a valuable asset that can mobilize support for products across sectors. In Chapter 6, bike builder Tony Pereira expressed this sentiment: "Portland has the potential (and may be well on its way) to become like a brand of its own within the industry, representing authenticity and quality within the international industry." For artisans like Pereria, making handcrafted products more widely available will only enhance the reputation of Portland as the place of artisan innovation, as well as elevate the status of other Portland-based artisans who are making things happen. This vibe will attract like-minded people to Portland, creating a positive cycle of development adding to the critical mass of artisans within and across industry clusters. Other artisans take a more critical view of Portland's reputation for "coolness." For these artisans, Portland is already being oversold as a region. They believe that hype and boosterism will undermine much that is authentic about Portland and lead to an elitist culture and saturated market of producers.

The global/local paradox is evident in markets for artisan products that are more dependent on sales outside the locality than expected. This paradox is especially present in the substantial use of web-based marketing. Artisans intuitively understand that the internet is more than a new marketing vehicle; it has fundamentally changed the ability of artisans and knowledgeable patrons to build and sustain a community of interest.

Scale and Authenticity

Determining the appropriate scale for an artisan enterprise remains problematic and unsettled as artisans find solutions that work for their product and their values.

Purist artisans remain small because this allows them to maintain autonomy and keep creative control. For these artisans scaling up is not an issue—they want to remain one- or two-person shops, unburdened by the complications of running a business or making a payroll. They desire to remain true to their craft and to those who appreciate what they do. In Chapter 9, music writer S. P. Clarke found this to be true of Portland's indie music scene: "most bands don't want to be on a major label" because "major labels can suck the vitality out of an artist."

Locality artisans are willing to expand within a given location but feel that other places should develop their own artisan enterprises. For example, in Chapter 7, Andrea Pastor of Cellar Door Coffee Roasters envisions their business growing only enough to provide "reasonable livelihood for ourselves and our employees." She and her partner Jeremy Adams believe that small scale roasters like themselves will emerge to fill the needs in other places.

Custom-stock artisans produce some handmade items in volume as well as one-of-kind specialty orders. They will grow sufficiently to meet demand but will not get so large as to lose touch with their artisan roots. Sacha White's company, Vanilla Bicycles, is an example of this approach. In 2007 they introduced the Speedvagen line of bikes. These cyclocross bikes are handmade and fitted for each customer, but they share basic design, materials, and paint job.

Scale-to-market artisans are willing to scale up and distribute their product as widely as possible as long as they can continue to create a craft-based, quality product. Widmer Brothers Brewing Company and Stumptown Coffee Roasters are both examples of this approach. Widmer, now considered a regional rather than local brewer, has entered into an agreement with corporate giant InBev to distribute its product nationwide. Stumptown Coffee Roasters has five locations in Portland, two in Seattle, and another in Brooklyn, New York. As Stumptown general manager Matt Lounsbury commented in Chapter 7, scaling up should not compromise quality: "We'll continue to do what we're really good at, which is roasting coffee for people and getting it to them within a day."

Lessons learned

ONE OF THE THINGS I have enjoyed most about this project is that student researchers took the idealized model of the artisan economy presented in Chapter 2, tested it in the field, and then honestly wrote about what they found. The stories presented in the chapters substituted real knowledge for abstract conceptions. As the material in this chapter shows, what they found was generally supportive of what we expected, but there were a few surprises, such as (a) artisans' awareness of the importance of social wealth and the role of collective actions and public decisions in creating it, (b) the importance of non-local sales and the role of the internet as a new marketplace, and (c) the multiple ways that artisans are resolving the issue of autonomy, locality, and scale.

While the results were supportive, it was refreshing and telling that the chapter authors also presented contrarian views, such as when Langlitz Leathers manager Dave Hansen dismissed ethical concerns about leather production and rejected the term artisan as more suitable to amateurs and hobbyists. I am reassured that chapter authors were not subverting the responses to make the data fit the theory.

Having said that, it is obvious that the research was not "objective" in the traditional sense. Far from it: researchers were interested in the people and their topic, and they framed their questions around a set of predispositions about how the world was organized. This, of course, is the reality of all research. You begin with what you think is important, gather the data, and try to extract some meaning from it. In the end, the chapter authors took the concepts and responses, played with them and challenged them, expanded them, and ultimately enriched us with the details and paradoxes of artisan work and life.

Chapter 19
Artisan Production
and Economic Development

Charles Heying

In this chapter, I recommend actions that can be taken to support an artisan economy. These recommendations flow from the lessons learned in the field about how artisans work and what they value. Many of the recommendations relate to issues specific to Portland, but they should also have general relevance.

Recommendation #1:
The artisan economy is just beginning; imagine other applications.

In 1997, when the internet was still in its infancy, my neighbor, an itinerant cellist who played in Baroque orchestras in Portland, Seattle, and San Francisco, became the u.s. distributor for Aquila, an Italian company that makes gut strings for fine instruments. He was your typical starving artist in need of money. He thought that creating a marketing website would allow him to connect to those musicians who were rediscovering the beauty of handmade gut strings. So he built a basic website, and his business was born.

A year later, I was looking for some shoestrings. Surprisingly, they are difficult to find. The markup is so slim that even shoe repair shops carry only limited stock. Then it hit me: gut strings, shoestrings, why not create a website that would offer unlimited varieties of shoestrings? It would be a perfect second job for an underpaid academic: minimal startup costs, flexible hours, off-the-shelf office technology, and shipping costs the price of a stamp and envelope.

I lost track of my neighbor when we moved, but recently I googled "gut strings Portland," and there was his website.[1] It's not fancy, but he remains the sole U.S. distributor of Aquila strings and still plays in Baroque orchestras. Obviously, it became a nifty side business for him. Unfortunately, I did not follow through on the shoestring idea. But someone else did. In 1999, Peas and Corn Company, a family-owned business in Glennville, Georgia, known for its specialty gift items like Reed Rocket Nutcrackers, Haws Watering Cans and thousand-dollar, custom-made knives, branched out to create ShoeLacesExpress.[2] Which one of the sons, daughters, or in-laws whose pictures grace the website thought of the idea, I don't know. But in the words of Arlo Guthrie, "you can get anything you want" at ShoeLacesExpress.

Having established my ability to spot opportunity, I am going to let you in on my next big idea—Bikes and Bounty Bank. You heard it here first. Bikes and Bounty Bank (more likely a credit union, but that lacked alliteration) is a financial service provider focused on the particular needs of cyclists and foodies. Need a loan for a bike? Bikes and Bounty is the place to go. Want to expand your vegan strip club (yes, Portland does have one)? Bikes and Bounty will go over your business and marketing plans and help you get the money you need. Looking for special discounts on cycling tours or nursery products? Bikes and Bounty has them. Need to know if AAA offers roadside assistance for cyclists? Bikes and Bounty will help you find out. Want your savings to be used by like-minded people who will build a stronger, more resilient local economy? Bikes and Bounty is the place to put your money.

Community banks and credit unions have been the one bright spot in the dismal banking fiasco. Perhaps they are just "too small to fail," but more likely they are too close to their members to take outrageous risks with their money. They tailor their business to the needs of their community, emphasizing hands-on, personalized service. In essence, they are the craft brew of the financial industry. While the total number of banks in the United States is declining because of consolidation, 648 new community banks have been created since 2005, including ninety-eight in 2008.[3] It is probably not coincidental that the resurgence of community banks is occurring simultaneously with large bank mergers. Since the big consolidations that have swept up regional banks, patrons have left in droves. For example, in 1997, when Wells Fargo bought out First Interstate and started charging fees to use a personal teller, it lost $9 billion in deposits.[4] Some of this money went to community banks and credit unions. But it seems the big banks hardly noticed, as the real money was not in providing personal service to small depositors, but in dealing in exotic financial instruments like derivatives and credit default swaps. We are all living with the consequences of that choice.

Bikes and Bounty represents a logical next step in the progression from geographically based community banks or credit unions to artisan enterprises that focus on the needs of particular communities of interest, like cyclists and foodies. It's another one of those back-to-the-future ideas. Recall that many financial institutions were created to serve special interest communities like religious or ethnic groups. Bank of America, for example, began as Bank of Italy, making loans to working-class Italians from San Francisco's North Beach neighborhood.[5]

The purpose of these stories is to suggest that we are just in the beginning of the artisan revolution. Ideas like this are everywhere. Clive Thompson of *Wired* magazine imagines "a one-of-a-kind revolution" where customized products are a click away.[6] He highlights the growth of sites like Etsy and the Instructables and imagines that programmable machines, like 3D laser cutters, will enable artisans to build all sorts of one-off products. If it were not for what we have seen in Portland's artisan sector, it would seem like science fiction. But with a little imagination, it is possible to conceptualize an artisan enterprise in even the most unexpected sectors, like gut strings, shoelaces, or financial services.

Recommendation #2:
Don't let economists design your economic development strategy.

I like economists—sometimes they say good things. But if you want an economy that looks more like an artisan economy, they are probably not the best choice to design your economic development strategy. Why? Because they are more likely to have disciplinary blinders that prevent them from seeing what is changing. For one, they are trained to use data that comes from sources that were designed to measure things that were important to an industrial economy, like standard industrial classifications and gross domestic product. And they focus on things like growth and jobs, concepts that are artifacts of an industrial economy, at least the way they are presently understood. Economic terminology also frames their worldview. Things like environmental impacts are described as "externalities," as if the economy operates in some abstract world and its connection to the physical world is tangential, even accidental. Pollution and resource depletion seem to come as a surprise to economists, something akin to "collateral damage." Likewise, the idea of wealth is bounded by what can be measured—money, privilege, and possessions—in order to compare individuals or economies.

One of the interesting discoveries from this research is that people can live on less as long as they live in a community with lots of "social wealth," including protected natural environments, affordable alternative transportation, lower-cost housing and retail spaces, a thriving public and cultural life, collaborative groups of artisans that share knowledge and resources, and a cluster of artisan-friendly, home-grown employers like Powell's, Stumptown, Grand Central, and New Seasons. Economists do not usually focus on creating "social wealth," because that runs counter to their disciplinary predisposition to maximize individual wealth and their nearly exclusive focus on flows of goods and services in the money economy. And when economists do consider something akin to "social wealth," it is usually framed as a vehicle for local exploitation, as in the "high-amenity city" that will attract high-income professionals and high-spending tourists. The idea that wealth is something that doesn't necessarily come from money and income, but is something that might come from mastering a craft, finding a manageable scale for your enterprise, and generally living a communally focused and engaged life, is not something they are likely to have learned.

It is unfair, of course, to single out economists for this critique. I could as easily include politicians, economic development professionals who are often urban planners, most of the private sector who depend on economic growth to create markets for new products, and all of the rest of us who clamor for better paychecks. When you really think about transitioning from an industrial economy to an artisan economy, the implications are challenging. At the very least, the concept of having a "steady job" working for a "stable institution" becomes problematic. But as many of us are realizing in the current economic downturn, that reality was a house of cards that has come crashing down around us in spite of our best efforts to prop it up. So it may be sensible to check out those who are testing alternative ways of working and living to get a sense of how we will find our way in the new reality.

So this is my recommendation: if you are looking for someone to direct your economic development efforts, consider hiring someone from Free Geek or City Repair or someone who helped start a farmers' market. These folks are schooled in the art of creating social wealth. Someone who initiated the transition from supermarkets to farmers' markets intuitively understands that economists are missing something when they say "[n]o state or metropolitan area can reasonably expect to expand its economy by developing a higher than average concentration of grocery stores."[7] They understand that adding more of the same will not do much for a community, but creating a new way for producers and patrons to interact will add value to a community. Economists' dismissal of the value of innovation in the non-traded sector seems to miss something fundamental about the multiple dimensions of innovation. Disruptive soft technologies like farmers' markets change the whole set of relationships that have been narrowly conceived as the one-dimensional act called "grocery shopping." Not only does a farmers' market provide a more diverse array of fresh produce, shorten chains of accountability, and reduce carbon footprint by shortening food miles, it also creates a new social space, changing the utilitarian act of shopping to something more like a social event, involving fun, education, and relationship-building.

That's the genius of wealth-building in an artisan economy, and the artisans that helped create Portland Farmers Market or Free Geek or City Repair understand that sort of alternative approach to city-building. Of course, if by some strange circumstance, an artisan was actually hired by the city's economic development agency, it might be a struggle for both the artisan and the agency, but the result could be surprising and transformative for both.

Recommendation #3:
The next big thing may be small.

Fifteen years ago, who would have predicted that craft brewers would be popping up in every little town in the country? My nephew, who is heading off to brewing school in Chicago, got his first break interning for Hub City

Brewing, located five miles outside of Oelwein, Iowa.[8] Oelwein is not exactly the heart of the artisan economy. Its population, currently numbering 6,129, is 7 percent smaller than it was in 2000.[9] But there's Hub City, a profitable and growing artisan enterprise, where you can take a pint of Oatmeal Stout, sit down in the middle of five hundred acres of tall corn, and take in the wonder of it all.

For those interested in creating the perpetually expanding economy, the idea that something would start small and only grow as much as necessary doesn't make sense and is certainly of little interest. From a traditional economic perspective, the notion of appropriate scale violates the truism that all enterprises must continuously grow or die. If an enterprise does not scale up, it's inevitable, logical, and efficient for some other more aggressive firm to take it over. And for the economic development professional, it is imperative that the triumphant firm be located in their fair city and not somewhere else. How very different is the attitude of the artisan firm, where you start small and get big enough to make it, and then let everyone else do the same thing wherever they are.

Strangely enough, given the reputation of artisan products for higher prices relative to mass-produced products, we heard comments from some artisans that handmade is not necessarily more expensive. Two reasons were mentioned. First, new low-cost information and production technologies help level the playing field and reduce advantages of scale. The second and related reason is that workers in artisan enterprises carry a lot fewer people on their backs than a traditional, large-scale enterprise where the worker on the shop floor is supporting high-paid management, expensive marketing, increasingly expensive shipping costs, and demanding shareholders, all of whom get their money before the worker does. Perhaps economies of scale are being rebalanced in favor of a thousand micro-enterprises doing their own thing in their own place. If that is the case, economic development strategies should be focused on helping support emerging artisan enterprises and helping them find an appropriate scale of operation.

Having made the case that appropriately scaled operations may be the way to go, I should recognize that this is one of those situations lamented by Benjamin Franklin as "the murder of a beautiful theory by a gang of brutal facts." We discovered in our research that the issue of scale is unsettled and problematic for artisans. The trade-offs described were complex: scale up but keep quality, scale up to locality but let other locations do their own thing, scale up to fit a specialty market that may be a mix of local and non-local buyers, don't scale up at all because it will undermine the artisanal value of the product. The one common idea coming out of these various responses is that the universal truism that advantages of scale trump every-thing is no longer true. So I stand by my recommendation that the next big thing may be small.

Recommendation #4:
Don't try to be cool if you're not.

Economic development professionals are hired to create jobs. They run with the pack. Whatever is hot, that's what they do. Richard Florida's cre-ative class idea is the current craze, and using the arts to stimulate the economy by attracting tourists is right up there. But trying to entice young creatives to your community or transforming the arts into vehicles for the tourist trade will not produce the long-term results desired by city leaders. Remember the story of Milwaukee, recounted in Chapter 1, where the city attempted to market its cool as a means of attracting young people back to the city.[10] The results were unspectacular and the reasons are obvious to any geek who has ever tried a similar strategy. Don't try to be something you are not. If you are an older industrial city, take stock of what you have and work with that. If there are some locals with good ideas, and they need a little help, check them out. Be like a prudent banker. Look at their track record, evaluate their risk, and give them a chance. Some will fail, but just the idea that you want to grow from within, that you trust your instincts and theirs and aren't relying on some outside guru that has the next big idea, may send a message that you are really interested in local talent. That message will be heard by young, creative people, and that may be enough to get them to stick around.

Artisans don't want fake cool. They are interested in those who are interested in what they do and will help them through the thicket to make a go of it. Yes, they have crazy ideas, and no, they don't have the foggiest notion how to start and run a business, but no one does at age twenty-five. Give them some advice; help them out; stick with them when they make mistakes. Who knows what amazing things might happen?

Recommendation #5:
Transformative ideas are devalued when they are oversold.

The idea of redirecting our economy toward self-reliance and sustainability is sound and necessary. There are many Portland artisans and enterprises that take these ideas seriously and are doing creative things to construct a society that minimizes its ecological impact by seeking abundance without exploitation. Unfortunately, sustainability is being transformed into another means for urban boosterism. When I hear that Portland decision-makers want the city to be the leader in sustainability, I am ready to help fashion designer Adam Arnold "strangle them with a sustainable rope." Why do we want to be the best, the first, the leader? If we have something to offer other than hype, we should be focusing on how we can share that with other communities so that they can take the lead in their own backyards. That is what we see happening in Portland's artisan economy: an open, collaborative approach where knowledge is freely shared and everyone is encouraged to pursue their own creative ideas. Why does the sustainability community seem caught up in trying to produce signature "firsts," such as an overly costly building that has all the green bells and whistles, or a supposedly cutting-edge sustainability program at a university? We should dial down the rhetoric of avarice and boosterism and dial up the discussion of the challenges of living sustainably. Hearing green economy projects promoted as the first, biggest, and best seems incongruous, like putting a green face on the pro-growth economy.

Recommendation #6:
Integrating hands, head, and heart is the best long-term strategy for supporting the transition to an artisan economy.

Remember the little buzz that seems to be happening about doing things by hand? To understand the incredible viability and creativity of the artisan economy, I would recommend that we explore that idea more. Richard Sennett's book *The Craftsman* is a place to start.[11] When the hands work, the brain works. When you get in there and do things, so many possibilities open up. We need to redesign institutions in ways that allow doing and thinking to become one again. People need to get down to the shop floor, get their hands dirty, and start making things. The Free Geek model described in Chapter 12 is an inspiring example. Open up those black boxes, change them from mysterious machines into helpful tools; mix and match, cobble and create until you feel like you're the master, not the servant. It's a metaphor for how the artisan economy works: creative, improvisational, and handmade. Every school kid should have some time at Free Geek. What better way to make science into a craft than to take things apart and put them back together again? If you want kids who love science, who think of science as something to be used to make useful things, then start with things they can manipulate with their hands. Of course, this isn't something new, and it's a long-term strategy for economic development, but young people schooled in the integration of hands, head, and heart, who combine a passion for knowing with respect for the sacredness of the things they touch, are likely to be the makers of a new economy.

Recommendation #7:
Don't fix it—you will only make it worse.

Gentrification is not inevitable, but to stop it we must resist our tendency to turn every neighborhood in this city into a clean, comfy, well-mannered place. Grunge is good; it keeps the rents low and yuppies out. This is probably the hardest lesson to learn. Portland has been lucky; we retained so many mixed-class neighborhoods with good housing stock and still-functioning business districts that artisans who have been priced out of one neighborhood can soon find another. But we may have run out our string. When the last neighborhood gets settled by its very own coffee shop, brewpub, funky art gallery, organic food co-op, and guerilla-radio-station-turned-music-label, we know that the frontier is at an end. Cute storefronts, new sidewalks, curb bump-outs, and neo-traditional street benches will soon follow. Somehow, we need to keep the entrepreneurs from sucking up Stark's Vacuums and spinning off another Bike Gallery, and the urban planners from making things too nice. I am hopeful that artisans are thinking about ways they can keep from spoiling their nest, but it's going to be tough. They do all these cute things and everyone wants to be where they are.

Recommendation #8:
Don't import bad ideas when we can grow our own.

There is something so wrong with this recommendation that it just seems right. Here is the situation. The Portland Trail Blazers hired a big-name eastern developer to revive the moribund Rose Quarter where the Blazers play their games. The bold, new idea is to create an "entertainment district" that will draw crowds from around the metropolitan area to brand name venues like ESPN Zone and the Hard Rock Café.[12] If you really believe this is a bold, new idea, try googling "entertainment district hard rock café" and follow the geography of your hits. The Rolling Stones have headlined in fewer cities than that.

Portland delegations have already been taking junkets to places like Kansas City to see their spiffy new Power & Light District, designed by the same developer. They were impressed—it all seemed so glitzy and upbeat. But behind the Power & Light is the dark shadow of underperformance. With nearly 30 percent of the project vacant and sales tax revenues 84 percent lower than projections, the city is $7 to $10 million short of revenues in just the first year. How many more subsidies from the city's general fund will it take to retire the $295 million in bonds that funded infrastructure and other costs? What streets won't be fixed? How many police officers will be laid off to make up for those lost revenues?

Sounds like a cautionary tale, but Portland Mayor Sam Adams and the Blazers seem undeterred. Both are pushing to use urban renewal funds to support the entertainment district concept. Worse, the mayor would like to link the Rose Quarter redevelopment to building a nearby convention center hotel, an idea whose economic viability is so questionable that every one of Portland's city, county, and metro governments has punted on it.[13] As with all these deals, the back-hall negotiations are even more complicated, involving bringing major league soccer to Portland and finding a new home for the Portland Beavers minor-league baseball team, but that is not the point. The point is that this is really old school. Barry Johnson, arts editor for the *Oregonian*, was on target with his analysis of the failure of this mindset in light of Portland's culture. Here is what he said:

> Last week, I was arguing with a colleague about the series of Major Projects that Mayor Adams has proposed or supported, including the entertainment district. At the end of our

discussion, exasperated at my denseness, he hotly asserted, "The White Eagle isn't the future!"

He is dead wrong.

Our future does rest with the White Eagle—and all of our other small clubs, restaurants, and bars. It depends on all the small businesses along Hawthorne, Alberta, Mississippi and every one of the city's working neighborhoods. And on our artists, of course, and the little creative-economy shops that design sailboards, shoes, dresses, trumpets, advertising campaigns, computer games and thousands of other things. The city's policies should encourage these activities, not harm them.[14]

Johnson expresses two equally dismal outcomes for the entertainment district. If it succeeds, it hurts the existing club scene; if it fails, taxpayer investment is wasted. The city should be paying Johnson good money for his profound insights. Instead they will probably pay an outside consultant to tell them what they want to hear. In any case, the politics of the deal will determine the outcome, not the analytics of the situation.

There just seems to be something needy about politicians who push big projects so they can claim credit for making things happen. Former Mayor Potter took a beating from the media for his failure to articulate his big vision for the city. Instead, he supported a citizen-led visioning project that, for all its organizational faults and delays, assembled the responses from thirteen thousand Portlanders who took the time to tell them what sort of city they wanted by 2030. Having read the summary from the *VisionPDX Input Report*, what I found remarkable was the absence of a single statement that identified the need for a new sports stadium, entertainment district, or a bigger convention center, or anything that even suggested that these were important icons of city identity.[15] What was in the report was a desire for vibrant neighborhoods, locally owned small businesses, economic equity, and sustainability. What came out of the community-visioning project was a call to action and a pilot project called the Vision Into Action Coalition Grant program.[16] This small grant program, which funded eighteen community projects in its first two years of existence, is a model of how to really help at the grassroots level. The program was very well run, extremely fair, and stimulated so much creative thinking that its effects will be felt for many years.[17] But the Vision

Into Action Coalition Grant program has since been cut from the city budget. I read its demise in the expressions of City Commissioners who listened politely but unresponsively while recipients pleaded for its continuance.

The deal to fund the boilerplate entertainment district has a long way to go, but with the big-money Blazers behind it and a pot of urban renewal money ready to use, it will probably happen. But what a wrong turn that would be. Perhaps my recommendation was correct after all. Why import bad ideas when we can grow our own?

Recommendation #9:
Do more, do less, do nothing, do something different.

Do more: The Portland Development Commission should do more of the good things it's doing. For example, it helped both the bicycle-frame makers and the distilled-spirits artisans form organizations to support and promote their crafts. In addition, it was instrumental in creating a fine display of handmade frames at the Portland International Airport. As the PDC staff and commissioners rethink their development strategy, they seem to be exploring ways to support the artisan sector. I urge them to continue exploring these alternatives.

Our research revealed some good examples of governments taking actions that were critical in helping alternatives get started. For example, the 1971 Oregon Bicycle Bill, which set aside 1 percent of state transportation funding to be used to promote bike and pedestrian alternatives, was important in stimulating Portland's bike culture and ultimately in preparing the ground for the handmade bike industry. Targeted efforts like this are helpful.

The creation of Portland's Office of Sustainable Development (OSD)[18] was instrumental in creating a focal point and providing legitimization for the many private and nonprofit efforts that have been emerging from citizen activists and entrepreneurs around sustainable development. While it is difficult to trace the lineage of the greening of building and zoning codes and other efforts such as procurement decisions, it is safe to say the OSD helped move these along.

The City has also been very supportive of creating spaces for community gardens, farmers' markets, craft markets, and food carts, as well as providing and maintaining safe and beautiful public parks. It provided Target Area Grants for business district renewals that were important first steps in the revival of many neighborhoods. It has continued to support and fund its neighborhood association system. These are only a few of the many positive examples of helpful government initiatives that we should see more of.

Do less: Our research provided numerous examples of the public sector responding to citizen initiatives to reduce fees or regulatory barriers. For example, changing laws relating to the production and distribution of liquor made it possible for brewpubs to operate legally. Brewpubs were an important innovation leading to the development of the craft-brewing industry. Lowering the cost of distilling permits has definitely lowered the barriers of entry for artisan distillers. A number of artisans remarked on the willingness of the city to be lenient in ways that help small enterprises—for example, not requiring business permits unless revenues reached a certain level, or permitting artisans to display work on sidewalks. In most of the gray areas of code enforcement, the city seems to want to make things work for small-scale enterprises rather than throw regulatory roadblocks in their way.

Public officials have regulatory roles that are critically important but that sometimes seem arcane and unnecessary to people who just want to get things done. When these regulations are important for public health and safety, they should be retained. But when they do little more than protect special interests, are residuals of values of a different era, or are artifacts from times when technology was different, government should be willing to stand aside and make adjustments. From what most artisans told us, Portland seems to have found a good balance between their responsibilities and their desire to encourage artisan enterprises. Sometimes less is more.

Do nothing: The case studies in this book demonstrate that much of the growth of the artisan sector occurred without the direct intervention, stimulation, or support of the public sector. This could be an argument for doing nothing. Certainly, the economic-development literature has struggled with the issue of the costs and benefits of government subsidies. The bulk of the current research on subsidies that are intended to get industry to relocate to a state or region suggests several types of problems. First, there is little evidence that the things that government provides—such as tax breaks, land assembly, job training, and outright subsidies—are critical factors in the decisions to locate a facility. Second, governments are caught in a competitive race that makes them spend more than they get. This is the pay-to-play dilemma. If governments don't get in the game, they have no chance to land the company. If they do get in the game, they will be forced to promise more direct and indirect support than the jobs will return. Third, the attempt to hold companies to agreements that link the creation of jobs to investments are seldom enforced. If the company underperforms or leaves, governments rarely attempt to enforce agreements because they don't want to reveal the cost of their subsidies or create the sense that they are anti-business. Besides, it is very costly and difficult to enforce contracts that are little more than statements agreeing to make good-faith efforts.

Finally, there is the problem of misdirected investments. For example, previous studies on investments by Olympic cities, some that I co-authored,[19] show that: consultants hired prior to games consistently overestimate the benefits; that the real public costs, especially for infrastructure and security, are often hidden; that the private interests who control Olympic organizing committees direct public investments to projects that distort long-term planning goals for the city; and that venues built for the Olympics frequently have maintenance costs that cannot be sustained. The list of Olympic stadiums that fail to attract sufficient events to be viable is long indeed, and the transportation projects that lead to nowhere is legendary.

Should government do nothing? I am inclined to agree that it should do nothing when it comes to trying to catch the big fish that everyone is fishing for. The convention center hotel is a case in point. To compete with other cities for convention and tourist revenue, every city decided to build a huge convention center, so they all went out and built one. Now they can't sustain them because everyone is competing for the same pool of large national conventions. The response to this problem has not been to step back and rethink the convention-center strategy. No, the response has been to up the ante by building an expensive convention center hotel. Cities have been encouraged to do this by consultants who argue that conventioneers want their hotel, entertainment, and convention hall close and convenient. Of course, these same consultants are telling every city exactly the same thing, creating the equivalent of a convention-business arms race. The results are remarkably similar for everyone: underperforming convention centers and underutilized hotel space.[20]

The alternative to thinking big is to think local. This research has shown an abundance of local, regional, and even international conventions that are bubbling up from Portland's artisan economy, like the North American Handmade Bicycle Show, Portland Zine Symposium, Platform International Animation Festival, Stumptown Comic Fest, Open Source Bridge Conference, Northwest Handmade Instrument Show, Oregon Potters Association Ceramic Showcase, and Wordstock, to name a few. It would seem that a good use of public funds would be to support local groups that sponsor and stage these important events. That investment would be wiser and more productive than building an unneeded convention center hotel or boilerplate entertainment district.

The alternative to investing in hard infrastructure is to invest in soft infrastructure: conventioneers will venture out of the tourist bubble and into the real city if given a little help. Why not subsidize a concierge-like service, or provide a local guide who could direct conventioneers to the great food and entertainment that already exists in the city, and why not give conventioneers a break on cab fare or a shuttle to get them there? Compared to backfilling payments on millions of dollars in revenue bonds for underperforming investments, this would seem like quite a bargain.

Do something different: The Portland Development Commission (PDC) should scale back on using its primary tool of urban renewal and consider developing a new set of tools more appropriate to twenty-first-century Portland. Urban renewal works like this: The PDC determines an area is "blighted." Once this designation is made, the PDC sells bonds to finance needed improvements, primarily infrastructure, that will encourage new private investment. The PDC pays off the bonds by capturing the new taxes that are generated by the new investments. It doesn't get all the property-tax revenue from an urban renewal district, only the taxes that come from the increased value created by the new investments. In theory, when the bonds are paid off, all of the taxes, including those from the higher valued properties, would go to the general fund and everyone would benefit. Then, paying for the schools, streets, parks, public safety would be less burdensome for everyone, because taxes from the higher-value properties would help carry the costs of urban services.

The problem with the theory is that it hasn't worked out that way. In the long history of urban renewal in Portland, almost none of the extra taxes from the improved properties have been returned to the general fund. In practice, these revenues are captured by existing urban renewal districts for even more improvement projects, or they go to fund the activities of the PDC. Essentially, urban renewal areas are allowed to reinvest in themselves while the rest of the city pays for a greater share of citywide public services than they should. It is unfair, and it reduces the revenues available for public services generally.

Portland should consider whether we really need more development. Is there a neighborhood left that wants to have the long arm of the PDC come in and make them into another Pearl District? Perhaps there are places that could use a scaled-back version of urban renewal, but I think there is growing sentiment in the city that we need less upscale development and more affordable housing, more funding for schools, more after-school programs, improved summer parks programs, more small grants for civic organizations and nonprofits, and more support for the many inventive and humane ideas that are just waiting to blossom.[21]

Cities and economic development agencies seem caught in structural traps. First, it's hard for them to escape the treadmill of growth and increased demand for urban services. The demand for better services requires more tax revenues, and the most painless way to get these is to build up the city. Unfortunately, more growth increases demand for services, and the treadmill keeps spinning. The second trap is that the tools available to cities and development agencies, such as property tax policy, land assembly, transportation planning, code enforcement, and bonding authority, are mostly connected to the physical aspects of the city.

Together, the treadmill and the tools push cities toward an interest in physical growth and development. Add to this the need of political leaders to take credit for highly visible projects, and the fact that those private sector actors who are involved in physical development of the city are also the ones most attentive to city politics, and you have a situation where all the tendencies are toward building high-value hard infrastructure. That is why sports stadiums, entertainment districts, convention centers, and urban renewal projects are so enticing. And that is why thinking in terms of soft infrastructure, such as more funding for school programs and affordable housing subsidies, small grant programs for grassroots efforts, summer parks, jobs programs, and increased funding for neighborhood associations, are a much harder sell to urban leaders. The message from our research is fairly clear: an affordable city with a lot of social wealth and soft infrastructure support is a city that will be attractive to artisans. An overdeveloped city of upscale neighborhoods with high rental costs, where public funding is not available for people-oriented programs, is not a place that artisans will be attracted to. The take-away message for economic development? Do something different.

CHAPTER 20
CONCLUSION

Charles Heying

"FURTHUR"

WHEN KEN KESEY got on his bus he was not particularly concerned about where it was going, but he was certain of its direction—Furthur.[1] So too, this project has taken us further than we expected, but in the direction we intended. Along the way, we learned enough to provide tentative answers to the three questions we posed at the outset, and to offer some insight as to what directions we should go in the future.

"Is Portland a frontier in the transformation of urban economies or a cultural anomaly representing a romantic, populist turn away from the global?" This was the first of three questions we asked in the introduction to this book. I can now conclude with certainty that the answer is yes and no. Portland is a cultural anomaly, but also a frontier. In *Better Together*, a book by Robert Putnam (who popularized the concept of social capital), Portland is described as an outlier, but in a good sense. Unlike nearly all other cities where the measures of civic engagement have declined over the last sixty years, Portland has experienced "a positive epidemic of civic engagement."[2] But Portland is a trendsetter in other, more negative ways. As this book is being written, Portland is experiencing the second-highest unemployment rate in the country. The higher numbers of young people moving here explain some of this, but not all. While Portland has a strong technology sector anchored by Intel, it has a weak bench of corporate headquarters.

The Minneapolis/St. Paul metropolitan region, with a population only 50 percent larger than the Portland region, has eighteen Fortune 500 companies. Portland has two. One of those, Nike, has no production facilities in Portland and none even in the United States. Portland is also a city where all of its homegrown banks, utilities, and corporations (save two) have been bought out by bigger rivals. As a result, Portland has a thin cadre of corporate leaders who involve themselves in civic affairs and philanthropy, leaving a community with very shallow pockets.

Perhaps the absence of elite leadership and Portland's backwater status as a branch-plant city has been its salvation. Citizens have come forward to fill the breach, and artisans have been forced to build a homegrown, self-sustaining economy. Something, other than job opportunities, continues to attract young people to the community. As Connor Dougherty reported in his *Wall Street Journal* feature on youth-magnet cities, "Portland has attracted college-educated, single people between the ages of twenty-five and thirty-nine at a higher rate than most other cities in the country. Only four other metropolitan areas had a higher ratio. Now the jobs are drying up, but the people are still coming."[3] These young people may be romantics, and they may lean toward a freewheeling populism, but they also are more likely to lean toward a future that is coming than the past that is fading. This book has provided numerous case studies of how that future, in the form of an artisan economy, is becoming a reality and changing how people work and live. So the answer is yes, Portland is a cultural anomaly, but it is also frontier in the transformation of urban economies.

The second question was this: "Is artisan production limited to a narrow range of expensive, high-end retail products, or are we observing a broader shift from homogeneous, mass-produced, mass-marketed products to hand-crafted, limited production products that engender a more personal relationship between producer and patron?" The answer is yes to the latter. We are observing a broader shift away from mass production and consumption and toward artisan goods purchased by more engaged and attentive buyers. In Portland, artisan products are widely available, and while they generally cost more, they are not inaccessible. In some cases, it may be that price differences are more a matter of perception than reality and reflect the fact that people are buying something that is more than a utilitarian product. The higher price for the artisan product represents an assurance of humane labor and safe practices, support for local producers who give back to the community in ways that distant corporations do not, and a more complex appreciation and enjoyment of the product. Paying a little bit more for these extra qualities indicates that the buyer has made a conscious decision to pay for a product that returns a higher value for cost. If that means the buyer decides to spend more on better food and make up the difference by riding a bike rather than buying a car, that is a rational trade-off to encourage a change in patterns of living that, in the end, are less expensive and produce a broader, more equitably distributed wealth.

The third question is one that we have considerable evidence to support, at least in Portland. Yes, "the artisan economy is part of a seismic shift in how we do things," and yes, "this transformation is grounded in a larger moral shift in values toward local, sustainable, self-reliant systems of making and using." The evidence from the case studies shows that artisans and Portlanders are attuned to the moral implications of their making and buying decisions. A cultural shift is taking place—one that has broad support.

MORE

IN RESEARCHING AND WRITING this book, I was surprised to find myself reconnecting to my previous research on Olympic cities. The research that Greg Andranovich, Matt Burbank, and I published about the process of bidding and preparing for the Olympics left us with a deeper knowledge of how elite interests drive the growth agenda in Olympic cities: who bears the costs, and who secures the benefits of these mega-event strategies. I have come away from that research profoundly skeptical that the best interests of citizens are served, and this research has confirmed that there is an alternative approach to urban development. Instead of the overblown spectacle of an international mega-event that displaces people and priorities, Portland has been creating an avalanche of homegrown mini-events, such as film festivals, bridge pedals, and comic fests. Portland has even re-invented the soapbox derby, changing it from a competitive, professionalized race to a wacky downhill scoot off the side of Mt Tabor. Unlike the Olympics, these homegrown events have no outrageous gate fees, no ubiquitous corporate logos, no doping or bidding scandals—just good, local fun that celebrates the local, handmade, and inventive.

This research has also led me to a deeper appreciation of how this research fits with the work of other scholars who have followed parallel lines of inquiry. The work of Shuman[4] and those who promote local sustainable economies finds broad support in this research. Our contribution is to show how "going local" is embedded in the values and actions of artisan enterprises. Lloyd's[5] study of Wicker Park highlighted the importance of the social spaces that were instrumental in sparking the arts and culture revival at that locality. We have provided a more nuanced picture of how social spaces are enacted and have addressed the notion of social wealth as an enabler of what Lloyd calls a neo-bohemian revival.

John C. Scott's[6] work on cultural clusters and the organization of work in the cultural economy was a major touchstone that this study supported. One important contribution of our work was to demonstrate that artisans, because they share values, lifestyles and often move fluidly between sectors, could be treated collectively as a cluster, one that transcends the individual industries that have traditionally been the focus of cluster research. This study also shares with works such as Sennett's *The Craftsman*[7] an emphasis on the integration of hand, head and heart as a way to heal the divisions between the intellectual and manual that were opened up during the ascendancy of industrial capitalism. And while this study has focused more on the production side of artisan work, it is clear that there are overlapping concerns addressed by authors such as Zukin,[8] who have examined "spaces of consumption." Obviously the questions are related, and this is an area that should be pursued.

There can be no escaping reference to Richard Florida and his creative-class thesis[9]; anyone who reads both works will discover common themes. However, there is a significant difference between what we recommend to support an artisan economy and the approach that Florida has taken to promote his creative-class thesis. We don't believe that cities should make cosmetic changes in order to make themselves more attractive to a narrow cadre of young well-educated people. Nor do we believe that attracting the so-called creative class is a panacea for economic revival. This one-size-fits-all mentality is the antithesis of an artisan approach to building with what you have and to close attention to locality, distinctiveness, and authenticity. Doing an extreme makeover of every city into a hive of youthful tolerance and hipness is the equivalent of biker shorts on a Sunday cyclist. I believe that the recommendations presented in our chapter on economic development are most compatible with those offered by Landry and Bianchi[10] and their creative-cities approach. Their basic lesson of providing support for initiatives that come from the grassroots resonates with what we have concluded. Having said that, I am not particularly enthused with Landry's tool-kit approach.[11] From my perspective, a more Zen-like approach is required: develop a right attitude, and the actions will follow.

A good place for Portlanders to find out what ideas have been bubbling up from the grassroots is to read the series of statements and reports that came from the Vision PDX process. Of course, the process of aggregating the responses has led to some statements that seem bland and generic, but if you read beyond that, you will discover what is meaningful to the people of Portland. I was particularly impressed with the energy and effort that led to the successful incorporation of a diversity of voices beyond those who usually participate in visioning exercises. So, look beyond the occasional generalities, and you will discover a rich tapestry of local knowledge and common-sense directions for the community.

BEYOND

THIS BOOK MAY REPRESENT the most thorough examination of artisan enterprises within a city. We looked broadly at artisan work and asked compelling questions of the 118 artisans we interviewed. If this exploratory work is of any value, others will perceive the problems and gaps of our research and will improve on what we have done. One of the areas that is rich with paradox and the promise of compelling research is asking how artisans are engaging the question of place, scale, and authenticity and how the process of scaling up will play out in sectors dominated by global corporations. Our research discovered a spectrum of responses that take us beyond the usual stereotypes of local good, global bad. It is more complex than that. While Budweiser/InBev does not seem like it will soon be displaced by a passel of regional Widmers, it is probably not wise to bet against it. In 2009, we have seen so many giants fall; prediction one way or the other seems risky.

The question of equity is still out there. Proposing a future where the focus shifts from creating jobs to encouraging vocations and from the accumulation of individual wealth to creation of social wealth may sound utopian, especially if your immediate need is a job to put food on the table. But for those who would use the equity issue as a stick to beat up on the artisan economy, I would argue that the current economic arrangement, which has destabilized communities with plant closings, pitted cities and regions against each other in a desperate chase for jobs, and sucked up homegrown industries into corporate monoliths that seem only responsive to the greed of the market for ever-higher returns, has not served the jobless all that well in terms of opportunity, stability, and the distribution of rewards. I guess I am more willing to trust my money to Bikes and Bounty Bank than Goldman Sachs. In these hard times, Bikes and Bounty Bank is not likely to be paying out its average employee the truly obscene amount of $770,000 a year and its higher executives $20 million or more.[12] Artisans may produce products of higher quality and price, but their incomes and attitudes show that they are far from the minions of privilege. So the equity issue is important, and it should be examined more closely, but it should be put in the larger perspective of who is really doing what to whom.

Early in this book, we described the purpose of our project. "First, it is a manifesto for the artisan economy as a path of resistance in a globalizing world, a path that is immediately accessible to individuals and communities who are looking for alternative futures. Second, it is a statement of expectations in a rather conventional research project." The research is completed, and I think we have done what we set out to do. We have argued for the artisan economy as a path of resistance, a way forward to an alternative future. In a more traditional sense we have interviewed artisans and asked them, as honestly as we could, whether this made any sense. We have reported what we found, with the intention of telling stories that would make their interests come alive. We have analyzed the results and presented the case as we saw it. We have offered some suggestions of how cities and citizens can support the move to an artisan economy. We have defended our ideas as well as we could, and now the defense is ready to rest.

Author Biographies

Compelled by experiences around the globe, **Renée Bogin**, MUS, researches concepts of global citizenship at Portland State University, including transnational civil society, alternative globalization movements, and multicultural sustainability.

Tracy Braden is fortunate enough to work as the student services coordinator at the Toulan School of Urban Studies and Planning. She has been in Portland since 2000, loves the city and the people who live there and is so glad to have been able to work on this project.

As a graduate student at Portland State University, **Alison Briggs** studies urban sustainability initiatives. She also coordinates the laptop refurbishment program at the nonprofit organization, Free Geek.

Melissa Cannon grew up in Northern Colorado and moved to Portland to study community development. Her research interests include creating healthy urban communities suitable for the needs of older adults.

Laura Cesafsky is completing a master's in urban studies at Portland State University. She enjoys bicycling around and indulging in the fruits of Portland's artisan economy where a grad school budget permits.

Shanna Eller is the Director of Community Environmental Services at Portland State University where she received her doctorate in urban studies in 2008.

Amanda Hess is a recent and happy transplant to Portland from Minnesota. She works in public policy at the Coalition for a Livable Future and aspires to better understand technology and craft-bicycle-churned ice cream.

Charles Heying is an associate professor of urban studies and planning at Portland State University. He has co-authored a book and numerous articles on the politics and development of Olympic cities. He fondly remembers his college days when he made the connection between his summer job and his artisan inclinations by building two electric guitars—a six-string from a shovel and a twelve-string from a pick—and formed his first band, Picks and Shovels.

Talia Jacobson completed her master's in urban and regional planning at Portland State University in 2009, specializing in transportation. She is cultivating the art of biking with large quantities of library books and groceries.

Lauren Larin is a doctoral student in urban studies at Portland State University. Her spare moments are filled tending her organic vegetable garden and cooking the harvest.

Born and reared a Portlander, **Serenity Madrone** graduated from Portland State with a bachelor's degree in community development and self-publishes zines of her art and poetry.

Lured by rain, coffee, fanzines, beer, and indie rock, **Moriah McSharry McGrath** moved to Portland in 2006. She researched artisan distilling as a doctoral student at Portland State University.

Rebecca Ragin is a professional writer whose work has been published in magazines such as *EatingWell*, *Natural Home*, and *Northwest Palate*, among others.

Josh Roll graduated from Portland State University with a master's degree in urban studies. He currently resides in Portland but works for Lane Council of Governments in Eugene doing land use and transportation planning. When not planning urban areas, Josh can be found on a local pitch with his rugby team, the Portland Rugby Club.

Marianne Ryder is an artist, researcher, and writer who spends too much time wondering how the world works. Currently an urban studies doctoral student at Portland State University, Ryder is studying community development and the role of artists in community building.

Oliver Smith is a doctoral student in urban studies at Portland State University and focuses on social and environmental issues related to transportation.

Bridger Wineman is a student of community development, equity planning, and alternative transportation in Portland, Oregon.

ENDNOTES

INTRODUCTION

1   Sharon Zukin, *Loft Living: Culture and Capital in Urban Change* (New Brunswick, NJ: Rutgers University Press, 1989), Sharon Zukin, "Urban Lifestyles: Diversity and Standardization in Spaces of Consumption," *Urban Studies* 35, no. 5/6 (1998).

2   Sharon Zukin, "Consuming Authenticity," *Cultural Studies* 22, no. 5 (2008): 736.

3   Elizabeth Currid, *The Warhol Economy: How Fashion, Art, and Music Drive New York City* (Princeton: Princeton University Press, 2007).

4   Richard D. Lloyd, *Neo-Bohemia: Art and Commerce in the Postindustrial City* (New York: Routledge, 2005).

5   Richard L. Florida, *The Rise of the Creative Class: And How It's Transforming Work, Leisure, Community and Everyday Life* (New York, NY: Basic Books, 2004).

6   Victor J. Tremblay and Carol Horton Tremblay, *The U.S. Brewing Industry: Data and Economic Analysis* (Cambridge, Mass.: MIT Press, 2005).

7   Oregon Brewers Guild, *Oregon Brewers Guild Fact Sheet* (cited June 10, 2009); available from http://oregonbeer.org/facts/.

8   Jim Robbins, "Think Global, Eat Local; the Sustainable Food Movement That Began with Berkeley Chef Alice Waters Has Blossomed in Portland, Ore. Are Its Proponents Just Dreaming? Or Is a Real Revolution Underway?" *Los Angeles Times*, July 31, 2005.

9   William Yardley, "In Portland, Cultivating a Culture of Two Wheels," *New York Times*, November 5, 2007.

10   Alta Planning + Design, "The Value of the Bicycle-Related Industry in Portland: September 2008" (cited June, 10 2009); available from http://bikeportland.org/wp-content/uploads/2008/09/2008-portland-bicycle-related-economy-report.pdf.

11   Ann R. Markusen, Yong-Sook Lee, and Sean DiGiovanna, *Second Tier Cities: Rapid Growth Beyond the Metropolis, Globalization and Community; V. 3* (Minneapolis: University of Minnesota Press, 1999).

CHAPTER 1

1   Ash Amin, *Post-Fordism: A Reader, Studies in Urban and Social Change* (Oxford; Cambridge, Mass.: Blackwell, 1994).

2   General Electric, *Products and Services* (cited June 11, 2009); available from http://www.ge.com/products_services/index.html.

3   Don Slater, *Consumer Culture and Modernity* (Cambridge, MA: Polity Press: Blackwell Publishers, 1997).

4   Bob Jessop, *The Future of the Capitalist State* (Malden, MA: Wiley-Blackwell, 2002).

5   Krishan Kumar, *From Post-Industrial to Post-Modern Society: New Theories of the Contemporary World*, 2nd ed. (Malden, MA: Blackwell, 2005).

6   Joel M. Podolny and Karen L. Page, "Network Forms of Organization," *Annual Review of Sociology* 24, no. 1 (1998).

7   Robert B. Reich, *The Work of Nations: Preparing Ourselves for 21st-Century Capitalism*, 1st ed. (New York: A.A. Knopf, 1991).

8   Michael J. Piore and Charles F. Sabel, *The Second Industrial Divide: Possibilities for Prosperity* (New York: Basic Books, 1984).

9   Allen, John Scott, *On Hollywood: The Place, the Industry* (Princeton, NJ: Princeton University Press, 2005).

10 Michael E. Porter, *The Competitive Advantage of Nations: With a New Introduction* (New York: Free Press, 1998).

11 Jessop, *The Future of the Capitalist State.*

12 Terry N. Clark, *The City as an Entertainment Machine*, 1st ed., Research in Urban Policy; V. 9 (Amsterdam [Netherlands] Boston [Mass.]: Elsevier/JAI, 2004), 1.

13 Deborah Stevenson, *Cities and Urban Cultures, Issues in Cultural and Media Studies* (Philadelphia, PA: Open University Press, 2003).

14 Ibid., 94.

15 Florida, *The Rise of the Creative Class: And How It's Transforming Work, Leisure, Community and Everyday Life.*

16 Ibid., 68–69.

17 Ibid., 250.

18 Jeffrey Zimmerman, "From Brew Town to Cool Town: Neoliberalism and the Creative City Development Strategy in Milwaukee," *Cities* 25, no. 4 (2008).

19 Richard Lloyd, "The Neighborhood in Cultural Production: Material and Symbolic Resources in the New Bohemia," *City & Community* 3, no. 4 (2004), Lloyd, *Neo-Bohemia: Art and Commerce in the Postindustrial City.*

20 Charles Landry and Franco Bianchini, *The Creative City* (London: Demos, 1995).

21 Charles Landry, *The Creative City: A Toolkit for Urban Innovator*, 2nd ed. (New Stroud, UK London; Sterling, VA: Comedia; Earthscan, 2008).

22 Ibid., xv.

23 Ibid., 133.

24 Ibid.

25 Ibid., 166.

26 Allen J. Scott, "Creative Cities: Conceptual Issues and Policy Questions," *Journal of Urban Affairs* 28, no. 1 (2006): 1.

27 Ibid.: 14.

28 Ibid.: 3.

29 Ibid.: 7.

30 Ibid.: 10.

31 Herman E. Daly, John B. Cobb, and Clifford W. Cobb, *For the Common Good: Redirecting the Economy toward Community, the Environment, and a Sustainable Future*, 2nd ed. (Boston: Beacon Press, 1994), R. J. Douthwaite, *Short Circuit: Strengthening Local Economies for Security in an Unstable World* (Dublin, Ireland: Lilliput Press, 1996), Michael Shuman, *Going Local: Creating Self-Reliant Communities in a Global Age*, 1st Routledge paperback ed. (New York: Routledge, 2000), Michael Shuman, *The Small-Mart Revolution: How Local Businesses Are Beating the Global Competition*, 1st ed. (San Francisco: Berrett-Koehler, 2006).

32 Sanford Schram, *After Welfare: The Culture of Postindustrial Social Policy* (New York: New York University Press, 2000), 91.

33 Daly, Cobb, and Cobb, *For the Common Good: Redirecting the Economy toward Community, the Environment, and a Sustainable Future*, 164.

34 Timothy Beatley, *Green Urbanism: Learning from European Cities* (Washington, DC: Island Press, 2000), Kent E. Portney, *Taking Sustainable Cities Seriously: Economic Development, the Environment, and Quality of Life in American Cities, American and*

Comparative Environmental Policy (Cambridge, Mass.: MIT Press, 2003).

35   Scott Lash and John Urry, *The End of Organized Capitalism* (Madison, Wis.: University of
     Wisconsin Press, 1987).

36   Juliet Schor, *The Overspent American: Why We Want What We Don't Need* (New York:
     HarperPerennial, 1999).

37   Thorstein Veblen, *The Theory of the Leisure Class* (Oxford; New York: Oxford University
     Press Inc., 2007).

38   Mike Featherstone, *Consumer Culture and Postmodernism*, 2nd ed. (Los Angeles: SAGE
     Publications, 2007).

39   Henry David Thoreau and Lily Owens, *Works of Henry David Thoreau*, 1981 ed.
     (New York: Avenel Books: distributed by Crown Publishers, 1981), 34.

40   Ibid.

41   Duane Elgin, *Voluntary Simplicity: Toward a Way of Life That Is Outwardly Simple,
     Inwardly Rich*, Rev. ed. (New York: Quill, 1993).

42   Slow Movement, *Making a Connection* (cited June 11, 2009); available from
     http://www.slowmovement.com/.

43   Jürgen Habermas, *The Theory of Communicative Action, Volume 2: Lifeworld and System: A
     Critique of Functionalist Reason* (Boston: Beacon Press, 1984), 196.

44   James C. Scott, *Seeing Like a State: How Certain Schemes to Improve the Human Condition
     Have Failed, Yale Agrarian Studies* (New Haven: Yale University Press, 1998).

45   Sue Clifford and Angela King, "Losing Your Place," in *Local Distinctiveness: Place,
     Particularity and Identity*, ed. Sue Clifford and Angela King (London: Common Ground,
     1993).

46   Lucy R. Lippard, *The Lure of the Local: Senses of Place in a Multicentered Society*
     (New York: New Press, 1997), William Vitek and Wes Jackson, *Rooted in the Land: Essays
     on Community and Place* (New Haven, Conn.: Yale University Press, 1996).

47   Timothy Beatley and Kristy Manning, *The Ecology of Place: Planning for
     Environment, Economy and Community* (Washington, DC: Island Press, 1997), Aldo
     Leopold, *A Sand County Almanac, and Sketches Here and There* (New York: Oxford
     Univ. Press, 1949).

48   Sim Van der Ryn and Stuart Cowan, *Ecological Design*, 10th anniversary ed.
     (Washington, DC: Island Press, 2007).

49   Helena Norberg-Hodge, *Ancient Futures: Learning from Ladakh* (San Francisco: Sierra
     Club Books, 1991).

50   John Ruskin and J. G. Links, *The Stones of Venice*, 2nd Da Capo Press ed.
     (New York: Da Capo Press, 2003).

51   Eileen Boris, *Art and Labor: Ruskin, Morris, and the Craftsman Ideal in America, American
     Civilization* (Philadelphia: Temple University Press, 1986).

52   Richard Sennett, *The Craftsman* (New Haven: Yale University Press, 2008).

CHAPTER 2

1   Allen J. Scott, "Creative Cities: Conceptual Issues and Policy Questions," *Journal of
    Urban Affairs* 28, no. 1 (2006).

2   Sue Clifford and Angela King, "Losing Your Place," *Local Distinctiveness: Place, Particularity
    and Identity*, ed. Sue Clifford and Angela King (London: Common Ground, 1993), 7.

3   Parker J. Palmer, *The Courage to Teach: Exploring the Inner Landscape of a Teacher's Life*, 1st
    ed. (San Francisco, Calif.: Jossey-Bass, 1998), 105.

4   Lloyd, *Neo-Bohemia: Art and Commerce in the Postindustrial City.*

5   Zukin, *Loft Living: Culture and Capital in Urban Change,* Sharon Zukin and Ervin Kosta, "Bourdieu Off-Broadway: Managing Distinction on a Shopping Block in the East Village," *City & Community* 3, no. 2 (2004).

6   Burros Marian, "Eating Well; in Oregon, Thinking Local," *New York Times,* January 6, 2006, New Seasons Market, (cited June 12, 2009); available from http://www.newseasonsmarket.com/homepage.aspx?location=H.

7   Joseph Cortright, "Making Sense of Clusters: Regional Competitiveness and Economic Development," in *The Brookings Institution Metropolitan Policy Program Discussion Papers* (Washington, DC: The Brookings Institution, 2006), 39.

8   New Seasons Market, (cited).

CHAPTER 3

1   Travel Portland, *Portland: The Center of the Beer Universe* (cited June 16, 2009); available from http://www.travelportland.com/media/mbmedkit/mb_beer.html.

2   Brewers Association, *Craft Brewing Statistics* (cited June 16, 2009); available from http://www.beertown.org/craftbrewing/statistics.html.

3   Stanley Wade Baron, *Brewed in America; a History of Beer and Ale in the United States, Technology and Society* (New York: Arno Press, 1972).

4   Ibid.

5   Tremblay and Tremblay, *The U.S. Brewing Industry: Data and Economic Analysis.*

6   Ibid.

7   Maureen Ogle, *Ambitious Brew: The Story of American Beer* (Orlando: Harcourt, 2006).

8   Tremblay and Tremblay, *The U.S. Brewing Industry: Data and Economic Analysis.*

9   "Another Round? Beer Mergers," *The Economist,* October 13, 2007.

10   Dan Bilefsky and Christopher Lawton, "SABMiller Has a U.S. Hangover; Overall Results Will Be Mixed, but Miller Keeps Losing Shares," *Wall Street Journal,* November 20, 2003.

11   Burce Aylward, August 8, 2008.

12   Tremblay and Tremblay, *The U.S. Brewing Industry: Data and Economic Analysis.*

13   Ogle, *Ambitious Brew: The Story of American Beer.*

14   Ibid.

15   Brewers Association, *About Us* (cited June 16, 2009); available from http://www.beertown.org/ba/index.html.

16   Chad Kennedy, personal interview, May 6, 2009.

17   Bill Schneller, personal interview, April 29, 2009.

18   Great American Beer Festival, *Beer Styles* (cited June 16, 2009); available from http://www.greatamericanbeerfestival.com/beer_styles1.html.

19   Brewers Association, *Craft Brewing Statistics* (cited).

20   Ibid. (cited), Oregon Brewers Guild, *Facts* (cited June 16, 2009); available from http://oregonbeer.org/facts/.

21   Hopworks Urban Brewery, (cited June 16, 2009); available from http://www.hopworksbeer.com/index.php.

22   Hopworks Urban Brewery, *Portland's Cw Profiles Hopworks Urban Brewery and Our Commitment to Sustainability— Online Video* (cited June 16, 2009); available from http://www.hopworksbeer.com/hop_vid1.php.

23   Brewers Association, *Craft Brewing Statistics* (cited).

CHAPTER 4

1   Ben Davis, personal interview, February 16, 2009.

2   These counts were estimated in summer 2008 through searches of online resources related to the Portland food economy. Each business was only counted once regardless of the number of retail locations.

3   Will Newman, *Proceedings from Portland Chapter of the Chef's Collaborative at the Farmer Chef's Connection* (2001 cited June 11, 2009); available from http://www.portlandcc.org/farmchef.pdf.

4   Cory Schreiber, personal interview, August 8, 2008.

5   *Oregon's Statewide Planning Goals: Goal 3: Agricultural Lands* (1994 cited June 11, 2009); available from http://www.oregon.gov/LCD/docs/goals/goal3.pdf.

6   Eric Asimov, "In Portland, a Golden Age of Dining and Drinking," *New York Times*, September 26, 2007.

7   James Beard Foundation, *About James Beard* (cited April 25, 2009); available from http://www.jamesbeard.org/index.php?q=about_james_beard.

8   Ibid. (cited).

9   Schreiber.

10 Asimov, "In Portland, a Golden Age of Dining and Drinking."

11 Schreiber.

12 Asimov, "In Portland, a Golden Age of Dining and Drinking."

13 Emily Eakin, "The Cities and Their New Elite," *New York Times* 2002.

14 Brian Rohter, personal interview, April 7, 2009.

15 Rebecca Larson, personal interview, September 15, 2008.

16 David Yudkin, personal interview, October 26, 2008.

17 Greg Higgins, personal interview, July 10, 2008.

18 Institute of Portland Metropolitan Studies, "Planting Prosperity and Harvesting Health: Trade-Offs and Sustainability in the Oregon-Washington Regional Food System," (Portland, Oregon: Nohad Toulan School of Urban Studies and Planning, Portland State University, 2008).

19 Berkeley Braden, personal interview, October 26, 2008.

20 Full disclosure, Berkeley Braden is the spouse of Tracy Braden, co-author of this chapter.

21 Institute of Portland Metropolitan Studies, "Planting Prosperity and Harvesting Health: Trade-Offs and Sustainability in the Oregon-Washington Regional Food System."

22 Integrity Systems Cooperative Co. & Sustainability Ventures Group, *Adding Values to Our Food System: An Economic Analysis of Sustainable Community Food Systems* (1997 cited May 6, 2000); available from http://www.ibiblio.org/farming-connection/foodsys/addval.htm.

23 The Hartman Group Inc., "Understanding Local from a Consumer Perspective: Presentation to the Food Marketing Institute," (2008).

24 Ecotrust, *About Us* (cited May 7, 2009); available from http://www.ecotrust.org/about/.

25 Institute of Portland Metropolitan Studies, "Planting Prosperity and Harvesting Health: Trade-Offs and Sustainability in the Oregon-Washington Regional Food System."

26 Laura McCandlish, *Slow Food Moves Faster on Social Activism* (Special to The Oregonian,

March 10, 2009 cited June 15, 2009); available from http://www.oregonlive.com/food-day/index.ssf/2009/03/slow_food_acts_on_social_activ.html.

27 Slow Food USA, *Good, Clean and Fair* (cited May 7, 2000); available from http://www.slowfoodusa.org/index.php/slow_food/good_clean_fair/.

28 McCandlish, *Slow Food Moves Faster on Social Activism* (cited).

29 Asimov, "In Portland, a Golden Age of Dining and Drinking."

30 Institute of Portland Metropolitan Studies, "Planting Prosperity and Harvesting Health: Trade-Offs and Sustainability in the Oregon-Washington Regional Food System."

31 Portland Farmers Market, *Pfm Information Booth* (cited May 7, 2009); available from http://www.portlandfarmersmarket.org/sec_InfoBooth/info_booth.php.

32 The Hartman Group Inc., "Understanding Local from a Consumer Perspective: Presentation to the Food Marketing Institute."

33 Institute of Portland Metropolitan Studies, "Planting Prosperity and Harvesting Health: Trade-Offs and Sustainability in the Oregon-Washington Regional Food System."

CHAPTER 5

1 Adam Arnold, personal interview, February 24, 2009.

2 Emily Katz, personal interview, February 8, 2006.

3 Wendi Martin, personal interview, March 22, 2006.

4 Anna Cohen, personal interview, March 4, 2009.

CHAPTER 6

1 Yardley, "In Portland, Cultivating a Culture of Two Wheels."

2 Aaron Hayes, personal interview, August 1, 2008.

3 Forbes Black, *Jonathan Maus on Bikes, Portland and Bikeportland.Org* (August 1, 2008 cited June 15, 2009); available from http://cycloculture.blogspot.com/2008/08/jona-than-maus-on-bikes-portland-and.html.

4 Alta Planning + Design, "The Value of the Bicycle-Related Industry in Portland: September 2008" (cited June 15, 2009); available from http://bikeportland.org/wp-content/uploads/2008/09/2008-portland-bicycle-related-economy-report.pdf.

5 Portland Department of Transportation, "Portland Bicycle Counts 2007," (City of Portland, Oregon, September 26, 2007).

6 Steven Reed Johnson, "The Transformation of Civic Institutions and Practices in Portland, Oregon, 1960–1999" (Dissertation, Portland State University, 2002).

7 Portland Department of Transportation, "Portland Bicycle Counts 2007."

8 League of American Bicyclists, *Bicylcle Friendly Community Master List* (cited June 15, 2009); available from http://www.bikeleague.org/programs/bicyclefriendlyamerica/pdfs/bfc_master_list_web.pdf.

9 World Carfree Network, *Towards Carfree Cities Conference Series* (cited June 16, 2009); available from http://www.worldcarfree.net/conference/.

10 Natelie Ramsland, personal interview, July 23, 2008.

11 Joseph Ahearne, personal interview, October 10, 2008.

12 Sean Chaney, personal interview, July 7, 2008.

13 Black, *Jonathan Maus on Bikes, Portland and Bikeportland.Org* (cited).

14 Shaun Deller, personal interview, July 9, 2008.

15   Pereira Cycles, Cyclocross (cited August 14, 2008); available from http://www.pereira-cycles.com/cyclocross.php.

16   Alta Planning + Design, "The Value of the Bicycle-Related Industry in Portland: September 2008" (cited).

17   Portland Department of Transportation, "Portland Bicycle Counts 2007."

18   Black, *Jonathan Maus on Bikes, Portland and Bikeportland.Org* (cited).

19   Jonathan Maus, *Booth, Speedvagen Mark New Direction for Vanilla Bicycles* (BikePortland.org, March 6, 2007 [cited June 15, 2009]); available from http://bikeportland.org/2007/03/06/booth-speedvagen-mark-new-direction-for-vanilla-bicycles/.

20   Alta Planning + Design, "The Value of the Bicycle-Related Industry in Portland: September 2008" (cited).

21   Chris King Precision Components, (cited June 16, 2009); available from http://chrisking.com/.

22   Elias Grey, personal interview, July 14, 2008.

23   Filmed by Bike, *Why* + (cited June 15, 2009); available from http://www.filmedbybike.org/about.html.

CHAPTER 7

1   Matt Milletto, personal interview, May 6, 2009.

2   Specialty Coffee Association of America, (cited June 16, 2009); available from http://members.scaa.org/default.aspx.

3   Stumptown Coffee Roasters, *Locations* (cited June 16, 2009); available from http://buystumptowncoffee.com/locations.

4   Matt Lounsbury, personal interview, May 7, 2009.

5   Julie Beals, personal interview, April 28, 2009.

6   Brent Fortune, personal interview, May 8, 2009.

7   Sarah Allen, "The Number 4," *Barista Magazine*, April/May 2009.

8   Din Johnson, personal interview, May 9, 2009.

9   Jeremy Adams, personal interview, May 8, 2009.

10   Milletto.

11   Andrea Pastor, personal interview, May 8, 2009.

12   Richard Reynolds, "Coffee's Third Wave," *Imbibe*, May/June 2006.

13   Kevin Fuller, personal interview, May 5, 2009.

14   Adam McGovern, personal interview, May 6, 2009.

15   Deeda Schroeder, "On a Roll," *Willamette Week*, May 7, 2008.

16   Allen, "The Number 4."

CHAPTER 8

1   *Imbibe Magazine*, "About *Imbibe*" (cited June 19, 2009); available from http://www.imbibemagazine.com/About.

2   Site Distiller, "Welcome" (Burning Still, October 29th, 2007 cited June 18, 2000); available from http://www.burningstill.com/?q=node/1.

3   Melissa Bearns, "New Spirits: Oregon's Microdistilleries Lead the Market," *Eugene Weekly*, March 9, 2006.

4   Mathew Kish, "Shot at Expansion," *Portland Business Journal*, March 5, 2007.

5   Lee Medoff, personal interview, July 31, 2008.

6   Blind Muscat's Cellarbook, *Walking/Drinking Tour of Portland* (cited).

7   Bearns, "New Spirits: Oregon's Microdistilleries Lead the Market."

8   Steve McCarthy, personal interview, August 1, 2008.

9   "At Oregon Watering Holes, It's Not Your Father's Beer," *Boston Globe*, January 21, 1999, Blind Muscat's Cellarbook, *Walking/Drinking Tour of Portland* (April 06, 2008 cited June 18, 2009); available from http://blindmuscat.typepad.com/tims_fine_wine_blog/2008/04/walking-drinkin.html, L. Johnston, "Portland Has Plenty of Froth and Bubble," *Sunday Mail*, November 9, 2003, Jessica Merrill, "In Oregon, It's a Brew Pub World," *New York Times*, January 13, 2006.

10   Oregon Public Broadcasting, "We've Got Spirits, Yes We Do!" (June 6, 2008 cited June 18, 2009); available from http://action.publicbroadcasting.net/opb/posts/list/1156812.page.

11   Anne Saker, "Portland Distillery Second in U.S. To Bottle Absinthe," *Oregonian*, July 9, 2008.

12   Heidi Dietrich, "Craft Liquor Startups May Stir Creation of New Industry in Washington State," *Puget Sound Business Journal*, July 4, 2008.

13   Northwest Agriculture Business Center, *Craft Distilling: Value Added Agriculture for Washington's Family Farm* (cited June 18, 2009); available from http://www.agbizcenter.org/FilesUploaded/file/distilling%20fact%20sheet.pdf.

14   Tom Kenworthy, "Peaks, Valleys Define Today's West," *USA Today*, May 18, 2001.

15   Eric Asimov, "An Orchard in a Bottle, at 80 Proof," *New York Times*, August 15, 2007.

16   McMenamins Hotels and Pubs, *Edgefield Distillery* (cited June 18, 2009); available from http://www.mcmenamins.com/index.php?loc=76&category=Distillery+Homepage.

17   A note on terminology: winery is the term for the location where wine is made, whereas vineyards are where grapes are grown. So while the McMenamins Edgefield Winery bottles some wines made from grapes grown in the Edgefield vineyard, others of their wines are made with grapes obtained from other sources. Many wineries grow no grapes whatsoever.

18   Oregon Public Broadcasting, "We've Got Spirits, Yes We Do!" (cited).

19   Clear Creek Distillery, *Additional Clear Creek Eaux De Vie* (cited June 18, 2009); available from http://clearcreekdistillery.com/other.html.

20   Nicole Krueger, "Distilling the Essence of the Fruit," *Statesman Journal*, July 20. 2008.

21   Clear Creek Distillery, *Breaking News* (cited September 8, 2008); available from http://clearcreekdistillery.com/distillery-news.html.

22   Asimov, "An Orchard in a Bottle, at 80 Proof."

23   Liz Crain, "Botanically Infused Libations Naturally Spice up Cocktail Hour," *Portland Tribune*, April 4, 2008.

24   Ibid.

25   Bearns, "New Spirits: Oregon's Microdistilleries Lead the Market."

26   Integrity Spirits, *Blog Archives* (cited June 19, 2009); available from http://integrityspirits.blogspot.com/.

27   Patrick Alan Coleman posting to Blogtown: The Mercury Blog, *Great American Distillers Festival: Wrap Up!* (Aug 25, 2008 cited June 18, 2009); available from http://blogtown.port-landmercury.com/BlogtownPDX/archives/2008/08/25/great-american-distillers-fest.

28   Ibid. (cited).

29   Toby Cecchini, "The New Bootleggers," *GQ*, July 2006.

30   Oregon Public Broadcasting, "We've Got Spirits, Yes We Do!" (cited).

31 New Deal Distillery, *Product* (cited June 18, 2009); available from http://newdealdistillery.com/Product/product_index.html.

32 Oregon Public Broadcasting, "We've Got Spirits, Yes We Do!" (cited).

33 Nick Fauchald, "America's Best New Whiskeys," *Food and Wine*, November 2007.

34 Oregon Public Broadcasting, "We've Got Spirits, Yes We Do!" (cited).

35 Danielle Centoni, "Mixmaster," *Mix*, June/July 2008. 23.

36 Oregon Public Broadcasting, "We've Got Spirits, Yes We Do!" (June 6, 2008 cited June 18, 2009); available from http://action.publicbroadcasting.net/opb/posts/list/1156812.page.

37 New Deal Distillery, *Product* (cited).

38 LOFT Liqueurs, *About* (cited June 18, 2009); available from http://www.loftliqueurs.com/index539a.html?q=node/2.

39 Oregon Public Broadcasting, "We've Got Spirits, Yes We Do!" (cited).

40 Ibid. (cited).

41 Oregon Public Broadcasting, "We've Got Spirits, Yes We Do!" (cited).

CHAPTER 9

1 Taylor Clark, "The Indie City: Why Portland Is America's Indie Rock Mecca.," *Slate*, posted September 11, 2007.

2 Mark Janchar, personal interview, July 23, 2008.

3 S. P. Clarke, personal interview, August 8, 2008.

4 Brandon Eggleston, personal interview, July 31, 2008.

5 Steve Schroeder, personal interview, August 4, 2008.

CHAPTER 10

1 Multnomah County Library, *About the Library/Library Fact Sheet* (cited June 22, 2009); available from http://www.multcolib.org/about/libraryfactsheet.html.

2 Powell's City of Books, *Store Description* (cited June 22, 2009); available from http://www.powells.com/info/places/burnsideinfo.html.

3 Rebecca Luxenburg, personal interview, July 22, 2008.

4 Dennis Stovall, personal interview, July 28, 2008.

5 Cameron Marschall, personal interview, August 12, 2008.

6 Literary Arts, *Fellowship Recipients – Publishers* (cited June 22, 2009); available from http://www.literary-arts.org/fellowships/past_publishers.php.

7 Chloe Eudaly, personal interview, July 18, 2008.

8 Justin Hocking, personal interview, August 8, 2008.

9 Victoria Blake, personal interview, August 12, 2008.

10 Kristi Turnquist, "Hollywood Says Hurray for Portland Comic Books," *Oregonian*, July 23, 2008.

11 Joseph Gallivan, "Spotlight's on Dark Horse," *Portland Tribune*, May 22, 2007.

12 As quoted in Ibid.

13 As quoted in Turnquist, "Hollywood Says Hurray for Portland Comic Books."

14 Chuck Moore, *Mayor Declares April Portland Comics Month* (Community@Comic Related, April 1, 2008, cited June 22, 2009); available from http://comicrelated.com/forums/index.php?s=c66c229fdeb06616c6f6885cd3a858f0&showtopic=1371&st=0&p=5501&#entry5501.

15 Matt Dryer, personal interview, July 7, 2008.

16 Andy Johnson, personal interview, July 25, 2008.

17 Steve Duin, *24 Hour Comics Day* (oregonlive.com blog, April 2, 2008 cited June 22, 2009); availablefromhttp://blog.oregonlive.com/steveduin/2008/04/24hour_comics_day.html.

18 Sarah Oleksky, personal interview, October 22, 2008.

19 Dark Horse, Company/Overview (cited June 22, 2009); available from http://www.darkhorse.com/Company/Overview.

20 Shawn Granton, ed., *The Zinester's Guide to Portland*, 4th ed. (Portland, OR: Microcosm Publishing, 2008).

21 Karen Gisonny and Jenna Freedman, "Zines in Libraries: How, What and Why?" *Collection Building* 25, no. 1 (2006).

22 Vance Nix, "DIY Zine Scene: Skip Those Pesky Editors and Publish Yourself," *Portland Sentinel*, May 6, 2008.

23 Alycia Sellie, "Baltimore County Public Library Zine Collection" (cited September 18, 2008); available from http://www.bcpl.info/centers/library/Zine.pdf.

24 Birar Levit, "Specular Preserves at Reading Frenzy" (Bitch Magazine blog, August 5, 2008 cited June 22, 2009); available from http://bitchmagazine.org/post/specular-preserves-at-reading-frenzy.

25 Martha Grover, *Somnambulist Number 10: The Portland Issue* (Portland, OR: Self Published, 2008).

26 Martha Grover, "Somnambulist Zine Blog Archive" (cited August 13, 2008); available from http://somnambulistzine.blogspot.com/.

27 Reading Frenzy, *Benefit for Martha Grover* (cited June 22, 2009); available from http://readingfrenzy.com/ledger/2008/06/benefit-for-martha-grover.

28 Grover, *Somnambulist Number 10: The Portland Issue*.

29 Sean Tejaratchi, *Crap Hound 7: Church & State Part One* (Portland, OR: Show and Tell, Press, 2008).

30 Ibid.

31 All Classical FM, Home (cited June 22, 2009); available from http://allclassical.org/index.php5.

32 KMHD 89.1 Jazz Blues and NPR News, *History* (cited June 22, 2009); available from http://www.kmhd.org/index.php?option=com_content&task=view&id=18&Itemid=69.

33 Barry Johnson, KMHD starts down a new path with OPB (cited January 17, 2010); available from http://blog.oregonlive.com/portlandarts/2009/09/kmhd_starts_down_a_new_path_wi.html.

34 KPSU 1450: Portland's College Radio, *Home* (cited June 22, 2009); available from http://kpsu.org/.

35 Patti MacRae, "KRRC: The (Barely Audible) Radio Voice of Reed College," *Reed Magazine*, August 2002.

36 Kenny Love, *College Radio: The Most Important Radio Level for Independents* (Streetdirectory.com, cited June 22, 2009); available from http://www.streetdirectory.com/travel_guide/31564/music/=college_radio_the_most_important_radio_level_for_independents.html.

37 Oregon Public Broadcasting, *OPB Radio* (cited June 22, 2009); available from http://opb.org/radio/.

38 PortlandIndependentMediaCenter,*PortlandIndymediaWebRadio—ArchivedLiveShows*(cited June22,2000);availablefromhttp://portland.indymedia.org/en/static/pdxradio.shtml.

39 Gerald Sussman and J. R. Estes, "Community Radio in Community Development: Portland's **KBOO** Radio," *The Portland Edge: Challenges and Successes in Growing Communities*, ed. Connie P. Ozawa (Washington, **DC**: Island Press, 2004).

40 **KBOO**, *About* **KBOO** (cited June 22, 2009); available from http://kboo.fm/node/4138.

41 Sussman and Estes, "Community Radio in Community Development: Portland's **KBOO** Radio."

42 **KBOO**, *The Underground* (cited June 22, 2009); available from http://kboo.fm/theunderground.

43 **KBOO**, *Youth Randomonium* (cited June 22, 2009); available from http://kboo.fm/YouthRandomonium.

44 Annie Soja, personal interview, July 28, 2008.

45 Erin Yanke, personal interview, July 28, 2008.

46 Charles Fairchild, *Community Radio and Public Culture* (New Jersey: Hampton Press, 2001).

47 Sussman and Estes, "Community Radio in Community Development: Portland's **KBOO** Radio."

48 Ibid.

49 Ibid.

50 Wikipedia, *Gus Van Sant* (cited June 22, 2009); available from http://en.wikipedia.Org/wiki/Gus_Van_Sant.

51 Simon Wakelin, *Ocularist Eyes Sundance* (Boards blog, December 18, 2002 cited June 22, 2009); available from http://www.boardsmag.com/articles/online/20021218/eyes.html.

52 David Walker et al., "Filming Portland: Four Emerging Local Filmmakers-and One Zany Group-Are Producing Must-See Cinema," *Willamette Week*, March 23, 2005.

53 Laika Entertainment House, Coraline (cited June 23, 2009); available from http://www.laika.com/entertainment/.

54 Platform International Animation Festival, *About* (cited June 23, 2009); available from http://platformfestival.com/content/thefestival.aspx.

55 Shawn Levy, *Comments: PIFF Dispatch. 1.* (GreenCiine Daily, February 12, 2007 cited June 22, 2009); available from http://daily.greencine.com/cgi-bin/gc-mt/mt-comments.cgi?entry_id=3244.

56 Film Action Oregon, *About* (cited June 22, 2009); available from http://hollywoodtheatre.org/about.html.

57 Film Action Oregon, *Educating* (cited June 22, 2009); available from http://hollywoodtheatre.org/educating/index.html.

58 The Clinton Street Theatre, *On the Marquee* (cited June 22, 2009); available from http://clintonsttheater.com/.

59 The Clinton Street Theatre, **PDX** *A. V. Club* (cited June 22, 2009); available from http://clintonsttheater.com/avclub.html.

Chapter 11

1 Community Live Journal, (cited July 25, 2009); available from http://community.livejournal.com/sew_hip.

2 Portland Saturday Market, *About Us, History* (cited June 25, 2009); available from http://www.portlandsaturdaymarket.com/Main%20Pages/About%20Us/history.htm.

3 Etsy Wiki, *Top Sellers* (cited June 28, 2009); available from http://www.etsywiki.com/index.php?title=Top_Sellers.

4   Cara Buchalter, personal interview, August 8, 2008.

5   Susan Beal, *A Short History of Craft in Portland* (**PDX** Super Crafty, cited June 25, 2009); available from http://www.pdxsupercrafty.com/about.html#history.

6   Dick Hebdige, *Subculture: The Meaning of Style* (London: Methuen & Co., 1979).

7   Ibid.

8   Nick Dyer-Witheford, *Cyber-Marx: Cycles and Circuits of Struggle in High-Technology Capitalism* (Urbana: University of Illinois Press, 1999). 163.

9   Ibid. 164.

10 As quoted in Jessica Herman, "Welcome to the Familia: An Explosion of Mafias, Collectives, and Co-Ops Shows That Crafting Is All in the Family," *Venus Zine*, June 1, 2005.

11 Inside a Black Apple, *Home* (cited June 25, 2009); available from http://www.theblackapple.typepad.com/.

12 Ramsland.

13 Hebdige, *Subculture: The Meaning of Style.*

CHAPTER 12

1   Free Geek, "Overview" (cited June 19, 2009); available from http://www.freegeek.org/about/overview/.

2   The Rebuilding Center, Home (cited June 19, 2009); available from http://www.rebuildingcenter.org/.

3   City Repair, About (cited June 19, 2009); available from http://cityrepair.org/about/.

4   Free Geek, Overview (cited).

5   Ubuntu, "What Is Ubuntu?" (cited June 19, 2009); available from http://www.ubuntu.com/products/whatisubuntu.

6   Free Geek, "Volunteer Build" (cited June 19, 2009); available from http://www.freegeek.org/volunteer/build/.

7   Richard Seymour, personal interview, January 1, 2009.

8   The Rebuilding Center, Home (cited).

9   Shane Endicott, personal interview, December 11, 2008.

10 Ian Demsky, "Deconstructing for Fema Dollars, New Orleans Gets a Lesson from Portland on Greening Its Katrina Cleaning," *Willamette Week*, June 28, 2006.

11 City Repair, About (cited).

12 Mark Lakeman, personal interview, December 19, 2008.

13 City Repair, About (cited).

14 City Repair, "Village Building Convergence" (cited June 19, 2009); available from http://cityrepair.org/events/vbc/.

15 City Repair, Projects (cited June 19, 2009); available from http://cityrepair.org/about/projects/.

16 Jennifer Anderson, "King Cob," *Portland Tribune*, June 13, 2006.

17 Ibid.

18 City Repair, About (cited).

CHAPTER 13

1   "For Serious Bikers, It's Gotta Be Langlitz," *Portland Tribune*, June 22, 2001.

2   Peter Korn, "Q & A with Dave Hansen," *Portland Tribune*, June 19, 2008.

3   Langlitz Leathers Inc., In the Press (cited June 18, 2009); available from
    http://www.langlitz.com/press.shtml.
4   Langlitz Leathers Inc., History (cited June 18, 2009); available from
    http://www.langlitz.com/history.shtml.
5   Dave Hansen, personal interview, July 17, 2008.
6   Nate Bagley, personal interview, July 17, 2008.
7   Talitha Leather, "Handmade Leather Bags, Purses, Wallets, and Journals" (cited June
    18, 2009); available from http://www.talithaleather.com/.
8   Elizabeth Robinson, personal interview, July 18, 2008

CHAPTER 14

1   Jeffrey Elliott, personal interview, March 17, 2009.
2   David King Bass Guitars, (cited June 20, 2009); available from http://kingbass.com/.
3   David King Bass Guitars, Bunnybass Interview with David King (cited June 20, 2009);
    available from http://kingbass.com/bunnybass.html.
4   David King Bass Guitars, "How I Build a Bass" (cited June 20, 2009); available from
    http://kingbass.com/build-a-bass.html.
5   David King Bass Guitars, Bunnybass Interview with David King (cited).
6   David King, personal interview, March 9, 2009.
7   eKalimba.com, Home (cited June 20, 2009); available from
    http://www.ekalimba.com/.
8   Ibid. (cited).
9   David Bellinger, personal interview, February 28, 2009.
10 eKalimba.com, Blog—"Darin Has Been Assisting Me for Awhile Now" (December 18,
    2008 cited June 20, 2009); available from http://apps.ekalimba.com/blog/.
11 Oregon Art Beat, "Monette Trumpets" (January 24, 2008 cited June 20, 2009); available
    from http://www.opb.org/programs/artbeat/segments/view/714.
12 Monette, "The Monette Approach to Design" (cited June 20, 2009); available from
    http://www.monette.net/newsite/monette_approach_00.htm.
13 Oregon Art Beat, "Monette Trumpets" (cited).
14 Cyndy Burton, personal interview, March 17, 2009.
15 Guild of American Luthiers, About Us (cited June 20, 2009); available from
    http://luth.org/aboutus.htm.
16 Elliott.
17 Guild of American Luthiers, About Us (cited).
18 Ibid. (cited).
19 Kurt Ungerer, personal interview, March 20, 2009.
20 Ibid.

CHAPTER 15

1   Rick Turoczy, personal interview, May 14, 2009.
2   Wikipedia, "Web 2.0—Definition" (cited June 20, 2009); available from
    http://en.wikipedia.org/wiki/Web_2.0#Definition.
3   Wiki Definition (cited February 13, 2010) available from
    http://en.wikipedia.org.wiki/Wiki.
4   Open Source Bridge, Home (cited June 20, 2009); available from
    http://opensourcebridge.org/.

5   Open Source Bridge, Blog—"Becoming an Open Source Citizen" (cited June 20, 2009);
    available from http://opensourcebridge.org/2009/02/becoming-an-open-source-citizen/.
6   Michael Richardson, personal interview, May 7, 2009.
7   Adam Lowry, personal interview, May 7, 2009.
8   Justin Kistner, personal interview, May 15, 2009.

CHAPTER 16

1   Alma Chocolate, About (cited June 25, 2009); available from
    http://www.almachocolate.com/about/.
2   Alma Chocolate, Chocolates (cited June 25, 2009); available from
    http://www.almachocolate.com/chocolates/.
3   Sahagun Handmade Chocolates, "Story" (cited June 25, 2009); available from
    http://www.sahagunchocolates.com/story.php.
4   Glass Art Society, About Us (cited June 25, 2009); available from
    http://www.glassart.org/aboutus.html.
5   As quoted in Pamela Koss, "A Glass Act," *Oregonian*, May/June 2008.
6   Bullseye Glass, About Us (cited June 25, 2009); available from
    http://www.bullseyeglass.com/aboutus/.
7   Bullseye Glass, Becon Presenters (cited June 25, 2009); available from
    http://www.bullseyeglass.com/becon/2009/presenters/.
8   Koss, "A Glass Act."
9   YOLO Colorhouse, Who We Are (cited June 26, 2009); available from
    http://www.yolocolorhouse.com/about_yolo.php.
10 YOLO Colorhouse, "Our Story" (cited June 26, 2009); available from
    http://www.yolocolorhouse.com/about_ourstory.php.
11 The Wall, Home (cited June 26, 2009); available from
    http://www.bythewall.com/index.php.
12 Portland Nursery and Garden Center, Home (cited June 26, 2009); available from
    http://www.portlandnursery.com/.
13 Pratt & Larson Ceramics, About Us (cited June 25, 2009); available from
    http://www.prattandlarson.com/about_us.php.
14 Randall Barton, "Back in Tile," *Portland Tribune*, November 6, 2007.
15 Ann Sacks, *History of Innovation* (cited June 25, 2009); available from
    http://www.annsacks.com/about/history.html.
16 Barton, "Back in Tile."
17 Ibid.
18 Design and Direct Source, Projects (cited June 25, 2009); available from
    http://www.designanddirectsource.com/projects.php.
19 Design and Direct Source, Sustainable Products (cited June 25, 2009); available from
    http://www.designanddirectsource.com/sustainable.php.
20 Amy Hsuan, "Tooling up for Tomorrow," *Oregonian*, July 16, 2008.
21 Leatherman, Oregon Proud (cited June 25, 2009); available from
    http://www.leatherman.com/about/oregonproud.asp?c=62.
22 Ibid. (cited).
23 As quoted in Inara Verzemnieks, "Strings Attached," Oregonian, November 23, 2007.
24 Ibid.
25 Tears of Joy Theatre, About Us (cited June 25, 2009); available from
    http://www.tojt.com/About_us.html.

26 Verzemnieks, "Strings Attached."
27 Portland Saturday Market, Artisans, Clothing and Accessories (cited June 25, 2009); available from http://www.portlandsaturdaymarket.com/Main%20Pages/Craft%20Pages/ClothingAndAccessories/Clothing.htm.
28 Pinkham Millinery, About (cited June 25, 2009); available from http://www.pinkhammillinery.com/about.
29 Vivian McInerny, "Portland's Mod Hatter Turns Some Heads," *Oregonian*, March 11, 2007.
30 Gamblin Artists Oil Colors, About (cited June 25, 2009); available from http://www.gamblincolors.com/about/index.html.
31 Gamblin Artists Oil Colors, "Torrit Grey Competition" (cited June 25, 2009); available from http://www.gamblincolors.com/torrit.grey/index.html.
32 John Foyston, "Gray, Green & Free," March 13, 2009.
33 Gamblin Artists Oil Colors, "Torrit Grey Competition Winners 2008" (cited June 25, 2009); available from http://www.gamblincolors.com/torrit.grey/winners.html.
34 Foyston, "Gray, Green & Free."
35 As quoted in Ibid.
36 Amy Sacks Eyeware, Bamboo Collection (cited June 25, 2009); available from http://www.amysacks.com/store.php?PRODUCT_CAT_ID=6.
37 SustainLane, "2008 U.S. City Rankings" (cited June 25, 2009); available from http://www.sustainlane.com/us-city-rankings/.
38 Amy Sacks Eyeware, Bamboo Collection (cited).
39 As quoted in Vivian McInerny, "Ai-Yai-Eye! Edgy Glasses!" *Oregonian*, July 22, 2008.
40 Oregon Potters Association, Home (cited June 25, 2009); available from http://www.oregonpotters.org/.
41 Oregon Potters Association, Members Links (cited June 25, 2009); available from http://www.oregonpotters.org/member_links.htm.
42 Chehalem Mountain Pottery, About Us (cited June 25, 2009); available from http://www.chehalemmountainpottery.com/aboutus/aboutus.html.
43 Ibid. (cited).
44 As quoted in Randall Barton, "All Roads Lead to Art," *Portland Tribune*, October 9, 2008

CHAPTER 17

1 Zukin, *Loft Living: Culture and Capital in Urban Change*.
2 Katherine Krajnak, "Spaces for Art: What We Can Learn and Do to Keep Portland Affordable for Artists" (Field Area Paper, Portland State University, 2007).10.
3 Milepost 5, *Showcase Pdx - Milepost 5 Video Biography* (cited June 24, 2009); available from http://www.milepostfive.com/video.
4 Bryan Suereth, email correspondence, May 5, 2009.
5 KPSU Radio, "Art Talk AM on the Radio—Interview with Bryan Suereth" (March 9, 2009, cited June 24, 2009); available from http://arttalkam.blogspot.com/2009/03/brian-sureth.html.
6 Ibid. (cited).
7 Brian Wannamaker, personal interview, April 29, 2009.
8 Ibid.
9 Krajnak, "Spaces for Art: What We Can Learn and Do to Keep Portland Affordable for Artists."
10 Ibid.

11   Artspace, Properties—Everett Station Lofts (cited June 24, 2009); available from http://www.artspace.org/properties/everettstation/.

12   Portland Art Studios, "A Guide to Portland's Creative Spaces" (cited June 24, 2009); available from www.portlandartstudios.com.

13   Brian Libby, "An Artistic Congregation at Milepost 5," *Oregonian*, May 28, 2008.

14   D. K. Row, "Gavin Shettler: Moving On" (oregonlive blog, February 29, 2008 cited June 24, 2009); available from http://blog.oregonlive.com/visualarts/2008/02/gavin_shettler_moving_on.html.

15   Milepost 5, Home (cited June 24, 2009); available from http://www.milepostfive.com/.

16   Quoted from **KPSU** Radio," Art Talk Am on the Radio—Interview with Bryan Suereth" (cited).

17   Patricia C. Scruggs, Joseph Cortright, and Marcia Douglas, "Designing Portland's Future: The Role of the Creative Services Industry," (A report written for the Portland Development Commission and the Industry and Professional Organizations of the Creative Services Cluster. Available at http://www.pdc.us/pdf/bus_serv/creative-svcs-report.pdf, June, 1999).

18   Portland Development Commission, News Release—September 13, 2000, "Creative Services Center Building Renovation Begins" (cited June 24, 2009); available from http://www.pdc.us/new/releases/2000/20000913_create_serv.asp.

19   Portland.com, "Regional Arts and Culture Council Announces Move to Creative Services Center" (cited June 24, 2009); available from http://www.portland.com/portland/press-releases/regional-arts-and-culture-council-announces-move-to-creative-services-center/.

20   Aimee Curl, "Portland Development Center Cuts Its Losses on Center," *Daily Journal of Commerce* (Portland, OR), January 12, 2004.

21   Ibid.

22   Aimee Curl, "**PDC** Moves Offices to Creative Services Center," *Daily Journal of Commerce* (Portland, OR), September 27, 2004.

23   Richard Ellison, personal interview, May 5, 2009.

24   Tool Shed—**PDX**, Home (cited June 24, 2009); available from http://www.toolshedpdx.org/.

CHAPTER 19

1   Aguila **USA**, (cited July 13, 2009); available from http://www.aquilausa.com/.

2   ShoeLacesExpress, (cited July 13, 2009); available from http://www.shoelacesexpress.com/index.asp.

3   Independent Community Bankers of America, Community Banking Facts (cited July 13, 2009); available from http://www.icba.org/files/ICBASites/PDFs/cbfacts.pdf.

4   Mark Calvey, "Wells Fargo Bank Recovering from Merger Hangover," *San Francisco Business Time*s, Friday, December 26, 1997.

5   Bank of America, History (cited July 13, 2009); available from http://newsroom.bankofamerica.com/index.php?s=community.

6   Clive Thompson, "A One-of-a-Kind Revolution," *Wired*, March, 2009.

7   Joseph Cortright, "Making Sense of Clusters: Regional Competitiveness and Economic Development," in *The Brookings Institution Metropolitan Policy Prog*ram *Discussion Papers* (Washington, **DC**: The Brookings Institution, 2006). 39.

8   Hub City Brewing Company, About (cited July 13, 2009); available from http://www.hubcitybrewingcompany.com/about.php.

9   City-Data.com, *Oelwein, Iowa* (cited July 13, 2009); available from http://www.city-data.com/city/Oelwein-Iowa.html.

10   Jeffrey Zimmerman, "From Brew Town to Cool Town: Neoliberalism and the Creative City Development Strategy in Milwaukee," *Cities* 25, no. 4 (2008).

11   Richard Sennett, *The Craftsman* (New Haven: Yale University Press, 2008).

12   Ted Sickinger, "Kansas City Here We Come?" *Oregonian*, Tuesday, May 12, 2009.

13   Ryan Frank, "Adams Pushes Convention Center Hotel," *Oregonian*, April 16, 2009.

14   Barry Johnson, "Entertainment District: Bigger's Not Better; Homegrown Reaps Rewards," *Oregonian*, April 27, 2009.

15   Vision Into Action, "Voices from the Community: The Visionpdx Input Report" (cited July 13, 2009); available from http://www.visionpdx.com/reading/inputsummary/.

16   Vision Into Action, "Vision into Action Grants" (cited July 13, 2009); available from http://www.visionpdx.com/action/grants.php.

17   Full disclosure, I am a board member of Café au Play, an organization that received one of the 2009 VIA grants.

18   The Office of Sustainable Development is now part of the combined Bureau of Planning and Sustainabiliity.

19   Greg Andranovich, Matthew J. Burbank, and Charles H. Heying, "Olympic Cities: Lessons Learned from Mega-Event Politics," *Journal of Urban Affairs* 23, no. 2 (2001), Matthew J. Burbank, Gregory D. Andranovich, and Charles H. Heying, *Olympic Dreams: The Impact of Mega-Events on Local Politics, Explorations in Public Policy* (Boulder, **CO**: Lynne Rienner Publishers, 2001), Charles H. Heying, Matthew J. Burbank, and Greg Andranovich, "Taking the Measure of the Games: Lessons from the Field," *Plan Canada* 45, no. 2 (2005), Holger Preuss, *The Economics of Staging the Olympics: A Comparison of the Games, 1972-2008* (Cheltenham, UK; Northampton, **MA**: E. Elgar, 2004).

20   Heywood T. Sanders, "Convention Myths and Markets: A Critical Review of Convention Center Feasibility Studies," *Economic Development Quarterly* 16, no. 3 (2002).

21   An extended list of these people-centered initiatives can be found in "Voices from the Community: The VisionPDX Input Report," available at http://www.visionpdx.com/reading/inputsummary/.

CHAPTER 20

1   "Furthur," an amalgam of the words "further" and "future," was the name of the bus used by author Ken Kesey and the Merry Pranksters whose travels were made famous by Tom Wolfe in *The Electric Kool-Aid Acid Test.*

2   Robert D. Putnam, Lewis M. Feldstein, and Don Cohen, *Better Together: Restoring the American Community* (New York: Simon & Schuster, 2003).

3   Conor Dougherty, "'Youth Magnet' Cities Hit Midlife Crisis: Few Jobs in Places Like Portland and Austin, but the Hipsters Just Keep on Coming," *Wall Street Journal*, May 16, 2009.

4   Michael Shuman, *Going Local: Creating Self-Reliant Communities in a Global Age*, 1st Routledge paperback ed. (New York: Routledge, 2000).

5   Richard D. Lloyd, *Neo-Bohemia: Art and Commerce in the Postindustrial City* (New York: Routledge, 2005).

6   Allen J. Scott, "Creative Cities: Conceptual Issues and Policy Questions," *Journal of Urban Affairs* 28, no. 1 (2006).

7   Richard Sennett, *The Craftsman* (New Haven: Yale University Press, 2008).

8   Sharon Zukin, *Loft Living: Culture and Capital in Urban Change* (New Brunswick, **NJ**: Rutgers University Press, 1989).

9   Richard L. Florida, *The Rise of the Creative Class: And How It's Transforming Work, Leisure, Community and Everyday Life* (New York, NY: Basic Books, 2004).

10 Charles Landry and Franco Bianchini, *The Creative City* (London: Demos, 1995).

11 Charles Landry, *The Creative City: A Toolkit for Urban Innovators*, 2nd ed. (New Stroud, UK London; Sterling, VA: Comedia; Earthscan, 2008).

12 Graham Bowley, "With Big Profit, Goldman Sees Big Payday Ahead," *New York Times*, July 15, 2009.

References

A

All Classical FM. Home. In, http://allclassical.org/index.php5. (accessed June 22, 2009).

Allen, Sarah. "The Number 4." *Barista Magazine*, April/May 2009, 10–11.

Alma Chocolate. About. In, http://www.almachocolate.com/about/. (accessed June 25, 2009).

———. Chocolates. In, http://www.almachocolate.com/chocolates/. (accessed June 25, 2009).

Alta Planning + Design. "The Value of the Bicycle-Related Industry in Portland: September 2008." In, http://bikeportland.org/wp-content/uploads/2008/09/2008-portland-bicycle-related-economy-report.pdf. (accessed June 15, 2009).

Amy Sacks Eyewear. Bamboo Collection. In, http://www.amysacks.com/store.php?PRODUCT_CAT_ID=6. (accessed June 25, 2009).

Anderson, Jennifer. "King Cob." *Portland Tribune*, June 13, 2006.

Andranovich, Greg, Matthew J. Burbank, and Charles H. Heying. "Olympic Cities: Lessons Learned from Mega-Event Politics." *Journal of Urban Affairs 23, no. 2* (2001): 113–31.

Ann Sacks. *History of Innovation*. In, http://www.annsacks.com/about/history.html. (accessed June 25, 2009).

"Another Round? Beer Mergers." *The Economist*, October 13, 2007.

Aquila USA. In, http://www.aquilausa.com/. (accessed July 13, 2009).

Artspace. Properties—Everett Station Lofts. In, http://www.artspace.org/properties/everettstation/. (accessed June 24, 2009).

———. "Streets Meet; So Can People." *Portland Tribune*, May 23, 2006.

Asimov, Eric. "An Orchard in a Bottle, at 80 Proof." *New York Times*, August 15, 2007.

———. "In Portland, a Golden Age of Dining and Drinking." *New York Times*, September 26, 2007.

"At Oregon Watering Holes, It's Not Your Father's Beer." *Boston Globe*, January 21, 1999.

B

Bank of America. History. In, http://newsroom.bankofamerica.com/index.php?s=community. (accessed July 13, 2009).

Baron, Stanley Wade. *Brewed in America: A History of Beer and Ale in the United States, Technology and Society*. New York: Arno Press, 1972.

Barton, Randall. "All Roads Lead to Art." *Portland Tribune*, October 9, 2008, B1.

———. "Back in Tile." *Portland Tribune*, November 6, 2007, B1–2.

Beal, Susan. A Short History of Craft in Portland. In, PDX Super Crafty, http://www.pdxsupercrafty.com/about.html#history. (accessed June 25, 2009).

Bearns, Melissa. "New Spirits: Oregon's Microdistilleries Lead the Market." *Eugene Weekly*, March 9, 2006, 4–5.

Bilefsky, Dan, and Christopher Lawton. "SABMiller Has U.S. Hangover: Overall Results Will Be Mixed, but Miller Keeps Losing Shares." *Wall Street Journal*, November 20, 2003, B5.

Black, Forbes. August 1, 2008. Jonathan Maus on Bikes, Portland and BikePortland.

Org. *In Cycloculture: A Journal for Real-World Cyclists*, http://cycloculture.blogspot.
com/2008/08/jonathan-maus-on-bikes-portland-and.html. (accessed June 15, 2009).

Blind Muscat's Cellarbook. April 6, 2008. Walking/Drinking Tour of Portland. In,
http://blindmuscat.typepad.com/tims_fine_wine_blog/2008/04/walking-drinkin.
html. (accessed June 18, 2009).

Bowley, Graham. "With Big Profit, Goldman Sees Big Payday Ahead." *New York Times*,
July 15, 2009.

Brewers Association. About Us. In, http://www.beertown.org/ba/index.html. (accessed
June 16, 2009).

———. Craft Brewing Statistics. In, http://www.beertown.org/craftbrewing/statistics.
html. (accessed June 16, 2009).

Bullseye Glass. About Us. In, http://www.bullseyeglass.com/aboutus/. (accessed June
25, 2009).

———. Becon Presenters. In, http://www.bullseyeglass.com/becon/2009/presenters/.
(accessed June 25, 2009).

Burbank, Matthew J., Gregory D. Andranovich, and Charles H. Heying. *Olympic Dreams:
The Impact of Mega-Events on Local Politics, Explorations in Public Policy*. Boulder, Colo.:
Lynne Rienner Publishers, 2001.

Burros, Marian. "In Oregon, Thinking Local." *New York Times*, January 6, 2006.

C

Calvey, Mark. "Wells Fargo Bank Recovering from Merger Hangover." *San Francisco
Business Times*, December 26, 1997.

Cecchini, Toby. "The New Bootleggers." *GQ*, July 2006, 112–14.

Centoni, Danielle. "Mixmaster." *Mix*, June/July 2008, 21–23.

Chehalem Mountain Pottery. About Us. In, http://www.chehalemmountainpottery.
com/aboutus/aboutus.html. (accessed June 25, 2009).

Chris King Precision Components. In, http://chrisking.com/. (accessed June 16, 2009).

City-Data.com. Oelwein, Iowa. In, http://www.city-data.com/city/Oelwein-Iowa.html.
(accessed July 13, 2009).

City Repair. About. In, http://cityrepair.org/about/. (accessed June 19, 2009).

———. Projects. In, http://cityrepair.org/about/projects/. (accessed June 19, 2009).

———. Village Building Convergence. In, http://cityrepair.org/events/vbc/. (accessed
June 19, 2009).

Clark, Taylor. "The Indie City: Why Portland Is America's Indie Rock Mecca." *Slate*,
posted September 11, 2007.

Clear Creek Distillery. Additional Clear Creek Eaux De Vie. In, http://clearcreekdistill-
ery.com/other.html. (accessed June 18, 2009).

———. Breaking News. In, http://clearcreekdistillery.com/distillery-news.html.
(accessed September 8, 2008).

Clifford, Sue, and Angela King. "Losing Your Place." In *Local Distinctiveness: Place,
Particularity and Identity*, edited by Sue Clifford and Angela King. London: Common
Ground, 1993.

Community Live Journal. In, http://community.livejournal.com/sew_hip. (accessed
July 25, 2009).

Cortright, Joseph. "Making Sense of Clusters: Regional Competitiveness and Economic
Development." *In The Brookings Institution Metropolitan Policy Program Discussion*

Papers. Washington, DC: The Brookings Institution, 2006.

Crain, Liz. "Botanically Infused Libations Naturally Spice up Cocktail Hour." *Portland Tribune*, April 4, 2008.

Curl, Aimee. "PDC Moves Offices to Creative Services Center." *Daily Journal of Commerce* (Portland, OR), September 27, 2004.

———. "Portland Development Center Cuts Its Losses on Center." *Daily Journal of Commerce* (Portland, OR), January 12, 2004.

Currid, Elizabeth. *The Warhol Economy: How Fashion, Art, and Music Drive New York City*. Princeton: Princeton University Press, 2007.

D

Dark Horse. Company/Overview. In, http://www.darkhorse.com/Company/Overview. (accessed June 22, 2009).

David King Bass Guitars. In, http://kingbass.com/. (accessed June 20, 2009).

———. Bunnybass Interview with David King. In, http://kingbass.com/bunnybass.html. (accessed June 20, 2009).

———. "How I Build a Bass." In, http://kingbass.com/build-a-bass.html. (accessed June 20, 2009).

Demsky, Ian. "Deconstructing for FEMA Dollars, New Orleans Gets a Lesson from Portland on Greening Its Katrina Cleaning." *Willamette Week*, June 28, 2006.

Depave. About Depave. In, http://depave.org/blog/about/. (accessed June 19, 2009).

Design and Direct Source. Projects. In, http://www.designanddirectsource.com/projects.php. (accessed June 25, 2009).

———. Sustainable Products. In, http://www.designanddirectsource.com/sustainable.php. (accessed June 25, 2009).

Dietrich, Heidi. "Craft Liquor Startups May Stir Creation of New Industry in Washington State." *Puget Sound Business Journal*, July 4, 2008.

Dougherty, Conor. "'Youth Magnet' Cities Hit Midlife Crisis: Few Jobs in Places Like Portland and Austin, but the Hipsters Just Keep on Coming." *Wall Street Journal*, May 16, 2009, A1.

Duin, Steve. April 2, 2008. 24 Hour Comics Day. In, oregonlive.com blog, http://blog.oregonlive.com/steveduin/2008/04/24hour_comics_day.html. (accessed June 22, 2009).

Dyer-Witheford, Nick. *Cyber-Marx: Cycles and Circuits of Struggle in High-Technology Capitalism*. Urbana: University of Illinois Press, 1999.

E

Eakin, Emily. "The Cities and Their New Elite." *New York Times*, 2002.

Ecotrust. About Us. In, http://www.ecotrust.org/about/. (accessed May 7, 2009).

eKalimba.com. December 18, 2008. Blog—"Darin Has Been Assisting Me for Awhile Now." In, http://apps.ekalimba.com/blog/. (accessed June 20, 2009).

———. Home. In, http://www.ekalimba.com/. (accessed June 20, 2009).

Etsy. Home. In, http://www.etsy.com/. (accessed June 25, 2009).

F

Fairchild, Charles. *Community Radio and Public Culture*, New Jersey: Hampton Press, 2001.

Fauchald, Nick. "America's Best New Whiskeys." *Food and Wine*, November 2007.

Film Action Oregon. About. In, http://hollywoodtheatre.org/about.html. (accessed June 22, 2009).

Filmed by Bike. Why +. In, http://www.filmedbybike.org/about. (accessed June 15, 2009).

Florida, Richard L. *The Rise of the Creative Class: And How It's Transforming Work, Leisure, Community and Everyday Life*. New York, NY: Basic Books, 2004.

"For Serious Bikers, It's Gotta Be Langlitz." *Portland Tribune*, June 22, 2001.

Foyston, John. "Gray, Green & Free." March 13, 2009, E1–6.

———. Educating. In, http://hollywoodtheatre.org/educating/index.html. (accessed June 22, 2009).

Frank, Ryan. "Adams Pushes Convention Center Hotel." *Oregonian*, April 16, 2009, C1–2.

Free Geek. Overview. In, http://www.freegeek.org/about/overview/. (accessed June 19, 2009).

———. Volunteer Build. In, http://www.freegeek.org/volunteer/build/. (accessed June 19, 2009).

G

Gallivan, Joseph. "Spotlight's on Dark Horse." *Portland Tribune*, May 22, 2007.

Gamblin Artists Colors. About. In, http://www.gamblincolors.com/about/index.html. (accessed June 25, 2009).

———. Torrit Grey Competition. In, http://www.gamblincolors.com/torrit.grey/index.html. (accessed June 25, 2009).

———. Torrit Grey Competition Winners 2008. In, http://www.gamblincolors.com/torrit.grey/winners.html. (accessed June 25, 2009).

Gisonny, Karen, and Jenna Freedman. "Zines in Libraries: How, What and Why?" *Collection Building* 25, no. 1 (2006): 26–30.

Glass Art Society. About Us. In, http://www.glassart.org/aboutus.html. (accessed June 25, 2009).

Granton, Shawn, ed. *The Zinester's Guide to Portland*. 4th ed. Portland, OR: Microcosm Publishing, 2008.

Great American Beer Festival. Beer Styles. In, http://www.greatamericanbeerfestival.com/beer_styles1.html. (accessed June 16, 2009).

Grover, Martha. *Somnambulist Number 10: The Portland Issue*. Portland, OR: Self Published, 2008.

———. Somnambulist Zine Blog Archive. In, http://somnambulistzine.blogspot.com/. (accessed August 13, 2008).

Guild of American Luthiers. About Us. In, http://luth.org/aboutus.htm. (accessed June 20, 2009).

———. Why Join? In, http://luth.org/why-join.htm. (accessed June 20, 2009).

H

"Hands Off Our Bud." *The Economist*, June 14, 2008.

Hebdige, Dick. *Subculture: The Meaning of Style*. London: Methuen & Co., 1979.

Herman, Jessica. "Welcome to the Familia: An Explosion of Mafias, Collectives, and Co-Ops Shows That Crafting Is All in the Family." *Venus Zine*, June 1, 2005.

Heying, Charles H., Matthew J. Burbank, and Greg Andranovich. "Taking the Measure of the Games: Lessons from the Field." *Plan Canada* 45, no. 2 (2005): 20–22.

Hopworks Urban Brewery. In, http://www.hopworksbeer.com/index.php. (accessed June 16, 2009).

———. Portland's CW Profiles Hopworks Urban Brewery and Our Commitment to Sustainability - Online Video. In, http://www.hopworksbeer.com/hop_vid1.php. (accessed June 16, 2009).

Hsuan, Amy. "Tooling up for Tomorrow." *Oregonian*, July 16, 2008, E1–2.

Hub City Brewing Company. About. In, http://www.hubcitybrewingcompany.com/about.php. (accessed July 13, 2009).

I

Imbibe Magazine. "About Imbibe." In, http://www.imbibemagazine.com/About. (accessed June 19, 2009).

Independent Community Bankers of America. Community Banking Facts. In, http://www.icba.org/files/ICBASites/PDFs/cbfacts.pdf. (accessed July 13, 2009).

Inside a Black Apple. Home. In, http://www.theblackapple.typepad.com/. (accessed June 25, 2009).

Institute of Portland Metropolitan Studies. "Planting Prosperity and Harvesting Health: Trade-Offs and Sustainability in the Oregon-Washington Regional Food System." Portland, Oregon: Nohad Toulan School of Urban Studies and Planning, Portland State University, 2008.

Integrity Spirits. Blog Archives. In, http://integrityspirits.blogspot.com/. (accessed June 19, 2009).

Integrity Systems Cooperative Co. & Sustainability Ventures Group. 1997. Adding Values to Our Food System: An Economic Analysis of Sustainable Community Food Systems. In, http://www.ibiblio.org/farming-connection/foodsys/addval.htm. (accessed May 6, 2009).

J

James Beard Foundation. About James Beard. In, http://www.jamesbeard.org/index.php?q=about_james_beard. (accessed April 25, 2009).

Johnson, Barry. "Entertainment District: Bigger's Not Better; Homegrown Reaps Rewards." *Oregonian*, April 27, 2009.

———. "KMHD starts down a new path with OPB." http://blog.oregonlive.com/portlandarts/2009/09/kmhd_starts_down_a_new_path_wi.html. (accessed Janurary 17, 2010).

Johnson, Steven Reed. "The Transformation of Civic Institutions and Practices in Portland, Oregon, 1960–1999." Dissertation, Portland State University, 2002.

Johnston, L. "Portland Has Plenty of Froth and Bubble." *Sunday Mail*, November 9, 2003, 630.

K

KBOO. About KBOO. In, http://kboo.fm/node/4138. (accessed June 22, 2009).
———. The Underground. In, http://kboo.fm/theunderground. (accessed June 22, 2009).
———. Youth Randomonium. In, http://kboo.fm/YouthRandomonium. (accessed June 22, 2009).
Kenworthy, Tom. "Peaks, Valleys Define Today's West." *USA Today*, May 18, 2001, 3A.
Kish, Matthew. "Shot at Expansion." *Portland Business Journal*, March 5, 2007.
KMHD 89.1: Jazz Blues and NPR News. History. In, http://www.kmhd.org/index.php?option=com_content&task=view&id=18&Itemid=69. (accessed June 22, 2009).
Korn, Peter. "Q & A with Dave Hansen." *Portland Tribune*, June 19, 2008.
Koss, Pamela. "A Glass Act." *Oregonian*, May/June 2008, 10–14.
KPSU 1450: Portland's College Radio. Home. In, http://kpsu.org/. (accessed June 22, 2009).
KPSU Radio. March 9, 2009. Art Talk AM on the Radio – Interview with Bryan Suereth. In, http://arttalkam.blogspot.com/2009/03/brian-sureth.html. (accessed June 24, 2009).
Krajnak, Katherine. "Spaces for Art: What We Can Learn and Do to Keep Portland Affordable for Artists." *Field Area Paper*, Portland State University, 2007.
Krueger, Nicole. "Distilling the Essence of the Fruit." *Statesman Journal*, July 20, 2008.

L

Laika House Entertainment. *Coraline*. In, http://www.laika.com/entertainment/. (accessed June 23, 2009).
Landry, Charles. *The Creative City: A Toolkit for Urban Innovators*. 2nd ed. New Stroud, UK London; Sterling, VA: Comedia; Earthscan, 2008.
Landry, Charles, and Franco Bianchini. *The Creative City*. London: Demos, 1995.
Langlitz Leathers Inc. History. In, http://www.langlitz.com/history.shtml. (accessed June 18, 2009).
League of American Bicyclists. Bicycle Friendly Community Master List. In, http://www.bikeleague.org/programs/bicyclefriendlyamerica/pdfs/bfc_master_list_web.pdf. (accessed June 15, 2009).
Leatherman. Oregon Proud. In, http://leatherman.com/about/oregon-proud.aspx. (accessed June 25, 2009).
———. In the Press. In, http://www.langlitz.com/press.shtml. (accessed June 18, 2009).
Levit, Briar. August 5, 2008. "Specular Preserves at Reading Frenzy." In, *Bitch Magazine* blog, http://bitchmagazine.org/post/specular-preserves-at-reading-frenzy. (accessed June 22, 2009).
Levy, Shawn. February 12, 2007. Comments: PIFF Dispatch. 1. In, *GreenCine Daily*, http://daily.greencine.com/cgi-bin/gc-mt/mt-comments.cgi?entry_id=3244. (accessed June 22, 2009).
Libby, Brian. "An Artistic Congregation at Milepost 5." *Oregonian*, May 28, 2008.
Literary Arts. Fellowship Recipients – Publishers. In, http://www.literary-arts.org/fellowships/past_publishers.php. (accessed June 22, 2009).
Lloyd, Richard D. *Neo-Bohemia: Art and Commerce in the Postindustrial City*. New York: Routledge, 2005.

LOFT Liqueurs. About. In, http://www.loftliqueurs.com/index539a.html?q=node/2. (accessed June 18, 2009).

Love, Kenny. "College Radio: The Most Important Radio Level for Independents." In, Streetdirectory.com, http://www.streetdirectory.com/travel_guide/31564/music/=college_radio_the_most_important_radio_level_for_independents.html. (accessed June 22, 2009).

M

MacRae, Patti. "KRRC: The (Barely Audible) Radio Voice of Reed College." *Reed Magazine*, August 2002.

Markusen, Ann R., Yong-Sook Lee, and Sean DiGiovanna. *Second Tier Cities: Rapid Growth Beyond the Metropolis, Globalization and Community*; V. 3. Minneapolis: University of Minnesota Press, 1999.

Maus, Jonathan. March 6, 2007. Booth, Speedvagen Mark New Direction for Vanilla Bicycles. In, BikePortland.org, http://bikeportland.org/2007/03/06/booth-speed-vagen-mark-new-direction-for-vanilla-bicycles/. (accessed June 15, 2009).

McCandlish, Laura. March 10, 2009. "Slow Food Moves Faster on Social Activism." In, Special to the *Oregonian*, http://www.oregonlive.com/foodday/index.ssf/2009/03/slow_food_acts_on_social_activ.html. (accessed June 15, 2009).

McInerny, Vivian. "Ai-Yai-Eye! Edgy Glasses!" *Oregonian*, July 22, 2008, D1–4.

———. "Portland's Mod Hatter Turns Some Heads." *Oregonian*, March 11, 2007, O6.

McKay, George. *DIY Culture: Party & Protest in Nineties Britain*. London: Verso, 1998.

McMenamins Hotels and Pubs. Edgefield Distillery. In, http://www.mcmenamins.com/index.php?loc=76&category=Distillery+Homepage. (accessed June 18, 2009).

Merrill, Jessica. "In Oregon, It's a Brew Pub World." *New York Times*, January 13, 2006, F1.

Milepost 5. Home. In, http://www.milepostfive.com/. (accessed June 24, 2009).

———. Showcase Pdx—Milepost 5 Video Biography. In, http://www.milepostfive.com/video. (accessed June 24, 2009).

Monette. "The Monette Approach to Design." In, http://www.monette.net/newsite/monette_approach_00.htm. (accessed June 20, 2009).

Moore, Chuck. April 1, 2008. "Mayor Declares April Portland Comics Month." In, Community@Comic Related, http://comicrelated.com/forums/index.php?s=c66c229fdeb06616c6f6885cd3a858f0&showtopic=1371&st=0&p=5501&#entry5501. (accessed June 22, 2009).

Multnomah County Library. About the Library/Library Fact Sheet. In, http://www.multcolib.org/about/libraryfactsheet.html. (accessed June 22, 2009).

N

New Deal Distillery. Product. In, http://newdealdistillery.com/Product/product_index.html. (accessed June 18, 2009).

New Seasons Market. In, http://www.newseasonsmarket.com/homepage.aspx?location=H. (accessed June 12, 2009).

Newman, Will. 2001. Proceedings from Portland Chapter of the Chef's Collaborative at the Farmer Chef's Connection. In, http://www.portlandcc.org/farmchef.pdf. (accessed June 11, 2009).

Nix, Vance. "DIY Zine Scene: Skip Those Pesky Editors and Publish Yourself." *Portland Sentinel*, May 6, 2008.

Northwest Agriculture Business Center. "Craft Distilling: Value Added Agriculture for Washington's Family Farm." In, http://www.agbizcenter.org/FilesUploaded/file/distilling%20fact%20sheet.pdf. (accessed June 18, 2009).

O

Ogle, Maureen. *Ambitious Brew: The Story of American Beer*. Orlando: Harcourt, 2006.

Open Source Bridge. Blog—Becoming an "Open Source Citizen." In, http://opensource-bridge.org/2009/02/becoming-an-open-source-citizen/. (accessed June 20, 2009).

———. Home. In, http://opensourcebridge.org/. (accessed June 20, 2009).

———. "Have a Beer, Launch a Tech Start-Up." Oregonian, May 2, 2009.

Oregon Art Beat. January 24, 2008. Monette Trumpets. In, http://www.opb.org/programs/artbeat/segments/view/714. (accessed June 20, 2009).

Oregon Brewers Guild. Oregon Brewers Guild Fact Sheet. In, http://oregonbeer.org/facts/. (accessed June 10, 2009).

———. Facts. In, http://oregonbeer.org/facts/. (accessed June 16, 2009).

Oregon Potters Association. Home. In, http://www.oregonpotters.org/. (accessed June 25, 2009).

———. Member Links. In, http://www.oregonpotters.org/member_links.htm. (accessed June 25, 2009).

Oregon Public Broadcasting. OPB Radio. In, http://opb.org/radio/. (accessed June 22, 2009).

———. June 6, 2008. "We've Got Spirits, Yes We Do!" In *Think Out Loud* [radio broadcast], http://action.publicbroadcasting.net/opb/posts/list/1156812.page. (accessed June 18, 2009).

———. June 6, 2008. "We've Got Spirits, Yes We Do!" In *Think Out Loud* [blog comments], http://action.publicbroadcasting.net/opb/posts/list/1156812.page. (accessed June 18, 2009).

Oregon's Statewide Planning Goals: Goal 3: Agricultural Lands. 1994. In, http://www.oregon.gov/LCD/docs/goals/goal3.pdf. (accessed June 11, 2009).

P

Palmer, Parker J. *The Courage to Teach: Exploring the Inner Landscape of a Teacher's Life*. 1st ed. San Francisco, Calif.: Jossey-Bass, 1998.

Patrick Alan Coleman posting to Blogtown: The Mercury Blog. Aug 25, 2008. Great American Distillers Festival: Wrap Up! In, http://blogtown.portlandmercury.com/BlogtownPDX/archives/2008/08/25/great-american-distillers-fest. (accessed June 18, 2009).

Pereira Cycles. Cyclocross. In, http://www.pereiracycles.com/cyclocross.php. (accessed August 14, 2008).

Pinkham Millinery. About. In, http://www.pinkhammillinery.com/about. (accessed June 25, 2009).

Platform International Animation Festival. About. In, http://platformfestival.com/content/thefestival.aspx. (accessed June 23, 2009).

Portland Art Studios. A Guide to Portland's Creative Spaces. In, www.portlandartstudios.com. (accessed June 24, 2009).

Portland Department of Transportation. "Portland Bicycle Counts 2007." City of Portland, Oregon, September 26, 2007.

Portland Development Commission. News Release—September 13, 2000, Creative Services Center Building Renovation Begins. In, http://www.pdc.us/new/releases/2000/20000913_create_serv.asp. (accessed June 24, 2009).

Portland Farmers Market. PFM Information Booth. In, http://www.portlandfarmersmarket.org/sec_InfoBooth/info_booth.php. (accessed May 7, 2009).

Portland Independent Media Center. Portland Indymedia Web Radio - Archived Live Shows. In, http://portland.indymedia.org/en/static/pdxradio.shtml. (accessed June 22, 2009).

Portland Nursery and Garden Center. Home. In, http://www.portlandnursery.com/. (accessed June 26, 2009).

Portland Saturday Market. Artisans, Clothing and Accessories. In, http://www.portlandsaturdaymarket.com/Main%20Pages/Craft%20Pages/ClothingAndAccessories/Clothing.htm. (accessed June 25, 2009).

———. About Us, History. In, http://www.portlandsaturdaymarket.com/Main%20Pages/About%20Us/history.htm. (accessed June 25, 2009).

Portland Zine Symposium. Home. In, http://pdxzines.com/. (accessed June 20, 2009).

Portland.com. "Regional Arts and Culture Council Announces Move to Creative Services Center." In, http://www.portland.com/portland/press-releases/regional-arts-and-culture-council-announces-move-to-creative-services-center/. (accessed June 24, 2009).

Powell's City of Books. Store Description. In, http://www.powells.com/info/places/burnsideinfo.html. (accessed June 22, 2009).

Pratt & Larson Ceramics. About Us. In, http://www.prattandlarson.com/about_us.php. (accessed June 25, 2009).

Preuss, Holger. *The Economics of Staging the Olympics: A Comparison of the Games, 1972–2008*. Cheltenham, UK; Northampton, MA: E. Elgar, 2004.

Putnam, Robert D., Lewis M. Feldstein, and Don Cohen. *Better Together: Restoring the American Community*. New York: Simon & Schuster, 2003.

R

Reading Frenzy. Benefit for Martha Grover. In, http://readingfrenzy.com/ledger/2008/06/benefit-for-martha-grover. (accessed June 22, 2009).

Reynolds, Richard. "Coffee's Third Wave." *Imbibe*, May/June 2006.

Robbins, Jim. "Think Global, Eat Local; the Sustainable Food Movement That Began with Berkeley Chef Alice Waters Has Blossomed in Portland, Ore. Are Its Proponents Just Dreaming? Or Is a Real Revolution Underway?" *Los Angeles Times*, July 31, 2005.

Row, D. K. February 29, 2008. "Gavin Shettler: Moving On." In oregonlive blog, http://blog.oregonlive.com/visualarts/2008/02/gavin_shettler_moving_on.html. (accessed June 24, 2009).

S

Sahagun Handmade Chocolates. Story. In, http://www.sahagunchocolates.com/story.php. (accessed June 25, 2009).

Saker, Anne. "Portland Distillery Second in U.S. To Bottle Absinthe." *Oregonian*, July 9, 2008.

Sanders, Heywood T. "Convention Myths and Markets: A Critical Review of Convention Center Feasibility Studies." *Economic Development Quarterly* 16, no. 3 (2002): 195–210.

Schroeder, Deeda. "On a Roll." *Willamette Week*, May 7, 2008.

Scott, Allen J. "Creative Cities: Conceptual Issues and Policy Questions." *Journal of Urban Affairs* 28, no. 1 (2006): 1–18.

Scruggs, Patricia C., Joseph Cortright, and Marcia Douglas. "Designing Portland's Future: The Role of the Creative Services Industry." 69: A report written for the Portland Development Commission and the Industry and Professional Organizations of the Creative Services Cluster. Available at http://www.pdc.us/pdf/bus_serv/creative-svcs-report.pdf, June, 1999.

Sellie, Alycia. "Baltimore County Public Library Zine Collection." In, http://www.bcpl.info/centers/library/Zine.pdf. (accessed September 18, 2008).

Sennett, Richard. *The Craftsman*. New Haven: Yale University Press, 2008.

ShoeLacesExpress. In, http://www.shoelacesexpress.com/index.asp. (accessed July 13, 2009).

Shuman, Michael. *Going Local: Creating Self-Reliant Communities in a Global Age*. 1st Routledge paperback ed. New York: Routledge, 2000.

Sickinger, Ted. "Kansas City Here We Come?" *Oregonian*, Tuesday, May 12, 2009, A1, A4.

Site Distiller. October 29th, 2007. Welcome. In, Burning Still, http://www.burningstill.com/?q=node/1. (accessed June 18, 2009).

Slow Food USA. Good, Clean and Fair. In, http://www.slowfoodusa.org/index.php/slow_food/good_clean_fair/. (accessed May 7, 2009).

Specialty Coffee Association of America. In, http://members.scaa.org/default.aspx. (accessed June 16, 2009).

Spencer, Amy. *DIY: The Rise of Lo-Fi Culture*. London: Marion Boyars, 2005.

Stumptown Coffee Roasters. Locations. In, http://buystumptowncoffee.com/locations. (accessed June 16, 2009).

Suereth, Bryan. Email correspondence, May 5, 2009.

Sussman, Gerald, and J. R. Estes. "Community Radio in Community Development: Portland's KBOO Radio." In *The Portland Edge: Challenges and Successes in Growing Communities*, edited by Connie P. Ozawa, 118–39. Washington, DC: Island Press, 2004.

SustainLane. 2008 US City Rankings. In, http://www.sustainlane.com/us-city-rankings/. (accessed June 25, 2009).

T

Talitha Leather. Handmade Leather Bags, Purses, Wallets, and Journals. In, http://www.talithaleather.com/. (accessed June 18, 2009).

Tears of Joy Theatre. About Us. In, http://www.tojt.com/About_us.html. (accessed June 25, 2009).

Tejaratchi, Sean. *Crap Hound 6: Deaths, Telephones, Scissors*. Portland, OR: Show and Tell, Press, 2006.

———. *Crap Hound 7: Church & State Part One*. Portland, OR: Show and Tell, Press, 2008.

The Clinton Street Theatre. On the Marquee. In, http://clintonsttheater.com/. (accessed June 22, 2009).

———. PDX A. V. Club. In, http://clintonsttheater.com/avclub.html. (accessed June 22, 2009).

The Hartman Group Inc. "Understanding Local from a Consumer Perspective: Presentation to the Food Marketing Institute." 2008.

The Rebuilding Center. Home. In, http://www.rebuildingcenter.org/. (accessed June 19, 2009).

The Wall. Home. In, http://www.bythewall.com/index.php. (accessed June 26, 2009).

Thompson, Clive. "A One-of-a-Kind Revolution." *Wired*, March, 2009, 34.

Tool Shed - PDX. Home. In, http://www.toolshedpdx.org/. (accessed June 24, 2009).

Travel Portland. Portland: The Center of the Beer Universe. In, http://www.travelportland.com/media/mbmedkit/mb_beer.html. (accessed June 16, 2009).

Tremblay, Victor J., and Carol Horton Tremblay. *The U.S. Brewing Industry: Data and Economic Analysis.* Cambridge, Mass.: MIT Press, 2005.

Turnquist, Kristi. "Hollywood Says Hurray for Portland Comic Books." *Oregonian*, July 23, 2008.

U

Ubuntu. "What Is Ubuntu?" In, http://www.ubuntu.com/products/whatisubuntu. (accessed June 19, 2009).

Urban Dictionary. "Twitterpated." In, http://www.urbandictionary.com/define.php?term=twitterpated. (accessed June 20, 2009).

V

Verzemnieks, Inara. "Strings Attached." *Oregonian*, November 23, 2007, 6–11.

Vision into Action. Vision into Action Grants. In, http://www.visionpdx.com/action/grants.php. (accessed July 13, 2009).

———. "Voices from the Community: The Visionpdx Input Report." In, http://www.visionpdx.com/reading/inputsummary/. (accessed July 13, 2009).

W

Wakelin, Simon. December 18, 2002. *Ocularist Eyes Sundance*. In, Boards blog, http://www.boardsmag.com/articles/online/20021218/eyes.html. (accessed June 22, 2009).

Walker, David, Becky Ohlsen, Brian Libby, Nancy Rommelmann, and Byron Beck. "Filming Portland: Four Emerging Local Filmmakers-and One Zany Group-Are Producing Must-See Cinema." *Willamette Week*, March 23, 2005.

"Where to Find Martha." *Martha Stewart Living*, July 2008, 102.

Wikipedia. Gus Van Sant. In, http://en.wikipedia.Org/wiki/Gus_Van_Sant. (accessed June 22, 2009).

———. Web 2.0 - Definition. In, http://en.wikipedia.org/wiki/Web_2.0#Definition. (accessed June 20, 2009).

World Carfree Network. Towards Carfree Cities Conference Series. In, http://www.worldcarfree.net/conference/. (accessed June 16, 2009).

Y

Yardley, William. "In Portland, Cultivating a Culture of Two Wheels." *New York Times*, November 5, 2007.

YOLO Colorhouse. Our Story. In, http://www.yolocolorhouse.com/about_ourstory.php. (accessed June 26, 2009).

———. Who We Are. In, http://www.yolocolorhouse.com/about_yolo.php. (accessed June 26, 2009).

Z

Zimmerman, Jeffrey. "From Brew Town to Cool Town: Neoliberalism and the Creative City Development Strategy in Milwaukee." *Cities* 25, no. 4 (2008): 230–42.

Zukin, Sharon. "Consuming Authenticity." *Cultural Studies* 22, no. 5 (2008): 724–48.

———. *Loft Living: Culture and Capital in Urban Change*. New Brunswick, NJ: Rutgers University Press, 1989.

———. "Urban Lifestyles: Diversity and Standardization in Spaces of Consumption." *Urban Studies* 35, no. 5/6 (1998): 825–39.

Zukin, Sharon, and Ervin Kosta. "Bourdieu Off-Broadway: Managing Distinction on a Shopping Block in the East Village." *City & Community* 3, no. 2 (2004): 101–14.

Index

Ooligan Press

Ooligan Press takes its name from a Native American word for the common smelt or candlefish. Ooligan is a general trade press rooted in the rich literary life of Portland and the Department of English at Portland State University. Ooligan is staffed by students pursuing master's degrees in an apprenticeship program under the guidance of a core faculty of publishing professionals.

Project Managers

Robyn Crummer-Olson
Rachel Gande
Kenny Hanour
Brian Kirk

Design Managers

Cory Freeman
Alan Dubinsky

Cover & Interior Design

Ellery Harvey

Editing Managers

Julie Franks
Dehlia McCobb
Katie Shaw

Editing Team

Jessicah Carver
Mary E. Darcy
Chelle Dey
Kenny Hanour
Maureen S. Inouye
Caroline Knecht
Lucy Softich
Kjerstin Johnson

Sustainability Consultants

Jessicah Carver
Natalie Guidry
Brian David Smith

Marketing Managers

Alex Tucker
Bryan Coffelt
Candice Peaslee

Marketing Team

Susan E. Wiget

COLOPHON

This book was lovingly set in Palatino, a typeface designed by Hermann Zapf in 1948 for the Linotype foundry. Based on the calligraphic style of the Italian Renaissance—and named after the 16th century calligrapher Giambattista Palatino—this typeface is acclaimed for its elegance and versatility.